From Anzio to the Alps

From Anzio to the Alps

An American Soldier's Story

Lloyd M. Wells

University of Missouri Press
Columbia and London

University of Missouri Press, Columbia, Missouri 65211
Printed and bound in the United States of America

First paperback printing, 2019

Library of Congress Cataloging-in-Publication Data

Wells, Lloyd M. (Lloyd Manning), 1919–2000.
From Anzio to the Alps : an American soldier's story / Lloyd M. Wells.
p. cm.
ISBN 978-0-8262-1537-6 (hardcover : alk. paper)
ISBN 978-0-8262-2206-0 (paperback : alk. paper)
1. Wells, Lloyd M. (Lloyd Manning), 1919–2000.
2. United States. Army. Armored Infantry Regiment, 6th.
3. World War, 1939–1945—Regimental histories—United States. 4. World War, 1939–1945—Campaigns—Italy.
5. World War, 1939–1945—Personal narratives, American.
6. Soldiers—United States—Biography. I. Title.
D769.30556th .W45 2004
940.54'215'092—dc22

2004004304

∞ This paper meets the requirements of the American National Standard for Permanence of Paper for Printed Library Materials, Z39.48, 1984.

Designer: Jennifer Cropp
Typefaces: Alcuin and Palatino

The University of Missouri Press offers its grateful acknowledgment to the National Archives for photos taken by the U.S. Army Signal Corps and to Robert Ferrell for his assistance in preparing this volume.

For my wife,
Carolyn

our son,
Randall Manning Wells,

our grandchildren,
Todd Manning Wells,
Randall Doyle Wells,
and Blythe Jane Wells,

and all the citizen
soldiers of World War II

Contents

Preface

This is a true story about a war which ended over forty years ago. It is based on a journal I kept during that war, on letters I sent home, on records in my army personnel file, and on recollections of men, women, and events. Standard works of military history and other treatments relating to the Italian campaign have been used to supplement my account and to place small-unit action in a larger, more understandable context.

There is much to tell, even about battles which have attracted the attention of other writers. Chapter 6, for example, reveals for the first time, insofar as I am aware, exactly what happened to 2/7 Queens when they came up to "the caves" at Anzio on the night of February 21, 1944. And there is even more to tell about actions not treated elsewhere. Chapters 13 and 14, "Eight Days in the Mountains" and "Twelve Days in the Valley," provide the only account available of what the last offensive in Italy was like for armored infantry troops on the thrusting perimeter of the attack.

But this is not just a story of battle actions. In a broader sense it is a personal story about the "Old Army" and how some of us tried to live in it and were transformed by it during one of the great upheavals in world history. Things happened to us, both on and off the line, and each of us was changed.

I can speak with certainty only for myself. In 1941 I was a one hundred and twenty pound–kid, somewhat bookish, more than a little immature, shy, truly a tender and callow fellow. By 1944 I was a one hundred and twenty-five–pound kid, still immature, still callow; but I had acquired an adult identity and a lifestyle related to that identity. Somehow, as improbable as it now seems, I had come to see myself as exactly what my military occupational specialty proclaimed me to be: an infantry unit commander. Consequently, on the line I tried to perform as I thought infantry unit commanders were supposed to perform, and off the line I allowed myself to behave as I thought they were entitled to behave. Since I had come to believe that there were not more than a dozen people in all of the outside world who really gave a good goddamn whether I lived or died, my loyalties were to myself, the platoon, the company, the battalion.

The journal material reveals something about how the transformation took place. Almost all of the material depicting battle actions was handwritten in rest areas or hospitals shortly after the events occurred and was copied by typewriter at the end of the war in Italy, when I was assigned to the battalion staff. This material is well preserved and indispensable for both prompting and disciplining memory. The uncopied material, on the other hand, is of considerably less, or no, use. Some of it has been lost; some is barely legible.

The material is uneven in other respects as well. There is no consistent time frame. Sometimes entries are on a day-by-day basis, but some months and some incidents are summarized in a paragraph. There are unexplainable gaps.

Nor, for several reasons, is the journal completely reliable with respect to exact dates. For one thing, there is a powerful tendency for men at the front not only to lose track of time but to develop a distorted sense of it. For another, some episodes remain stark in memory but were confusing and difficult to locate in chronological sequence even when experience was fresh. I have tried to confirm dates by cross-checking but have not always been successful. Inaccuracies likely remain.

Very little of the narrative is presented in terms of day-to-day happenings; I have condensed, expanded on, and omitted journal entries in the interest of a shorter, smoother, more understandable story.

There is something else to explain. I knew from the beginning that I couldn't provide an honest account without treating sensitive aspects of stress-related behavior both on and off the line. And telling this part of the story presents a common problem which I have tried to solve in the usual way.

While the tone and substance of conversations recorded here are accurate within the limits of fallible memory, and the geographical locations are, or were, real places, the names of persons have been changed and their identities otherwise disguised to avoid intrusions on privacy. The right simply to be left alone is a fundamental one, and I would not want to reveal anything, whether unfavorable, innocuous, or even praiseworthy, which my associates of that period would prefer not to have told.

After 1945 my journal notes and other records lay fallow through four decades as I tried to establish a new identity and carve out another career. I joined no veterans' organization, attended no reunions, and made no efforts to continue old friendships. Once upon a time I had much in common with the officers and men of the battalion, but that was in another existence, in an entirely different, almost unreal world of long ago. We were different people then. I tried for some time and with some success to put the war behind me.

Shortly after my retirement as a professor at the University of Missouri, I began a systematic examination of my records and recollections. Reading carefully for the first time what I had written when I was young brought both pleasure and pain. There were feelings of guilt and shame at things done and things left undone. There was sadness in reliving the deaths of a few special friends. There was frustration at not being able to find answers to all of the questions which had lingered in my mind. And there was painful longing for lost youth.

But there was pleasure, too, in remembering how we were and some of the things we had done. There was pleasant surprise at retrieving information long forgotten and other information about which my unaided memory had been in error all of those years. There were feelings of accomplishment at being able to reconstruct in general outline the sequence of major events. And there was insight. In the end I thought I had gained a somewhat better understanding of why my first life turned out as it did, and that had been part of my original purpose.

But I had other things in mind as well. I wanted to leave behind a document of at least modest scholarly interest as well as an account evocative of a simpler time and of the funny, sad, terrorizing, and tender moments of a war which, with the death of each man or woman who lived through it, recedes just a little bit further into the nation's past. I hope you will agree that I have accomplished these things.

Lloyd M. Wells
(1919–2000)

In Memoriam

Our colleague of many years, Lloyd Manning Wells, professor emeritus of political science at the University of Missouri–Columbia, passed away on January 4, 2000, after a lingering illness. He was eighty years old. Lloyd was born in the small community of Clever, Missouri, in 1919. He was drafted into the army in June of 1941. After attending OCS (Officer Candidate School) he was commissioned second lieutenant and later promoted to first lieutenant with the First Armored Division. Lloyd saw action in North Africa, Italy, and Germany. He was awarded the Combat Infantry Badge, the Purple Heart with two oak clusters, and the Bronze Star. After leaving the service, he received a B.A. from Southwest Missouri State College in 1948 and an M.A. from the University of Missouri in 1950. He was awarded a Ph.D. from Princeton University in 1955, and while a student there, he worked for the Legislative Reference Bureau of the New Jersey State Legislature. He was a member of the Southern Methodist University faculty from 1955 to 1958 and served on the University of Missouri faculty from 1958 until he retired in 1985.

Lloyd's research centered on the Supreme Court and the bureaucracy. He coauthored *The Supreme Court and Public Opinion*. Other published research appeared in such sources as the *Social Science Quarterly,* and the *Public Administration Review,* as well as in anthologies. His greatest contributions, however, were as a teacher, an administrator, and a colleague. He taught courses ranging from the auditorium course of American government to advanced undergraduate courses and seminars in public administration. He received high praise for his teaching. He was known for his ability to stimulate thought and for his gentle sense of humor. One-on-one, he dealt with students in a sympathetic and encouraging manner.

At one time or another, he held every administrative position in the department, and he carried out all assignments with aplomb. He was elected to serve as chair from 1967 to 1970. As chair he was sensitive to the needs of the faculty for discretion in teaching and research. He was one of a vanishing breed of academic administrators who believed that community scholars could behave in a collegial and responsible way, and he conducted himself in a manner as to bring those values out in others. As a faculty member, he was known for his integrity and fairness. He brought his good judgment and mediation skills to departmental committee and faculty meetings to help the department work its way through potentially divisive problems. And withal, there was his clever wit to liven the meetings.

He is survived by his wife of fifty years, Carolyn, and three grandchildren. A son, Randall, preceded him in death.

Lloyd will be missed by his family, his colleagues, and his students. However, we are content that his was truly a life worth living.

DEAN L. YARWOOD
DAVID M. WOOD

The Italian Campaign: 1943–1945

1943

January–June

January 14–24:	Casablanca Conference, Morocco. Agreement reached for the invasion of Sicily.
May 11–25:	Trident Conference, Washington, D.C. Preparations made to attack Italian mainland.

July–October

July 10:	Operation HUSKY, the Allied invasion of Sicily, initiated.
July 26:	Mussolini removed from power.
August 17–31:	Allied-Italy negotiations for surrender
September 3:	Surrender agreement signed. Operation BAYTOWN kicks off as the British Eighth Army crosses the Strait of Messina.
September 9–17:	During Operation AVALANCHE, U.S. Fifth Army troops land at Salerno. After eight days of intense fighting, Germans withdraw to the north.
September 10:	Rome falls to Germany.
September 27:	British Eighth captures airfields at Foggia.
October 1:	Naples seized.
October 3–6:	British Eighth battles for Termoli.
October 12–15:	U.S. Fifth crosses Volturno River.

November–December

The Italian campaign reaches its first winter stalemate.

Axis forces withdraw to the Gustav Line.

British Eighth slowly advances north on the Adriatic coast toward the Gustav Line, but stalls at the Sangro River. U.S. Fifth pushes north on the western side of Apennines mountain range, approaching the town of Cassino and Liri Valley.

1944

January–June

January 4–15:	On the drive toward Cassino and the Gustav Line, the U.S. Fifth captures Mt. Porchia and Mt. Trocchio.
January 12:	Directive issued for Operation SHINGLE, an Allied campaign to take Rome.
January 20–22:	Phase one of SHINGLE. U.S. Fifth Army troops fail to break the Gustav Line.
January 22–30:	Phase two of SHINGLE proceeds as the U.S. Sixth Corps leads an amphibious landing at Anzio, which ends in a 125-day stalemate on the beachhead.
January 24–February 10:	First Battle of Cassino.
January 25:	Allied breakout from Anzio halted at Campoleone and Cisterna.
January 30:	Second attempt to end containment fails.
February 11:	New Zealand Corps assumes control on Cassino front.
February 15:	Benedictine Abbey of Monte Cassino bombed.
February 16–18:	Second battle for Cassino.
February 19:	German counterattack at Anzio fails.
March 3:	Second German counterattack at Anzio defeated.

March 15–23: Third battle for Cassino.

April 17: Directive issued for DIADEM and BUFFALO, operations designed to end stalemates at the Gustav Line and Anzio beachhead.

May 11: Operation DIADEM launched on Cassino front to break through the Gustav Line and take control of Highway 6, the most direct route to Rome.

May 17–18: Allies capture abbey and the town of Cassino.

May 23: Breakthrough at Gustav Line. Germans retreat.

May 23–28: In Operation BUFFALO, the Sixth Corps leads the breakout from Anzio via Cisterna.

June 4–5: British and American troops capture Rome.

June 6–7: Operation OVERLORD. The invasion of Normandy.

August–September

August 4: Allies reach Arno River at Florence, twenty miles south of Germans' Gothic Line.

August 13: Directive issued for Operation OLIVE. Plans for breaching the Gothic Line and taking the Po River Valley.

August 15: Operation ANVIL/DRAGOON. The Allies invade southern France.

August 25–September 21: The Eighth Army launches Operation OLIVE. Allies capture Rimini but fail to advance.

September 13–27: The Fifth Army begins attacking German positions along the Il Giogo and Futa Passes in the Apennines in an effort to break through the Gothic Line, and take control of the Po Valley.

October–December

Despite the Allied troops' persistent hammering at the Gothic Line, the German defensive position holds. There is another winter stalemate.

1945

January–February

Axis and Allied forces make preparations for spring offensives. The U.S. Tenth Mountain Division is able to make headway, capturing strategic positions in the northern Apennines, overlooking the Po Valley.

January 30–February 2: Malta Conference. Planned redeployment of Allied forces from Italy and Greece to northwest Europe.

April

April 9–14: Allied forces begin final offensive.

April 19: Allies push toward Bologna.

April 21: Allies troops capture Bologna and lay chase to German forces retreating across the Po River.

April 28: Mussolini killed.

April 29: Negotiations for surrender open in Caserta.

April 30: Hitler commits suicide.

May

May 2: German forces in Italy surrender. Berlin falls.

May 7: Germans sign unconditional surrender.

From Anzio to the Alps

Chapter 1

In the Beginning There Was Basic Training

It has been called "the good war." I don't know about that. It depends, I guess, on a lot of things, including where you were then and how you were before the whole thing started. For my parents it meant trading one kind of war for another. As mobilization for global conflict gained momentum, the domestic depression which had dominated the land for a decade was driven into retreat. By June of 1941, when I was drafted, the harsh realities of unemployment had given way to worry about what a shooting war might bring. Dad, age forty-three, had landed a steady job as a pipe fitter with Springfield Gas and Electric. Mom, thirty-nine, was still working as a saleslady at Kresge's Five and Ten, as she had been since I was eleven.

My only brother—Dad called him "Pete," Mom called him "Bitty Burr," Grandma called him "Frank," while his classmates and I called him "Carl" most of the time—was two years younger. Over the years he and I had become increasingly involved in the struggle to keep us fed, housed, clothed and in school. We were working people, Dad and Mom taught us, and a working person has nothing better going for him than his name. Even our childhood promise to help keep the Wells name clean was beginning to take on new meaning.

For the past year and a half I had been working as an usher at the Landers Theater from 5:00 p.m. until midnight six days a week and hurrying off to morning classes at what is now Southwest Missouri State University on five of those days. My job also required attendance at Saturday morning staff meetings, but, of course, we didn't get paid for those.

According to the prevailing logic, we were not working then; we were learning how to improve our work performance. If I didn't become a world-class usher, it was not for lack of instruction.

The job competed with school. When the draft notice came, I had completed a little less than half of the requirements for a degree and was planning to go to summer school to make up for those terms in which I had indulged myself with a light load. My puny plans would have to be set aside. Why, I wondered, did my so-called friends and neighbors on the draft board need me so soon when we were still at peace.

But there were compensations. My routines had become a bit wearing and my job more than a bit frustrating. While, as a halfhearted and self-interested pacifist, I was not eager to go into the army, the order to report to Ft. Leavenworth was neither wholly unexpected nor entirely unwelcome. I was getting restless.

Late in the afternoon of the day before I had to report, a small group of relatives and close friends waited in the crowded Frisco station to see me off. Mom and Dad were there, of course, and old Bitty Burr must have been there too. I don't remember seeing him, but that is probably because I was paying so much attention to my high school sweetheart. She was easy to look at, five feet two, very blonde, very pretty, and very, very well stacked.

Our relationship had progressed beyond the hand-holding stage. I was in love, I had told her, as no one had ever been in love before. We were not formally engaged but didn't need to be for we both knew, as everyone else knew, that we were meant for each other.

So there we were, assembled for the kind of farewell I quickly came to hate—everybody standing around through an interminable wait trying to make lighthearted conversation long after there was anything left to say. Why couldn't my folks just drop me off at the station with a hug, a good-bye, and good luck? Why did my mother insist on hanging around for one last wave as my train pulled out of the station?

But that first time a feeling of terminal loneliness came over me shortly after the crowded troop train got under way. My car was filled with a band of loud and convivial draftees having a last fling at freedom. I felt out of place, a boy among men. The guy sitting across the aisle offered me a drink. I thanked him politely and declined, hinting broadly that I was completely burned out after several days and nights of wild debauchery. Then to give my act some semblance of credibility, I tried to sleep.

The high point of my brief stay at Leavenworth came the next day at the end of a long, fast-moving production line devoted to what were called "physical exams." I stood bareassed naked in front of the final table behind which sat what I later concluded was an army psychiatrist. At the time I don't think I had more than a vague understanding of the word. It is certain I didn't know what this man's specialty was. In appearance he was set apart from the other doctors primarily by the thick lenses of the glasses he wore. I thought they might be a part of his professional equipment. They magnified his eyes to the point of grotesqueness. Maybe they gave him some kind of X-ray vision or something.

After hurriedly consulting the papers I handed him, he raised his eyes, blinked a couple of times, and looked me up and down.

"Hello, Lloyd," he said.

That was a switch. I hadn't been called anything better than "Mac" all day. I acknowledged his friendly overture with a tentative "hello."

He glanced down at his papers, looked up, and blinked as he surveyed me again.

"Lloyd," he asked, "do you like girls?"

I was not visibly moved by his question, if that is what he had expected, but I managed a hesitant, barely audible, "Yes, sir." I also believed the world was round, but if the army held a different opinion. . . .

There was brief silence. We blinked at each other. He may have had some doubts about me but made a little check on his paper and waved me on. Apparently I had passed his test, and he had found, I was about to say "uncovered," another guy who said he liked girls.

Later I thought of several clever answers I could have given to his question, but at the time the encounter was more confusing than anything else. Everything was confusing, nothing more so than the apparent hostility and verbal abuse. I went to sleep that first night with the thought, "My God! I have to put up with this for a whole year." The expression *little did I know* fit my total situation rather well.

The first few weeks at Leonard Wood, where I was shipped for basic training, brought more of the same. It was clear from the outset that I was not a natural-born soldier. But nobody had ever thought I was. My familiars would tell you, and have what they considered funny stories to illustrate the point, that I was never what you would call "handy." In basic training I had trouble mastering such things as how to roll a full field pack and pitch a pup tent in the approved manner. I also had problems on the rifle range and was classified as a "bolo" on my first try with the M1. When I finally qualified with the rifle, learned to field strip, clean, and reassemble it, all while blindfolded, I thought I had passed a major milestone. My respect for the army went up a notch, from a minus one to an even zero. If they could teach me that stuff, they could teach anyone.

I had far less difficulty mastering the rhetorical conventions and the improbable idiom of the infantry. I knew most of the words; it was largely a matter of stringing them together for maximum effect. But I didn't know, for example, that the post you were on was always the anus of creation. Nor had I realized there were so many different kinds of fornicators.

It was easy to detect the soldier's fondness for alliteration (in winter you could get as cold as a "whore's heart") and the demand for the extravagant and scatological greatly outweighed any concern for the probable. In those distant and unprogressive days "son of a bitch" remained the epithet of choice. And in the army I knew, a string of expletives or an interspersed expletive was considered the most appropriate way of supplying emphasis and feeling to a statement.

Consider, for example: "You're goddamn fuckin' well told" and "I'll guaran-fuckin'-tee you." The former, in its primary meaning may be translated as, "You are extremely well informed," while the latter signifies, "You have my absolute assurance in this matter." One or both these expressions might be anticipated, for example, if you were to say to a disgruntled acquaintance, "I understand you're putting in for a transfer." A simple positive or negative would not suffice. The softer language might suggest that your respondent was either halfhearted or indecisive, characteristics unbecoming a soldier. If, however, he didn't wish to reveal his plans, he might simply say, "Oh, blow it out your ass," another general-purpose expression which could be used as a substitute for or a supplement to an invitation for you to go have sexual intercourse with yourself.

It is not surprising that this language was sometimes enshrined in the record of court-martial proceedings. I found that out a little over a year later as a brand-new second lieutenant taking retreat with an infantry company at Camp Breckinridge, Kentucky. After the preliminaries were completed and before the flag was lowered, it was my duty on this occasion to read the results of recent courts-martial in the division for the spiritual uplift of the troops. Couched in formal military legalese, the document which I read at the top of my best military voice went somewhat as follows:

"Charge: Violation of the Ninety-sixth Article of War. Specification: In that on or about October 1, 1942, in the vicinity of Camp Breckinridge, Kentucky, Pvt. John Doe, 1234567, Co. A, 745th Infantry, did respond to a lawful order given by Corp. Richard Roe, 89101112, Co. A, 745th Infantry, a noncommissioned officer who was then in the execution of his office, by saying. 'Oh, blow it out your ass,' or words to that effect."

In the general laughter which followed I was unable for some time to finish reading the document. It gave the findings: guilty as charged. And the sentence: six months in the guardhouse with a forfeiture for six months of two-thirds of all pay and allowances.

A second example comes to mind. Toward the end of the war in Italy, a company commander in search of relaxation after a hard stint on the line found his way into a rear echelon, members-only officers' club. He was made to feel unwelcome there. In the fight which ensued, the military police were called and the captain taken into custody. He stood accused of a long train of abuses: using vulgar language in the presence of American nurses and WACs, starting a fight, resisting arrest, and referring to the arresting officer, among other things, as a "piss-complected muff diver."

My sympathies were, of course, with the company commander, whom I had always known to be a keen observer and a reliable informant. Under the circumstances I was glad that the captain had not been entirely content with the more familiar expressions of disesteem; I was disappointed the record did not provide relevant information about the arresting officer.

But all of this gets me ahead of my story, and I now return to basic training at Leonard Wood. As I became more proficient in the language, I began to make friends. In a chance encounter the first week, I met a man who had more problems than I. It was after supper. I was in the dayroom, scanning the next day's duty roster to see whether I had drawn KP or some other choice assignment. A voice behind me asked, "Is my name up there, Slim?" He gave me his name.

I looked around. Standing there was this little guy, about five feet, five inches tall and, I would guess, about thirty years old. To say that his uniform didn't fit would be the equivalent of saying that King Henry VIII was "the marrying kind." Without putting too fine a point on it, this recruit might well have been the original model for the "sad sack." The sleeves of his shirt and legs of his pants had been rolled up haphazardly. There was a hurt look in his watery, pale blue eyes. I moved aside so that he could get a better look at the board.

He asked again, "Is my name up there?" and added apologetically, "I never did learn to read."

I felt surprise and sympathy in about equal measure. To my knowledge I had never met a grown man who couldn't read his own name. "What was the name?" I asked, trying to conceal my reactions. He told me again. I looked back at the list and reported that both of us seemed to have escaped this time.

I saw him several times after that. He was not in my platoon, which meant that he didn't live in my barracks. We usually met in the dayroom after supper. One night we found a reasonably private spot, and I read him a letter which he had just received from his bride. The handwriting and the spelling were a bit difficult to make out, and the contents were neither memorable nor affectionate. It was as if his wife of a few weeks had, by the painful act of writing, made the ultimate sacrifice in demonstrating the great depth of her love. Although I offered to write a response if he would tell me what to say, he replied only that he would "study on it."

I didn't see him for several days after that and more or less forgot about him. When finally I made inquiries, I was told that he had gone "over the hill." Perhaps there were hidden meanings in that letter, some secret message which had escaped me. I never found out.

Going over the hill was not a live option for most of us. We stayed around. We complied. We adjusted. And—apart from the punishing hikes, the Mickey Mouse discipline, the endless repetition of training exercises, the spit-and-polish inspections, KP, guard duty, working in the pits on the rifle range, all interspersed with frequent examples of institutional madness—it was a breeze.

The infamous hikes provided the greatest physical stress. They were seldom more than twenty miles at a stretch, and I know that in the present athletic age people run that distance before breakfast every morning; but permit me to issue a challenge to anyone looking for new physical fitness worlds to conquer: Try marching twenty miles in army fatigues with a full field pack on a single canteen of water when the temperature is at one hundred degrees. You will need special equipment available at any army surplus store. And now permit me to specify the contents of the pack and to offer some advice.

Start with an extra pair of shoes and socks, a raincoat, a blanket, toilet articles, a face towel, a tent pole and pegs all rolled up neatly in a shelter half. To this you add a mess kit with utensils, a bayonet, a gas mask, a short-handled pick or shovel, a web belt containing at a minimum a canteen, canteen cup and first aid kit. And by all means, don't forget your "piece," which in my case was an M1 rifle. Consult your local arms dealer for this item. He is sure to have one in stock. Total weight of this *impedimenta*? How the hell should I know? We're talkin' about a pack I carried fifty years ago. You can't expect a man of my age to remember everything. To be on the conservative side, let's just say the pack weighed two hundred pounds, more if you carried field rations.

Before you move out, inspect your equipment carefully to see there are no straps which pinch, rub, or bind and nothing which can work loose to pound or gouge your flesh. Pay special attention to your feet, your toenails, your shoes and socks. Be advised that a condition to which you attach no significance at the outset can, after five miles, become a focus of attention, after ten miles a preoccupation, and after fifteen miles an agony. You don't want to fall out of the line of march, because I never fell out, and surely you can do as well as I.

You will move out at a slow and steady pace calculated to yield two and a half miles per hour, walking fifty minutes and resting ten. But your experience won't be comparable to mine unless you assemble a column of marching men extending as far as the eye can see to front and rear. Your squad and platoon will be marching around you, of course. It is only with such a contingent that you will be able to experience the full effect of the accordion movement which has afflicted marching troops since, as they say, "time immemorial." That, as I understand, extends back even before World War I.

The accordion movement operates somewhat as follows: The column in front will slow without warning and for reasons which will forever remain a mystery. You will then be forced to shorten your stride and reduce your cadence to avoid running over the man in front. The slower movement will continue for several minutes until you have become adjusted to it. Then, suddenly, for reasons which again you cannot fathom, the column in front will take off, as we used to say, "like a big-assed bird." Now you must lengthen your stride to its fullest extent and break into a run to catch up. So much for the slow and steady pace.

This movement can be repeated until you feel yourself lurching rather than hiking down the road. In the best of times, it is tiring and irritating; under the worst conditions, when you think you are already taxed to the limits of human endurance, it can be "the last fuckin' straw" and produce a kind of paranoia which manifests itself in the suspicion that such tricks have been cunningly devised as a means of developing your killer instinct.

I don't mean to suggest that your hike will be all blood, tears, toil, and sweat. The early-morning coolness of the first couple of hours should be reasonably pleasant. There will be adequate time to view the picture-postcard scenery typical of military reservations. There will be opportunity to banter with friends, to catch up on the latest latrine rumors, and perhaps to originate a few wild stories yourself. The dominant mood in the ranks will be lighthearted. It should not be difficult to avoid tapping your canteen during this period.

As the sun nears its zenith, however, conversation will lag, and the irrepressible comics in the ranks will have to work harder for their laughs. Now you will be thrown back on your inner resources. You may want to recite poetry to yourself, work on the multiplication tables, try to list in chronological order the presidents of the United States, anything to keep your mind off the heat and your need for water. You should realize that when your canteen is empty, you can neither ask for nor expect anyone to give you a drink from theirs. Such things are not done. If a weaker squad member is tottering and in obvious danger of going down, it is legitimate, even commendable, to give him a breather by carrying his piece or his pack for him, but altruism ends at water's edge. And don't let anyone carry your equipment for you.

By the middle of the afternoon at the latest, the sick, lame, and lazy will begin to drop out. They await an uncertain fate. Your resolve to continue the march will harden at the sight of them. Have not the noncoms said this hike will separate the men from the boys?

By late afternoon your canteen will be empty. You won't be able to keep your mind off water any longer. You may find yourself fantasizing about your next weekend pass, when you plan to take a comfortable hotel room, fill the bathtub with water, add ice cubes to taste, climb into the tub, and sip the water while you luxuriate in its coolness. When you reach this stage, you are in a position to appreciate the lines in Kipling's *Gunga Din* which proclaim:

> You may talk of gin and beer when you're quartered safe out here,
> . . . .
> But when it comes to slaughter, you'll do your work on water.
> And you'll lick the bloomin' boots of 'um that's got it.

When you close into your bivouac area, drink as much water as you want as soon as it is available. I have never known anyone to suffer from such indulgence. If the PX tent has preceded you into the field, you may want to purchase and drink several bottles of soda. Four bottles should be about as much as you will want and all you can carry conveniently in your two hands. All of this liquid may not restoreth the soul, but it does wonders for the body.

You will have learned some simple lessons from the hike: the central importance of perseverance, your capacity to go on longer than you thought you could, and, above all, you will have learned, not at just an intellectual but at a gut level, that water is truly a precious, life-giving commodity. And so good luck and good marching while I take a well-deserved rest in the shade and return to my story.

When basic training was over, we were "turned to duty" and moved to Little Rock, Arkansas, for participation in the Louisiana maneuvers, said at the time to be the largest such peacetime exercises in the history of the Republic. For all I know the high command may have drawn intellectual stimulation and greatly enhanced professional competence from these war games; for the rest of us there was almost unrelieved boredom and strenuous exertion in meaningless movement from one bad bivouac area to another. We marched and countermarched through some of the most desolate parts of Arkansas, Louisiana, and Texas, pretending we were in the presence of an enemy other than the heat and our officers and non-coms. To the daytime rigors of the hike were added the nighttime discomforts of prickly heat, insect bites, and patches of skin exposed to poison ivy while we were creeping and crawling through the underbrush.

But nothing lasts forever. When the games were over, we moved back to Leonard Wood for advanced training. I received my first furlough. Back on the post by the middle of October, I drew a winter uniform and decided to take advantage of my limited educational experience. Since I had worked on my high school newspaper, I applied for and became, without any competition, insofar as I know, company correspondent for our regimental publication *Semper Primus.* And since I had lettered in football as an undersized and substitute running back for what is now Springfield Central High School, I drew equipment and was looking forward to a season in which I would be relieved from KP and other mundane features of garrison life.

Things didn't turn out that way. I didn't have access to a typewriter for my newspaper work, and the football squad, for some reason, never even assembled for practice. It is written: "You can't win them all," but verily, verily I say unto you that you can't win any of them with luck such as that.

I was much more fortunate in securing frequent weekend passes to visit Springfield, some ninety miles down Highway 66 to the southwest. In those uncomplicated days hitchhiking was a safe, economical, rapid, and dependable mode of travel for a man in uniform. If I passed Saturday morning inspection under the less than benign eyes of our company commander, I could usually get a pass, be on the highway outside the post by noon, and in Springfield before sundown. The return trip was usually made on Sunday night by the last Greyhound bus, which left for the post at about 9:30 p.m.

I was on a weekend pass when Pearl Harbor permanently changed all of our lives. The momentous news was slow to reach me. On that gloomy, overcast Sunday afternoon, I had taken my first and only girl to see Lillian Hellman's *The Little Foxes.* About 9:15 p.m. I made my way to the Greyhound station. My darkened bus, already almost full, was waiting on the side ready for its trip back to the post.

I had come to expect on these occasions that my fellow passengers, exhausted from a weekend of strenuous relaxation, would be sleeping quietly throughout the journey. That night was different from all other nights. As I climbed aboard, I heard a low buzz of conversation overridden from time to time by louder voices commenting on the still-unfolding events and speculating on the shape of things to come. When it became clear to me that the Japanese had attacked at a place called Pearl Harbor, my first impulse was to get off the bus and return home for one last, long, lingering farewell. My more rational self prevailed, however, and I sank back in my seat to ponder dismally on my uncertain future.

On Monday morning, December 8, the company assembled in the mess hall after breakfast. Our company officers now emphasized, somewhat gleefully, I thought, the indefinite extension of our military obligations and the increased severity of penalties for violating certain Articles of War. There was no information about the division's plans for the immediate future. They didn't tell us much of anything we didn't already know.

Training continued more or less as usual. The weather took a turn, and bivouacs in the snow became an added feature of infantry life. Actually these campouts were not so bad unless you happened to have a preference for keeping warm at night.

In the early spring of 1942 our first sergeant announced at a retreat formation that a call for infantry officer school candidates had come down. There was no mention of the requirements for candidacy. I heard the announcement without any thought that it had implications for me. I didn't see myself as officer material.

No one ever consulted me about OCS, and I was considerably surprised one day to find I had been nominated to attend. I don't even remember how I was notified. I think the first sergeant called me in to let me know. He probably wanted to see what I looked like. Lacking the capacity to attract attention by my positive qualities as a soldier, I had sought the protection which anonymity brings in all large organizations. "Maintaining a low profile" is, I believe, the current expression for it.

It was my "college education" which had to be the determining factor in my selection since I had nothing else going for me. I learned at this time that in a company of two hundred men I was one of two people who had any college credit whatsoever. The other man was our company clerk. I knew him only on sight because I had consciously avoided the orderly room where he worked. He was already a noncommissioned officer; I held the almost automatically granted rank of private first class. In a flurry of paperwork, I was promoted to corporal and thereby, I gather, made eligible for admission to OCS.

Knowing a little more now than I knew then about the operation of bureaucracies, I have concluded that the first sergeant, wanting to score points with higher headquarters and assure that his unit had at least token representation in the officer candidate pool, had gone to the extreme of nominating me. He probably consulted my platoon sergeant to find out if I could be spared. I don't suppose the sergeant had to agonize very long before giving his answer. In any case, according to *Semper Primus* in a story I had nothing to do with, let me say, the regiment furnished a total of thirteen candidates to the Ft. Benning class scheduled to begin on May 20, 1942. I was one of the thirteen.

I felt no elation at having been selected. While I didn't underestimate the advantages of officer status, I had serious reservations. By that time I had found a home in the First Infantry Regiment. My friends, Wilhelm, Treem, Gaunt, "Hoot Owl," Jaspering, "Indian," et al. were in my squad. I knew at least by sight most of the unusual characters in the regiment. They included, for example, an improbable high-ranking, white haired officer who, conducted by his jeep driver and with an umbrella held carefully above his head to ward off the sun, would sometimes appear as unexpectedly as an apparition at summer time training sites to give us the benefit of his grandfatherly advice on such subjects as water discipline and venereal disease. I would miss such people. Besides, I had picked up on the idiosyncratic speech patterns of our first sergeant and could, on appropriate occasions, provide a pretty fair imitation. All this would be lost when I shipped out.

Other things would be lost as well. There were certain advantages to being a private first class, a certain freedom in being unfree. I had begun to develop a small modicum of confidence that I might be able to acquit myself in combat honorably enough to keep the Wells name clean, but I was not at all sure that I could, or that I wanted to lead other men. More importantly, I was not at all sure I could pass the course. That was really the bottom line.

Once the selection had been made, however, the thought of trying to decline never entered my mind. Having developed a kind of fatalism which enabled me to go where I was told, I regarded OCS as another assignment. I had not volunteered for it; I would make no objections to it. If my superiors wanted me to go to Ft. Benning, I would go to Ft. Benning. And it might turn out all right.

Chapter 2

Ninety-Day Wonder

In the early summer of 1942 the Infantry Officer Candidate School at Ft. Benning, Georgia, was engaged in a crash program to turn out a new cohort of second lieutenants of infantry every three months. Sometimes derided as "ninety-day wonders" by the skeptical and irreverent, the graduates of Benning were to become the platoon leaders, the company executive officers and the company commanders of World War II. Only very rarely could an OCS graduate realistically aspire to a rank higher than that of captain; but it was equally rare to find an infantry officer at the company level who had not been commissioned at Benning.

My most glaring weakness at OCS was, as I had anticipated, a lack of leadership experience. Almost all the other candidates had been buck sergeants or staff sergeants, and there was at least one former first sergeant on the class roll. Some were National Guard, others regular army. All of them seemed older than I.

School regulations prevented a candidate from openly flaunting his prior rank. Although I saw one guy adjusting to the new democracy by rather ostentatiously removing his staff sergeant stripes with a razor blade, such a show was not necessary to establish the identity of the seasoned noncoms. Their behavior on the drill field told the story. They had the confidence which goes with the experience of saying to one man, "Go," and he goeth, and to another, "Come," and he cometh. It was equally obvious that I and three or four other former pfcs lacked that experience.

We were told at the outset we would be subjected to "peer evaluation," and that information tended to make us self-conscious. I don't know how else to explain the subdued behavior of the candidates on my floor of the barracks.

There was little joking, no "pissing and moaning," and almost no horseplay during the entire three months. Conversation, usually carried on in well-modulated tones, never reached out to include everybody on the floor. We were in bed by lights out. Apart from two New York National Guard candidates who seemed to be the best of friends and the aggressors in a rather childish feud with southern boys in another barracks, social relationships on my floor tended to be highly impersonal. The almost sedate atmosphere was in sharp contrast to the life I had known in the enlisted barracks at Leonard Wood.

I made no close friends at Benning and missed the ones I had left behind. On the weekends I slept, wrote letters, read, studied, and went to the movies. Others seemed to be doing much the same. Sometimes we teamed up for excursions to the post exchange or the theater, but our conversations never got beyond bland superficialities. We never exchanged confidences, admitted doubts or confessed weaknesses, fearing, I suppose, that anything we said or did might be used against us.

There were other psychological pressures. The tone was set in the first couple of weeks when the uncertainty of successfully completing the course became obvious to us all. The daily barracks inspections, carried out while the candidates were in the field, began to produce a rather strange result as revealed by the record of our derelictions posted on the bulletin board.

The former first sergeant seemed to be singled out for special attention. He began to collect demerits for nonobvious reasons. The black marks mounted alarmingly. The man was gigged almost every day for something, a slight misalignment of his bed, a speck of dust on his shelf, an unbuttoned shirt in his footlocker, etc. For the rest of us, the inspections seemed only a little more rigorous than usual and the sergeant appeared to be anything other than a sloppy soldier. The whispers were that they were "out to get old sarge," who looked to be in his mid-forties.

One morning after breakfast the announcement came into the barracks over the loudspeaker that he was to report to the orderly room at 0900 hours or some such time. He didn't accompany us to the field. When we returned to the barracks at the end of the day, he was gone. His cot had been removed and all traces of him obliterated. There were whispers but no general talk about either the man or the incident. It was as if he had become a nonperson.

As the course progressed, other candidates who didn't have a large number of demerits were held back for reasons you could only speculate about. They, too, were instructed to report to the orderly room and sometimes they, too, had disappeared without a trace by day's end. At other times, however, they would either join us in the field or we would find them waiting in the barracks on our return, acting as if nothing had happened. Neither the disappearances nor the miraculous second comings were talked about openly.

One day, two or three weeks before graduation, I was held back. Reflecting on the worst-case scenario, I immediately surmised I had ranked consistently low on peer evaluation and the tactical officers had decided I was too immature, too shy, too much of a loner to be trusted with the lives of others. I could have made out a good case against myself.

By this time I very much wanted to finish the course and get my commission. The stigma of failure was more than enough to outweigh earlier ambivalence. Among other things, expectations had been built up on the home front. Upon my admission to OCS, the occasion was duly noted by my hometown newspaper, the *Springfield Leader and Press,* which included in its account a picture of the smiling candidate, a picture supplied, no doubt, by my proud parents. What now, o promising young man?

I went to the orderly room at the appointed time. A panel of four or five tactical officers sat behind a long table looking very official, very stern. I saluted, reported in the prescribed manner, and was invited to sit down.

The interview took an unexpected turn from the outset. My judges immediately began to chastise me because my belt buckle didn't have a high shine. They asked if I really wanted to be an officer; I told them I did. Then why in the name of all that is holy had I appeared before them so shabbily dressed?

When they persisted in this line of questioning, I remember telling them I had assumed a decision to dismiss me might already have been made on more substantial grounds. What would those grounds be, they wanted to know. Well, I suggested, academic performances might be more important. I was trying to deflect the inquiry into an area where I knew I had done at least passably well.

They would have none of that. Did I think that becoming an officer required only the ability to pass a few simple written tests? Of course, I didn't think that. The tactical commander insisted that no decision had been made in my case; but now . . . well! It was obvious I didn't understand how important it was for an officer to set an example for his men.

Having settled that matter to their satisfaction, they moved on to other considerations. One member of the panel presented me with a tactical problem and wanted to know what orders I would give as a platoon leader for dealing with the situation. I brightened a little. Now was my chance to show I had learned something. I might be able to redeem myself. But when I gave them my answer, they acted as if they could hardly credit their ears. An embarrassing silence followed. There were no follow-up questions.

They gave me a second chance with another problem. Same results. The impatience of the panel was becoming evident. How, their attitude seemed to ask, did this clown ever get here in the first place?

At this point the tactical commander asked whether I still thought I was capable of leading a platoon. I told him I thought I was just as capable as any second lieutenant I had ever seen. That was a truthful answer although I didn't know I felt that way until the words were out of my mouth. Apparently it was also a safe answer. There were no second lieutenants on the panel.

There was more thrust and parry. I don't recall that anything was ever said about my academic standing or the results of my peer evaluations. After about an hour, the tactical commander terminated the ordeal, insisting again that no decision had been made in my case but shaking his head sadly over the sorry figure I had cut in the interview. I rejoined the company.

I wasn't sure of getting my commission until the very last moment. On the night before graduation, however, I accompanied another candidate into Columbus for what must have been the tamest celebration in the annals of military history. It was not a night to remember, although it was my first trip off the post in three months. We probably had dinner and went to a movie. I recall only stopping at one of the local bars for a nightcap and startling the cocktail waitress by ordering a whiskey sour. It was the only mixed drink I had heard of.

Next morning I reflected briefly on the possibility that I might be pulled out of ranks before the commissioning ceremony. It was a bit late in the game but anything could happen. I thought about the fate of the former first sergeant. His example demonstrated that anyone could be dismissed. Did the school now want to show that a candidate could be dismissed at any time? Would I become an object lesson for future classes? Would my sad story become a legend to be told and retold at future class reunions? I could just hear someone saying, "Remember that poor little bastard—what was his name? Washed out on the last day and they shipped him off to Guadalcanal."

We assembled after breakfast. The company was called to attention, and the tactical commander proceeded to inspect the ranks. He stopped in front of me only long enough to say, "I see your brass is well polished this morning," to which I replied, "Yes, sir." Then and then only was I sure that the prize had been won. I would become a ninety-day wonder, the only wonder being that I had made it through.

I went home on leave for a couple of weeks, adequate time to show off my new uniform. My parents took me around to call on their close friends. I visited my grandmother, who called me "her little soldier boy." My exalted rank failed to impress her. She wouldn't have known a second lieutenant's uniform from that of a grand admiral in the Swiss navy. In a major step upward in our relationship, my dad bought me a beer. The friendly bartender asked him, jokingly, I hoped, whether I was old enough to drink.

But I spent most of my time, as I had intended, with my intended. Neither of us wanted to get married in the uncertainty facing us. We parted with our understanding fully intact but without making excessive demands on each other. She got ready to go back to school; I left for my first assignment.

When I reported to Camp Breckinridge in September of 1942, I found a post less than half completed. In the infantry regiments a small cadre of officers and noncoms was in place. Additional officers to fill out the table of organization were arriving daily, but the recruits had yet to put in an appearance. There was no place to house them, no mess halls to feed them, no supply rooms to equip them. We had been hurried to Breckinridge to wait.

Several weeks elapsed before the basic structures were in place. During this time the company officers had little to do. Calisthenics and a training schedule of sorts kept us somewhat busy in the mornings. In the afternoons we slept and gambled. A few enterprising young officers, no doubt operating on the principle of first things first, busied themselves with fashioning a bar, complete with jukebox, in our battalion officers' quarters. And at night we drank and caroused in Evansville, Indiana, which lay just across the Ohio River about thirty miles from the post.

In those days before the troops came in, Evansville was a fun place for soldiers. There were plenty of respectable and not so respectable bars, hotels, and restaurants. There were big city amenities which I had never known, a racetrack, a major nightclub and gambling casino. And there were more unattached females than I had ever seen in my life.

Women of all ages were employed at the shipyards, where "liberty ships" were being turned out at what was said to be a fantastic rate. And then there were the coeds at Evansville University. By this time, of course, the draft had affected Evansville as it had other places. Most of the eligible men were gone from both the town and the campus. Under the circumstances members of the Breckinridge cadre were welcomed almost everywhere, I think it more or less accurate to say, "with open arms." I was glad I wasn't married.

On my first trip into Evansville, another junior officer and I had dinner in one of the better restaurants in town. Shortly after we were seated, a representative of the management came over to welcome us. After a brief conversation, he urged us to order anything we wanted on the house. When we chose steak, he turned to our waiter and said, "Bring these gentlemen the very best steaks we have and put it on my account." We thanked him, of course. It was good to be appreciated. "Lieutenant" sounded ever so much better than "Mac." As we waited for our dinner, we drank Rum and Coca-Cola and listened to the jukebox play "That Old Black Magic." Yes, I reflected, it was good to be "an officer and a gentleman."

When, finally, the recruits came into camp, most of us were glad to see them. The long layoff had left us bored, jaded, and physically out of shape. With the beginning of basic training the frequency of our visits to Evansville lessened and our physical condition rapidly improved.

My initial experience as a platoon leader was a confidence builder, primarily because I was blessed with an outstanding platoon sergeant and excellent squad leaders. With few exceptions the recruits were also of first-rate quality. I liked and respected them; they seemed to reciprocate. Under the direction of the noncoms, the platoon more or less operated itself.

We got our first look at enemy soldiers with the arrival at Breckinridge of a contingent of German POW's, remnants, we were told, of Rommel's *Afrika Korps.* We eyed them with curiosity as they marched down the roads in perfect step, singing in harmony. They, in turn, watched us with what I interpreted as a mix of amused tolerance and haughty disdain as we marched by when they were taking a break in the fields by the side of the road.

The German troops were impressive. They appeared to be of uniform height, about five feet, nine inches tall, young, husky, tanned, disciplined. Someone at our higher headquarters, influenced, perhaps, by the German marching songs, decided that American soldiers should sing too. They designated as our marching song a then-popular little ditty called "This Is the Army, Mr. Jones." Whatever the tune may have had to recommend it as a popular song, it sounded lightweight and frivolous coming halfheartedly from the discordant voices of a column of raggedly marching men. I never ordered my platoon to sing in the presence of the enemy. I didn't want to be accused of giving aid and comfort to the *Afrika Korps.* They didn't seem to need either.

Training curtailed but did not eliminate the social life to which we had become accustomed. Many of us still made our weekend trips to Evansville, which by now was clogged with troops and experiencing the usual problems which attend that kind of commercial success. For those who chose to stay on the post, the battalion officers' bars were always open, and there must have been regimental, division, and post officers' clubs as well. I never had occasion to inquire.

What in an earlier day would have been called Bachelor Officers' Quarters housed at Breckinridge the unmarried, the nominally married, and the truly married, although the latter group was by far the smallest of the three. We unmarrieds were quartered two to a room. There were two closets, space for two cots, two footlockers, two nightstands. We shared a single window. My roommate, a relatively quiet man in his late thirties, was regular army and had given up a master sergeant's stripes in dubious exchange for a second lieutenant's bars. He had been in Panama, in Hawaii, in the Philippines, and on every domestic post you could think of. He had used up more ink signing the payroll, he told us, then we had drunk GI coffee. At Breckinridge he was having second thoughts about his decision to go to OCS. Being quartered with me after having been accustomed to considerably more privacy and deference may have had something to do with his soul-searching.

Smitty, as he was called, usually stayed on the post. He was too wise and mature to party very much with the other platoon leaders, but he sometimes enlivened our otherwise dull routines in unexpected ways. On one memorable evening in the line of duty, he and I took advantage of a once-in-a-lifetime opportunity to chew out a colonel, our regimental commander.

Let me try to keep a short story short. On the weekend before the events of which I speak, the MP's in Evansville had picked up a number of our enlisted men for being out of uniform, failure to salute, etc. Someone at a higher headquarters, we assumed it was the colonel in question, had seen fit to blame the laxness of junior officers for these offenses. Our battalion, and perhaps others for all I know, was restricted to the post for the following weekend, and company officers, including Smitty and me, were assigned MP duty in Evansville for the purpose of putting on report any other soldiers so poorly trained as to disgrace the uniforms they wore.

Early Saturday evening, pursuant to our assignment, Smitty and I tied MP bands around our arms and checked out a jeep with Smitty as driver. Taking a bottle along against the night air, we drank judiciously and managed to stay reasonably sober. As we cruised Evansville, we stopped to admonish a few of the worst malefactors, but I don't recall that we took any names. About 0200 hours we started back to the post.

Before turning in, one of us had the idea of checking out the Trocadero, the rather swanky nightclub and gambling casino alluded to earlier. It was on our way out of town, in an area along the river known as "no man's land" because neither Kentucky nor Indiana took responsibility for law enforcement there, or so we had been told by the locals.

By the time we arrived at the Trocadero in the cool, cool, cool of the evening, singing filled the air, and the party had a tad more than a glow on. There was interesting activity on the long portico which marked the entrance to the club. Some people were just arriving, others leaving, while still others were lingering unpredictably. One of the first things I noticed was a solitary officer leaning off the portico, puking into the grass. The odds were six to five that he would be going back inside after he had emptied his belly. Nearby a young couple, heterosexual as was the custom in those days, were bearing public witness to the very high regard in which they held each other. I would have bet ten to one that they would be leaving soon. Sitting on the steps off to one side was a full colonel, indeed, one could say with accuracy, a very full colonel.

His cap was off, his thin hair awry, his coat unbuttoned. The collar of his shirt had been loosened, allowing his tie to hang down almost to his navel in a most unmilitary manner. The colonel was out of uniform. No question about it. As Smitty and I got back into the jeep, I inquired "Do you know who that was?"

"Who?" asked my roommate.

"That," I reported, "was Colonel Demerest."

"Are you sure?" asked Smitty.

To which I replied, "You have my absolute assurance in this matter," or words to that effect.

"Then let's go back and arrest that old son of a bitch," was the unhesitating response.

It had been a rather dull evening. Arresting the colonel seemed to me just the thing to do. I followed dutifully along, allowing my partner to do the talking.

"On your feet, soldier," ordered the fearless second lieutenant as we stood above the colonel.

"I'm sick," moaned the poor colonel.

"I don't give a damn," sneered my partner. "Get on your feet."

The colonel struggled to comply.

"What's your name?" Smitty demanded.

"I am Colonel Demerest," his victim mumbled.

My partner ignored this meek confession. "Button your coat. Straighten your tie. Where's your cap?" The words were snapped out just as if we were dealing with a raw recruit. The colonel complied as quickly as he could. When at last he had retrieved his cap and straightened it on his head, Smitty appraised his appearance with a critical eye.

"That's better," he acknowledged gruffly. "Now if you are who you say you are, I suggest that you go home or at least get off the street. You're a disgrace to the uniform." With that parting shot, our duty having been discharged with fine impartiality, we went home to bed.

We heard no more of the incident and felt no repercussions from it. Nor did I fear we would. My confidence in my roommate's assessment, representing as it did the judgment of an experienced old army hand, was complete. As Smitty sized it up, there was a good chance the colonel wouldn't even remember the encounter in the morning. Even if he did recall it, he could not be sure of who had accosted him and could have no interest in publicizing the incident.

Life went on. My tour at Breckinridge continued into the summer of 1943. Somewhere along the line I and most of the other second lieutenants who were commissioned when I was were promoted to first lieutenant. As far as I was concerned, it was much like being promoted from private to private first class. I assume others looked at it the same way. With the exception of the officer candidates at Benning, there were very few people of my acquaintance, either in the States or overseas, who were bucking for promotion. The higher rank of first lieutenant meant, of course, a slight increase in pay but made little difference in assignments. (In my division in Italy almost all platoons and some companies were commanded, at least temporarily, by first lieutenants.) The big jump was from first lieutenant to captain, and relatively few made that leap. As a rule, it came, I should say, only to those who were both capable and lucky enough to be in the right place at the right time.

In midsummer, we were sent once again on maneuvers. This time the state of Tennessee was graced by our presence. Operations were on a somewhat smaller scale than I had experienced as an enlisted man, but being an enlisted man or a junior officer made little difference. I recorded only two incidents which relieved the hard work and boredom.

One of these, the high point of the exercises as far as I was concerned, was the time in the wilderness when, on a taut army blanket, I broke up a crap game by winning all the money anyone was foolish enough to bet against me. Such was my confidence in my luck that, toward the end, I was shooting "all or any part" of $100 against a collection of dispirited but still unbelieving friends. It was a big game, and since there was nothing else to break the monotony, it attracted an audience. I came away with something like $1,200, most of which I wired home to the girl I was absolutely sure I would marry if I lived long enough to marry anyone.

The other incident had more profound and longer lasting consequences. Toward the close of maneuvers, I and several other junior officers in the division received orders pulling us out of the field and directing us to report to Ft. Meade, Maryland, some ten days later. We knew we were slated for overseas duty, presumably to the African or European theater. That, at the very least, was a big break. No one I knew wanted to go to the Pacific. From what we heard, they were fighting a miserable and bloody war out there.

On balance, I was not sorry to receive the call. I had, after all, been in the army over two years and had been around the block twice, once as an enlisted man, once as a ninety-day wonder. If I was ever going to be ready, I should be ready now. Just as actors, actresses, and athletes must find it difficult to maintain enthusiasm for their work when they are called upon to rehearse constantly for a play which is never performed or to practice for a game which is never played, I would have found it difficult to continue playing soldier for the remainder of the war. In the past year I had been cast in the role of instructing enlisted men on how to conduct themselves in combat and was keenly aware that I really didn't know what I was talking about. It was time to find out. It was time to undergo the test.

It was not that I wanted to be a hero. Nor was I eager to do my bit for the war effort. I had no burning hatred for the enemy. Insofar as I had thought about it at all in the past two years, I had assumed without question that the war we were fighting was a just war, but I never doubted we would win it with or without my help. Not patriotism but boredom, some sense of obligation, perhaps, but, more important, a sense of adventure, of curiosity, and a desire to prove myself allowed me to accept my orders without regret.

If other junior officers felt differently, and some of them probably did, they said nothing about it. All of us had time to visit home for the purpose of "putting our affairs in order," as was said. A few availed themselves of the opportunity. But my affairs, never very complicated, were already in order. Most of my salary had already been allotted to my mom and dad. I had the usual $10,000 GI insurance policy with them as beneficiaries. My prospective bride and I understood each other. What else was there to arrange?

Under the circumstances, a brief trip home could only culminate in a series of tearful farewells, an ordeal for all concerned. I quickly joined the large group of junior officers who had decided to head straight for New York City. We would have time for one last fling, working our way down the coast as time permitted. It might just be the only opportunity we would have to see a vital part of our native land.

Chapter 3

Innocent Abroad

For the first twenty years of my life, almost all of my travel had been within a small area of southwest Missouri. We had close relatives on farms in Christian County and in the nearby towns of Clever, Republic, and Billings. Grandparents, great-uncles Jim and Enoch, aunts Mary, Ethel, and Veva, along with innumerable cousins lived in this area. Every thirtieth of May without fail we decorated family graves and held an informal reunion at Wise Hill Cemetery just north of Clever. Sometimes, later in the summers, we took brief but exciting excursions into Harold Bell Wright's *Shepherd of the Hills* country between Branson and what is now Silver Dollar City.

Longer trips were rare occurrences. Some were subsidized, as was my high school football travel to Coffeyville, Kansas. Prior to 1941 I had never been north or east of St. Louis nor west of Tulsa, Oklahoma, although I had ventured south into Arkansas a few times and once got as far as Springdale to visit a cousin. Two years in the military had broadened my horizons: the army had sent me farther east to Evansville, Indiana, and, at government expense, I had traveled south to Ft. Benning, Georgia. Nor was that all. On several occasions I had been to dimly lit restaurants where cocktails were served. I had learned to order steak, medium well, vinegar-and-oil dressing on the salad, and a baked potato, dry, please. Would the lieutenant like an after-dinner drink? Well, bring me a Napoleon brandy. No, on second thought, better make that a Courvoisier.

Still, I knew there was an even bigger world out there. As an infantry unit commander in transit to serve his country, I would now have opportunities to visit faraway places with romantic sounding names, places such as New York, New York, Washington, D.C., and Ft. Meade, Maryland. I looked forward to the great adventure of just being in such exotic places.

Unlike the railroads of the postwar period, the passenger train which took us to the East Coast in the summer of 1943 was not troubled by problems of "idle capacity." It was packed with a mixed crowd of service people whose destinations and reasons for travel could easily be surmised and a few civilians whose purposes remained a mystery. All the seats were filled. People were sitting on their luggage in the aisles. Although it was not easy to negotiate passage from one car to another, the mood of passengers was friendly, cooperative, and gay (in the earlier sense of the word).

I still remember the face and the figure of the attractive older lady—she must have been at least thirty-five, maybe forty—who made a place for me at her table in the lounge car. I lingered there as the train sped through the night. I don't know how long the trip took, but despite the crowding and inconvenience, it was the most exciting train ride of my life.

New York City was partially blacked out when I saw it for the first time. German submarines, we were told, lurked offshore and preyed on merchant ships with supplies bound for England, North Africa, and elsewhere. Since the lights of the city silhouetted our ships to the advantage of the U-boat marauders, a partial blackout had been decreed. It mattered little to me. It was enough just to be in New York. The blackout simply added to the excitement.

At this time my circle of companions was constantly changing, expanding, contracting, and changing again. A chance encounter could lead to an invitation for drinks and subsequently to an expedition into the night for dinner, more drinks, new encounters, new adventures. Despite all that was said, I found New Yorkers to be friendly people. At least they were kind to servicemen. One night I had four or five other junior officers bedded down in a double room at the Governor Clinton Hotel. The management knew of our arrangement and made no objections. Much later I read some place that two Nazi saboteurs put ashore by submarine at about this time had found their way into the city and to temporary lodging at the Governor Clinton. Apparently, unknown to either the hotel or ourselves, my companions and I had enjoyed the hospitality of an equal opportunity hostelry.

On another occasion I fell in with a young officer who had friends at

Yank magazine headquartered in Manhattan. We went there, were provided with female companionship and treated to a guided tour of some of the more interesting nightspots in the vicinity.

But shortly the clock, as they say in closely contested football games, became a factor. By my calculations, I had two time-outs left, so I moved on down the coast to Baltimore and then to Washington.

In Baltimore there was an unpleasant encounter with some sailors in the blackest blackout possible. I will never know why they started throwing punches when one of our party accidentally jostled one of their party in the dark. And, then, there was the sorry emotional state of a newly found companion who, in the course of barhopping around town, became preoccupied with a fortune teller's prediction that he would soon find "a watery grave." He would not be consoled even by the thought that the fortune teller was probably an enemy agent. Deciding that Baltimore was a sailor's town, I quit that city by the dawn's early light.

In Washington I met four or five old friends from home, unfortunate contemporaries who, for one reason or another, had been classified as 4F in the draft. Having been rejected for military service, they had taken government jobs and moved to the already overcrowded District of Columbia. Their problems did not end with apartment hunting. They had just about given up going out, they told me, because they could no longer face the question, "Why aren't you in uniform?" It was an inquiry which came trippingly to the tongues of waitresses, cashiers, unattached females, and others with whom they had more than momentary contact. My friends to a man expressed regret that they were not going with me. Knowing them, I didn't doubt their sincerity. Neither they nor I wanted to be shunted aside from the greatest adventure of a lifetime. I was the lucky one.

When I reported to Meade at the appointed time, I found, as I had more or less expected, that going off to war was no simple matter. We were confined to the post for processing. That meant more physical exams, more immunizations, more papers to fill out. In what the army must have regarded as due course, we were moved to Newport News, Virginia, where there was more waiting, new equipment to be drawn, more instructions. Finally after the bureaucratic machinery had exhausted its efforts on our behalf, we were herded into liberty ships bound, we were told, for Oran, Algeria.

The trip compared unfavorably with most others I had taken under military auspices. Perhaps I had expected too much. As a Missouri high school boy I had acquired, primarily through the poetry of John Masefield, a most unrealistic view of the sea and of the men who go down to the sea in ships. This voyage destroyed forever my romantic illusions about the seafaring life. We had barely cleared the harbor when I was led to reflect that John Masefield had never crossed the Atlantic on a crowded liberty ship in wartime.

Contrary to all my expectations, the sea around us had a dirty, greenish cast. The frequent oil slicks and the garbage floating in the water combined with the slow, seemingly aimless movements of the ship to give one the impression of being adrift on a cesspool. The voyage was prolonged for almost a month as we moved in convoy, zigging and zagging at the speed of the slowest ship, quite possibly, someone suggested, the *Nina,* the *Pinta,* or the *Santa Maria.* Most of our time was spent below.

Our sleeping accommodations consisted of canvas hammocks suspended one above another from the floor to the ceiling. They hung so close you couldn't raise your knees without bumping the rump of the guy above. For the most part we slept in our uniforms, which quickly became soiled by the grease which had been applied generously to the exposed machinery of the ship. We were supplied with much-used, greasy life jackets, which we were supposed to wear, or at least to keep near us, at all times. A thin skim of oily dirt covered the floor. Showers were available at scheduled times; but the only thing coming from the shower heads was a cold, brackish, salt water, and it came in irregular and unpredictable bursts.

For four or five hours each day at carefully assigned times groups of us were allowed to occupy narrow spaces on the deck. In good weather this respite was most welcome. Even in less than good weather many of us went on deck when allowed to do so to escape the stale air and the foul smells below. On the basis of impressionistic, but I thought, very convincing evidence, I estimated that roughly two-thirds of the American army was uncontrollably flatulent.

Sometimes during our periods on deck, sleek destroyers operating at some distance from our ship would provide brief excitement by knifing through the water at high speed to positions on the periphery of the convoy. We could then hear the dull booms of their depth charges and sometimes the sharper crack of their surface weapons. At first we assumed that our friends in the navy were waging a heroic struggle against enemy submarines. But when their activity persisted on a somewhat regular schedule and failed to produce any observable results, we more or less concluded that we were witnessing routine naval exercises and target practice. That took the edge off our interest.

There was a storm. Our ship pitched and tossed like a raft in white water. During all of one night I heard the sounds of crockery breaking in what the sailors called the galley. Daylight brought no relief. Many of my fellow travelers became seasick, and the smell of their vomit did nothing to improve the quality of the air. I avoided contributing to the common misery only by remaining in a prone position on my bunk until the storm subsided.

To cap it all off, there was more than adequate reason to complain of the food. Army personnel were fed in more or less continuous shifts, two meals a day, each meal consisting for the most part, or so it seemed to me, of dehydrated eggs and dehydrated potatoes. I knew we were in real trouble the second day out when I began to wish for a can of cold hash or a can of meat and beans, both of which were staples in the army C ration. Feeling hunger pangs, I was shocked to learn that members of the crew, eating three meals a day, and experiencing the taste of real meat, were selling steak sandwiches to army personnel at the outrageous, unheard-of price of one dollar per sandwich. Such was my contempt for these ignoble transactions, reflecting as they did on both seller and buyer, I resolved to accept nothing from the crew even if offered free. My resolve was never put to the test.

When we passed through Gibraltar and entered the Mediterranean, we knew our journey was at last nearing its end. At this point one member of the crew told us he and his fellow entrepreneurs were praying for an air raid or a submarine attack because either of these occurrences would mean additional hazardous-duty pay for the merchant marine sailors. Since army personnel had no such pecuniary interest, we remained dubious as to the advantage of any kind of attack. In this case the spirit of free enterprise went unrewarded. We docked at Oran without incident.

Although I didn't know it at the time, the regiment to which I would later be assigned had preceded me to Oran by about a year. It, however, had come in the hard way, over the beaches as a part of Operation Torch, the Allied plan for the invasion of North Africa. The landings took place in early November of 1942, and in two or three days resistance had ceased. Most historical accounts report that Allied casualties were light, but there was at least one major exception. An entire battalion of my future regiment temporarily ceased to exist as a combat unit following an abortive attempt to seize Oran Harbor by direct assault while other elements of the invasion force landed at various beaches both east and west of the city.

No one tells the story better than George F. Howe in his book *The Battle History of the First Armored Division* (Washington: Combat Forces Press, 1954). Here I shall note only his report on the casualties. Out of a battalion total of 393 officers and men, 189 were killed, including the battalion commander, and 157 were wounded. A few made it ashore only to be captured. Only 47 men escaped unharmed.

By November of the year I arrived in Oran, the Sixth Armored Infantry Regiment, having fought through Algeria and Tunisia, was already moving or had moved to Italy with the division. I lagged behind the regiment by one continent, one campaign, and two more replacement depots, known as "repple depples" to the officers assigned. It was to take me a bit over two months to catch up with it.

Our long sea voyage had taken the edge off our physical conditioning, and we stayed in Oran long enough to restore it. Up to a point, I welcomed the opportunity for increased physical exertion through calisthenics and jogging, but climbing the seawall at Canastel every day was a little much. No point in being fanatical about the matter.

There was plenty to see but little to do in Oran. In the course of several trips, I visited a French Foreign Legion post, prowled around the fringes of the native quarter, walked the streets where it was safe to walk, and found my way down to the waterfront on more than one occasion. I was fascinated by the sights and sounds of an ancient city where you could hear a babel of languages: French, English, something I took for Arabic, and other unidentified dialects. At first I tried to make modest contributions to Arab beggars who had learned at least enough English to plead, "Alms for the love of Allah." I wanted it clearly understood that I had no quarrel with Allah but soon found that the request for alms in his name greatly exceeded my meager supply of cash. I gave up the effort.

In recalling my first experience on foreign soil, I find that two incidents are still vivid to me. One of these involved a barbershop, the other a bar. Both were located in Oran. I entered the barbershop with mixed motives. There was the legitimate need for a haircut combined with some vague, unformed notion of coming on to the pretty young French-Arabic woman who could be seen through the window acting as both barber and cashier. There was another barber, also a woman, in the establishment, but my eyes had fallen on the lady who seemed to be the owner. Through a mix of pidgin French, American baby-talk, and sign language, I made known to her my wishes for a haircut, very cleverly concealing my ulterior motive. I was conducted to a barber chair.

I soon found that the shop featured more than haircuts. An old Arab man entered and conversed with the cashier. Money changed hands. This didn't surprise me. Man of the world that I had become, I realized that business establishments were sometimes used as fronts for prostitution. It was the way of the world. One had to accept such things with equanimity.

But now events began to move in mystifying ways. The old man was ushered into an alcove resembling a large clothes closet, partially concealed by a drawn curtain but within plain sight of the chair on which I sat. The cashier drew back the curtain and furnished the old man with a funny-looking water pipe from which he took several deep drags. He then stretched out full length upon what looked to be a shelf in the alcove. The curtain was drawn, and the cashier again became my barber.

From time to time two small children, coming out of a back room, would run through the shop, pause to tug at the curtain, peer in at the old man, and giggle. Each time my barber, whose children they seemed to be, would shoo them out gently.

I didn't know what in hell was going on. As I reflected on the puzzle, I somehow became convinced that I was about to witness some perverse sexual act performed in front of my very eyes, especially if the children pulled the curtain at just the right time. For all I knew those seemingly innocent little kids might be involved in some unspeakable way. Thus when my haircut was finished and the young lady asked very sweetly in broken English whether I "desired" anything else, I rather forcefully denied that I did. Saying "oh, no, no, no," several times, I thrust some occupation currency into her hand and dashed out of the shop much as I would have done had it been on fire. Having made my escape, I reflected that if this was the way they practiced sex in North Africa, I wanted no part of it.

The other incident took place in more familiar surroundings and involved more readily understandable behavior. One night in a bar frequented by British and American soldiers and by merchant seamen from various countries, my attention was drawn to an American seaman surrounded by a small group of four or five much younger British and American soldiers.

The old salt, about fifty years old, was a big man, somewhat overweight but vigorous, healthy, and apparently in the prime of life. He had a big, ruddy face, a blondish mustache, prominent eyebrows of the same color, and twinkling blue eyes. If it would mean anything to anyone, I would say that he looked very much like Alan Hale, an American movie actor of the day who specialized in the macho kind of role this real-life seaman was playing to the hilt as he leaned back against the bar with a glass of gin and orange in his hand.

For the benefit of his less experienced companions, the man of the sea was discoursing on the sexual talents of the women of the world. He rated the American women as among the most sexually gifted. The women of Oran ranked somewhere around the median for all ports of call in his vast experience, while those of the British Isles were, unfortunately, to be found only in the lowest quintile.

When this part of the analysis brought mild protest from the British soldiers, our cosmopolitan sailor became an advocate and adduced evidence to support his conclusion. He reminded his listeners, both immediate and further removed, that Edward the Eighth of Great Britain, unable to find sexual satisfaction either at home or in the empire, had abdicated his throne to possess the woman he loved, a Baltimore divorcée. "That just proves," he concluded, "that right there in Baltimore, Maryland, we have pussy fit for a king." We will never know how many voyages this man of the sea had to wait through before he could deliver his punch line. Or why he bothered, for that matter.

In a relatively short period of time as these things go, a number of us were shipped to a repple depple near Mateur in Tunisia. This trip was made on a narrow-gauge railroad in 40/8 boxcars familiar to veterans of World War I as conveyances designed to transport either forty men or eight horses. There were no horses on this trip unless you wanted, as I did, to count as parts of horses some of the supposed human beings aboard.

The journey took several days. There was starting, stopping, waiting, and moving forward at a pace which could have been greatly exceeded for a significant span by a Missouri jackrabbit. When I was told that on previous shipments troops had to be restrained from firing at telephone poles and wandering Arabs, I could understand without condoning their actions. The repple depple in Tunisia seemed to fit the description which soldiers used promiscuously to characterize any post they were on. The phrase "out in the boondocks" does not do justice to the isolated region in which the camp was located. Apart from the American tent colony, there were no signs of human habitation for miles around. The ground in our immediate vicinity was strewn with small rocks; the topsoil was thin and anemic. The scant vegetation, including a few stunted trees, contributed to a quick conclusion that life here was hard and pleasures few.

The only place which held promise of relieving the boredom was a British officers' club at Bizerte, several kilometers up the road. Army trucks maintained a regular shuttle, but the last transportation out of Bizerte in the evening came before midnight, helping to assure that socialization would not be prolonged. I made one trip into Bizerte and found the club somber, dark, and dismal. When I entered early in the evening, the place was deserted except for a few British officers, some conversing quietly, others sitting alone, mournfully sipping their gin and orange.

The scene was enlivened a bit later when a contingent of Canadian officers in British battle dress entered and soon scandalized the establishment by their raucous horseplay. They were more rowdy, more American, than the Americans. One of them set fire to a newspaper which a British officer was reading. During the flap which ensued, I left, half-fearful that our neighbors to the north might turn on the few Yanks present before trashing the place. Besides, it was time for me to catch my ride back to camp.

One aspect of the scene on the ride up to Bizerte had attracted my attention. I got a second look on the way back. Stacked higher than a tall man's head on both sides of the road for a distance of several miles were crates of American supplies now abandoned by the army. Since the nomadic Arabs had earned a reputation for being great pilferers, and there had been plenty of time for pilfering these unguarded treasures, I concluded that the remaining crates must contain equipment too heavy to be transported by hand, donkey, or camel and/or material unsuitable for any use except killing people.

I was shocked by the obvious waste. It was second only, in my mind, to the great waste involved in the massive consumption of manpower by the rear echelon military bureaucracy. In the circles in which I moved, there was general agreement that the United States could not permanently afford a military establishment in which such a large tail wagged such a small dog. Now, in the course of that bouncy ride to and from the officers' club in Bizerte, I was led to the conclusion that only sheer necessity could bring about reform. Wasteful practices were too deeply ingrained, interests too firmly vested. There may well have been logistical, strategic, and other considerations which made abandonment of those supplies perfectly rational at the time; still, military waste was the norm from which economy and efficiency were deviant cases. Since the war, I have never been able to contemplate proposals for large increases in military appropriations without reflecting on the appalling examples of waste I observed.

Just a day or so after that trip to the officers' club, I passed through Bizerte again, this time as part of a shipment bound for Naples and my last repple depple assignment of the war. From the deck of the ship I took a long last look at the African shoreline. Despite evidence of war damage, including hulks of partially sunken ships in the harbor, Bizerte, with its palm trees, white sand, and inviting beaches, struck me as an ideal vacation spot for more peaceful times. I realized, of course, that in all probability I would never return here. Better absorb the scene now while the weather was perfect, the sea smooth and shimmering in the late afternoon sun. We moved slowly out of the harbor. Night came on. The convoy proceeded to blackout, although somehow the possibility of an air raid or submarine attack seemed rather remote to me. Despite the cramped quarters, my sleep was restful. The entire trip was uneventful.

When we entered the Bay of Naples, I came on deck eager for my first look at Italy. Once again the sun was shining, the sky was blue, the temperature mild in marked contrast to the winter weather to come. I located Vesuvius and took in the beauty of the distant landscape. Soon I could see in outline the great amphitheater which was the city, the hills to its back, its main street a long middle aisle running down to the cluttered stage of the waterfront. See Naples and die? My God, let's hope not.

As we approached the shore, it became increasingly clear we were entering an active theater of war. Barrage balloons floated overhead. The dock area had been severely damaged by a combination of Allied bombing and German demolition. The hulls of sunken ships were still visible in the harbor. A number of twisted cranes as well as other broken and burned-out unloading machinery were also in evidence. In places the destruction extended from storage facilities to what must have been bars, shops, hotels, and tenements two or three hundred yards in back of the landing sites. Nor, as we would find out later, was damage limited to the harbor area. Allied bombers had leveled the main railway station and its environs; the Germans had mined the main post office building, had destroyed the few large manufacturing plants and many of the smaller ones. Hundreds, perhaps thousands of Italians were homeless and hungry. Some, we were told, were living in caves in back of the city.

Buffeted on all sides, Naples was still very much alive, a vibrant and an exciting city. I sensed some of its energy, its misery, its sorrow, its joy in the activities of a small army of street vendors who crowded the shore as the troops began to stream off the ship. They were trying to sell "Noche, Noche," fruit, and various kinds of souvenirs, both sacred and profane, some very profane, to the rich Americans.

I could see some of our men hiring Italians as porters to carry their packs. Most embarrassing. I couldn't imagine the German troops who had occupied this city just a few weeks before engaging in such a practice. Nor would the British officers have tolerated it. The symbolism was all wrong and especially bad for our forces. It seemed to confirm the stereotype of the American army as soft, undisciplined, overly concerned with creature comforts, ready to flaunt its wealth, ready to reduce everything to the cash nexus. I shrugged off my sensitivity. Nothing I could do about all that. Both the Germans and the British were better disciplined, more "soldierly" than we were. So what? The British could not win without us, and the Germans couldn't win with us aligned against them. We would show them a better side later on. At least I hoped so.

I lingered bareheaded at the rail, trying to memorize every aspect of the scene. This moment was a turning point. I was opening a new, and perhaps final, chapter in my life. Powerful, conflicting feelings churned up inside. Never had I had a deeper appreciation of the preciousness of life; never had my prospects for keeping mine been more uncertain. It was good, it was exhilarating to be in this beautiful place at this exciting time, about to embark on a great adventure. But a wistful sadness caused me to say a silent prayer for my deliverance, not for my sake, I told myself, but for the sake of those at home who loved me. And, then, when the time came, I saddled on my pack, moved into line and off the ship.

Christmas Day 1943 found me in a repple depple on a racetrack just outside the city. I had long since reclaimed my sleeping bag, which had miraculously appeared in a shipment from Bizerte—score one for the much-maligned rear echelon—and had stretched out my belongings on the concrete floor under the racetrack stands. It was a cozy hideaway, not far from what had been pointed out to me as the royal box from which, in happier times, the Italian royal family had watched the races. In other words, right there in Naples, Italy, I had found shelter fit for a king.

When I awoke on Christmas morning, I thought briefly of home and of Christmas past. This morning there was no tree, no Christmas music, no presents, no loving family. I quickly dismissed these thoughts as unworthy of a first lieutenant of infantry in the army of the United States. After all, a soldier's life was not supposed to be an easy one. I hitched a ride into Naples for the day.

At that time the front was still a considerable distance ahead. The Fifth Army, under Lt. Gen. Mark Clark, was safely headquartered at Caserta, some thirty miles to the north. At various points considerably farther up, Allied troops were slowly, painfully, and at great cost slogging their way toward Cassino. It had taken them three months to move from the beaches at Salerno to their present positions. It was to take an additional five months to breach the Cassino line.

Rumors and reports of the fighting filtered back to the repple depple. They were not reassuring. Before Christmas we were hearing about the rain, the mud, the cold, and the tenacity of the *Tedeschi,* as the Italians called the Germans. I heard the words *trench foot* for the first time along with bitter complaints that every whore in Naples owned a pair of waterproof GI mountain boots intended for the front but diverted to rear echelon uses. We also heard about the 88s, about the severity of enemy artillery, mortar, and small-arms fire, about "booby traps," about "battle fatigue," and about men, our men, running away. As the King James version might have phrased it, I thought on these things and was sore afraid.

Chapter 4

Mt. Porchia:
The Legacy of a Battle

My status as a repple depple orphan was terminated abruptly in the middle of January when I was assigned to the Sixth Armored Infantry Regiment of the First Armored Division. The regiment had suffered heavy casualties on the Cassino front just a few days earlier. I wasn't the only replacement sent forward. Despite my fears, I left the repple depple, as I think most did, without enthusiasm but without regret. Being an unemployed infantry unit commander was a dreary, demoralizing experience, a bit like being on the dole. A part of me wanted to get out of the rear echelon, to earn my keep, to "see the elephant" as my great-grandfathers had done in the American Civil War.

Although I didn't realize it immediately, my posting to a distinguished armored infantry regiment was a piece of good luck. Not the least of the practical advantages was that, unlike straight infantry units, our companies had their own organic transportation even if it was mostly in the form of half-tracks. By present-day standards these were rather primitive troop carriers which provided tracks for the rear wheels, a thin plate of armor on the sides and rear, and a .50-caliber machine gun mounted next to the driver's seat in the front.

The tracks were designed for a war of movement, but it was not their speed which appealed to us. Neither was it their firepower nor their protective armor. Indeed, according to the old Africa hands they were worse than useless in combat because they attracted artillery fire and bombs without providing protection against either. But they did give some assurance we wouldn't have to hike our guts out, and they gave the outfit a certain cachet, a certain flair, don't you know.

On the day I was assigned, a First Armored Division jeep transported me down to a rain-soaked area around Bellona where different divisional units were bivouacked. I was accompanied by two other lieutenants, both assigned to the company I was going to. One was Lt. Francois Lebec, with whom I developed a close friendship. The other was a lieutenant who was killed before I got to know him well.

Frank was several inches taller than I and moved about with the lithe grace of a jungle cat. He was a Louisiana man who enjoyed acting the part of a simple Cajun. His name, his complexion, his knowledge of the Cajun dialect and traditions were consistent with the role he created, but Frank was far from being a simple man. For one thing, he was an honors student and a university graduate. For another, he was a tough, low-key individual with a deceptive inner strength which helped to sustain him and others in trying situations.

We were given routine welcomes at a number of headquarters. At regiment the commanding officer tried to give us a pep talk as we stood before him wearing our steel helmets and trying to maintain a respectful attitude. I don't remember much of what he told us. He began by saying, "I have already been at those bastards once this month, and, by God, before the month is out I'll be back at the sons of bitches again." After that, I tuned him out.

The receptions became more informal and realistic as we went down the line. At battalion we were informed that both Frank and I, by virtue of our dates of rank, were senior to the acting commander of the unit to which we were assigned. It was tactfully suggested, however, that we might not want to pull rank just yet because the acting CO was a seasoned combat officer. Frank and I readily agreed that, under the circumstances, accidents of date of rank should not be determining and that we would be happy to serve under the incumbent.

Our stay at battalion was short. Then it was out in the air and down the muddy road for a few more miles past even muddier bivouacs until the driver found the company headquarters we were looking for. Here we stopped and got out. The weather was raw and disagreeable, the wind somewhere between chilly and downright cold. Our surroundings were dismal. A few bedraggled men, some rather badly in need of a shave and resembling characters in a Mauldin cartoon, wandered around the company area, going to or coming from the large pyramidal tents under which the company was sheltered. Their boots squished on the sodden vegetation when they detoured to avoid the muddier spots on the paths. Some of the men eyed us with curiosity; others seemed too dispirited to take notice. There were no greetings, no saluting. A few ragged, half-dressed Italian kids, their bare legs blue with cold, were prowling around the company garbage cans which had already been picked clean after the noon meal.

Inside the big tent which served as company headquarters, we shook hands with two lieutenants, the acting CO and his executive officer. They were the only company officers still on their feet following the attack on Mt. Porchia. The acting CO was a big, ponderous man, slow of movement, slow of speech. Sometimes a small hint of a smile would play across his face, but his habitual look, then and later, was one of great solemnity. There was a pained expression in his eyes. That afternoon he appeared abstracted, his thoughts, perhaps, on the battle he had recently survived.

Second Lieutenant Bricker was serving as company executive officer. He was responsible for supervising a lot of the paperwork and practical details involved in requisitioning, receiving, supplying and assigning the enlisted replacements who were coming in. I had no doubt he was good at his job. In appearance and manner the exec was, in most respects, the opposite of the company commander. While the CO was massive and phlegmatic, his assistant was small, intense, and active with an apparent abundance of nervous energy. His speech was clipped, his language precise. But he, too, seemed completely devoid of humor, and I had occasion just a few weeks later in a dugout at Anzio to observe a rather curious display of temper. Or was it nerves?

The incident involved "Axis Sally," a German propagandist who affected a sultry voice and a lighthearted radio personality. She and a partner identified only as "George" broadcast each night from a station in Rome some twenty-five or thirty miles away. While George specialized in telling, in Alfred Hitchcock tones, ghoulish stories about injuries inflicted on Allied troops, Sally provided the all-important sex interest. Had it not been for Sally, I doubt we would have listened.

She played nostalgic American popular songs interspersed with sexually suggestive comments and little news items for the beachhead defenders. There was frequent speculation about how "wealthy Jewish bankers" and other privileged males were enjoying our women at home. One night Sally welcomed our outfit to the beachhead, correctly identifying our location. Each night she or her partner would read off the names of soldiers, identified by serial number, rank, unit, and sometimes hometown, who had surrendered and were now, as Sally put it, "Safe as Jerry's guest." She ended each broadcast with, "Easy boys, there's danger ahead."

To me the broadcasts were a curiosity and, in the absence of any other entertainment, I enjoyed listening to them. So, apparently, did a number of others in the big CP dugout. We hooted one night when Sally reported that the Luftwaffe had carried out "successful" bombing raids against troops in the pine forest. We had experienced the raids, suffered no damage, and considered the attack inconsequential. We were impressed, I suppose, and, perhaps, a little startled that Sally and George were so well informed about our movements. George's stories about how Private Smith had lost a leg when he stepped on a mine and Private Jones had left his guts strewn on the barbed wire did not make for pleasant listening. But there were no "wealthy Jewish bankers" in my hometown, and I had complete trust in my girl in any case. As far as I know the broadcasts didn't have a significant impact on troop morale. But, for some reason, they disturbed Lieutenant Bricker. As we listened to Sally one evening, Bricker snapped. He could stand it no longer. "Shut that bitch off!" he shouted suddenly. When his startled listeners made no move to comply, he jumped up, moved to the set, and executed his own command. There was a stunned silence followed by mild complaints. But we never tuned into that broadcast again when Bricker was present. It didn't mean that much to the rest of us.

Neither of the lieutenants we met that first day was destined to remain permanently with the company. When I returned from the hospital after being hit on the breakout at Anzio, both were gone. One had been reclassified and sent back to the States. Nobody seemed to know what had happened to the other one, and locating him never became one of my preoccupations.

Despite some negative impressions when I reported to the company, I took heart from my initial contacts with several enlisted men. One of these was Pfc. Jeremy Bozart, company runner, general handyman, and unofficial battalion historian. Bo was a short, squat, friendly individual of indeterminate age who had been with the First Armored when it shipped out for Northern Ireland in 1942. He was the one who first told me about the regiment's tragic failure to take Oran Harbor by direct assault and about its recent costly success in taking Mt. Porchia.

Bo seemed grateful for his association with officers and noncoms. He aspired to no higher rank and no better job, but spoke in awed tones of certain battalion heroes both dead and alive. He was an incorrigible gossip and in a position to pick up small items of information, which he promptly relayed to all who would listen. As a rule, carrying messages didn't take up a good deal of his time, so he made himself useful around company headquarters by turning his hand willingly to a variety of chores such as cleaning the company commander's equipment or, as on the day I met him, helping replacement officers to get settled in. As he hefted my barracks bag and headed in the direction of the unit I was to command, he told me I had a good platoon, that I would like Platoon Sergeant Antonio, that if I needed anything to let him know, etc.

In the platoon area we were met by a relaxed, self-assured young guy of average height and olive complexion. There was a look of quick intelligence in his brown eyes. Although he wore a pfc stripe, this was Platoon Sergeant Antonio. He had been a pfc at Porchia and hadn't yet sewed on his staff sergeant's chevrons. Bo introduced me as "the new Lieutenant." Antonio and I shook hands.

"Where you from, Lieutenant?" he asked, initiating the second part of the ritual.

"Springfield, Missouri," I told him.

"Never been there," he said. "That's a long way from New Jersey."

"You from New Jersey? What part?"

"White House," he replied.

"White House?" I wasn't sure I had heard it right.

"White House," he confirmed.

"Can't say I've ever been there."

"Not many people have," he said. His grin widened.

"Well, that's nothin'," I said. "Right here in this army we got grown men who never even heard of Springfield, Missouri, the Queen City of the Ozarks. Can you imagine that?"

"I never would have believed it." He startled me with his peculiar laugh. First there was a sharp intake of air through his nose. The resulting sound was that of a suddenly interrupted snore. Then came a short burst of deep-throated laughter. I soon found I could gauge the depths of his amusement by the number of snorts. Three was tops. This was a one-snort laugh.

With the preliminaries out of the way, Antonio continued the conversation.

"Well, I'm sure Bo has filled you in. Probably nothin' left for me to tell you."

"He may have left out one or two things," I replied, "but he did tell me this was the best platoon in the company."

"Just the company?" Antonio seemed incredulous. "Why not the battalion? Why not the division? Why not the entire raggedy-assed Fifth Army? I'm surprised at you, Bo, for not tellin' the lieutenant the whole truth."

Bo's grin was a bit uncertain. He didn't say anything.

Actually, Antonio told me after Bo left, there were so many changes—so many new men and so many old men in new positions—it was hard to know what kind of a platoon we had left. We had one first-rate squad leader, he said, and two others who were untried but should turn out OK.

He thought we could depend on most of the old timers, but we had our share of eight balls. On balance, he concluded, the platoon should be as good as most and better than some. I told him I would have to feel my way for awhile.

"Sure," he replied. "Take your time. You're gonna find out we're all alike in one way. We're all homesick and we're all scared."

"That goes for me too," I said, "but I'll hafta go up front with you people before I can really take hold."

He nodded sympathetically. "Sure," he said, "after the first time, you'll be OK."

I hoped he was right.

Unfortunately I wasn't able to keep Antonio long. In the continuing reorganization of the company it was decided his talents were needed to fill the first sergeant's position. I was sorry to lose him but grateful he was with the platoon long enough to see me through my first trip to the front just a few days later.

Before we moved up, I got to know other key members of the platoon. The senior squad leader was Sergeant Loman. He had been with the company in Africa and had most recently won praise for his performance at Porchia. Both officers and enlisted men had confidence in him. Loman's appearance was not exactly imposing. He was a slight man of about my height or, perhaps, an inch shorter. With his thinning hair, creased, weather-beaten face, and yellow teeth he looked to be fifty years old, but I knew he must be fifteen years younger.

His health was not good. He coughed and wheezed a lot; because, he told me, he only had one lung that was "worth a damn." And he told me how he had lost the other one. It involved an incident in his youth before the war. Loman was a farm boy from Arkansas. He and a male companion were attending some social function which, I gathered, was not sponsored by the Future Farmers of America or the 4-H Club. There was drinking and hell-raising that night. At the end of the evening a dispute arose with some other young men about who had the faster car. Loman's companion was driving a "Something, Something" of which he was very proud. He offered to bet that, given a two-minute head start, nothing, but nothing, could catch him.

His challenge didn't go unanswered. A match was arranged. Loman got in the car with his friend. They raced the motor—I'm sure they did, whether Loman mentioned it or not—and sped off into the night.

They were on a gravel road familiar to all parties. Behind them Loman could hear their competitor, who was driving a "Something, Something, Else." As they sped along, Loman thought about a sharp turn which lay ahead and mildly observed that they could never make it at the speed they were going. The driver assured him that they damn sure would make it and continued on, trying to coax even more speed from his car. As they approached the turn, Loman said he told the driver once again they were not going to make it. "Shit," he said in telling the story, "I knew goddamn well there was no way we could make it."

He was right; they didn't make it. The car skidded on the gravel, left the road, and turned over. Loman was pinned under the wreckage. After a period of hospitalization, he was released minus one lung but with his honor intact. I don't remember what happened to his friend, and I never did know how Loman got into the army, but I was glad to have him succeed Antonio as platoon sergeant when the time came.

I must go back in time now to events at Porchia because they became part of company legend and had lasting effects for both good and ill. And to go back to Porchia, I must say something about the approaches to Cassino which had to be cleared before Allied troops came up against the German main line of resistance centering in Cassino town and the mountains above.

I believe it was the British General Alexander, Mark Clark's nominal superior, who was quoted at about this time as saying, "It may be true that all roads lead to Rome, but, unfortunately, all roads are mined."

If the commander of the Fifteenth Army Group did not say that, he could have. Not only were all roads mined, the troops' passage was contested by the force of German arms. On every major terrain feature and many minor ones between Salerno and Cassino the German high command under Field Marshal Kesselring had carried out what is generally conceded to be one of the most successful delaying actions in military history.

The terrain gave the defense distinct advantages. Cassino and the peaks to its south barred entry into the Liri Valley where the Fifth Army hoped to bring the full weight of its armor to bear. The main road from Naples to Rome at that time was Highway 6, the old Via Casalina of the Roman Empire. It approached Cassino from the south through the Mignano Gap, a narrow valley six or seven miles long bordered by mountain ridges on both sides. This highway and these heights are what is meant by the "approaches to Cassino."

Mt. Porchia was the last ridge but one on the road leading into the town. Only Mt. Trocchio barred the way ahead. In the rear of Porchia lay Mt. Lungo, Mt. Rotondo, Mt. La Difensa and numerous other heights all now safe in Allied hands. They had been taken by other units of the Fifth Army most frequently against determined opposition from veteran German divisions not yet compromised by the impossible demands which Adolf Hitler saw fit to impose on the resources of his country. At Porchia, it was my regiment's turn to spearhead the advance.

The regiment did not, of course, go after Porchia without assistance. It simply provided the infantry component around which Task Force Allen was assembled. Other units of the task force included tank and tank-destroyer battalions, division artillery, an engineer combat group, and assorted other outfits, including a contingent of medical personnel whose services were to be much in demand.

There are differences in the historical accounts of this battle, even differences, rather surprisingly, as to specific times and dates. Not surprisingly, there are differences between what the men experienced and what the historians saw fit to record. Faced with a jumble of documentary and testimonial evidence, it is never possible for anyone to know exactly what happened in any large engagement. Nonetheless, the broad outlines of this action are reasonably clear.

Shortly after dark on January 4, 1944, or thereabouts, the regiment came down from the heights on Mt. Lungo and formed up with First Battalion on the right, Second Battalion on the left, and Third Battalion in reserve, a standard attack formation. Tank and tank destroyers were in support of both assault battalions, and engineers were assigned down to the company level to clear paths through the mine fields which lay ahead.

According to Jerry Bozart and others in the company, the distance from the base of Mt. Lungo to Mt. Porchia was about two or three miles over ground which looked flat but was partially cut through by concealed ditches and streams. It was not easy going in the dark, but the infantry moved out across the field rather than risk a daylight movement under direct observation.

The First Battalion ran into early trouble and was held up. Second Battalion paused at the first phase line, much closer to Lungo than Porchia, waiting for its sister battalion to come on line. Here the troops were struck by a massive artillery and mortar barrage, more deadly than any the veterans of Africa had ever seen. Casualties were so high that Second Battalion had to be pulled back to regroup. The Third Battalion was sent forward in its place. If this account is correct—and both officials and unofficial reports confirm it—the regimental reserve had been committed long before the troops could reach a point from which to launch the final assault.

The next day the contending forces traded punches. The Germans launched a counterattack in the morning. It was beaten back. In the afternoon, the Americans resumed their advance against continuing heavy artillery and mortar fire. They made slow progress but by nightfall were finally in a position to make a direct assault on Porchia itself. The attack began at first light the next day. The approach across the fields, difficult and costly as it was, had been only a preliminary to the main event. Close to the base of Porchia, the troops were met by heavy volumes of small-arms fire coming from stone farmhouses which had been converted into defensive strong points. Tank and bazooka action reduced these positions one by one. The infantry also encountered in some profusion the deadly *Shu* mine which, because its destructive core was encased in wood or plastic, could escape the mine-detecting equipment carried by the engineers. Small wonder the movement was slow.

Early in the afternoon, however, elements of the First Battalion reported back to regimental headquarters that they were on top of the objective with something like two dozen men. The almost inevitable enemy counterattack, carried out in battalion strength, just as inevitably pushed them off. At this stage, according to all reports, General Allen inserted into the regiment troops from the Forty-eighth Engineer Combat Battalion to serve as riflemen for the next assault. Before daylight on January 7 or thereabouts, the First Battalion, with engineers attached, was back on top to stay. The other two battalions of the Sixth Armored fought their way up the slopes within their respective boundaries to join the First Battalion on the ridge. The enemy counterattack did not come until the next afternoon. By that time the regiment with supporting engineers was well dug in. The attack was beaten off.

Our men waited on top of Porchia for another four days before they were relieved. There were no more counterattacks; and, to the surprise of everyone it seems, the German command decided to abandon Mt. Trocchio almost without a fight after the capture of Porchia had left it exposed. On January 12 the regiment came down the hill. On the thirteenth it moved farther back to Bellona where I joined the regiment two days later.

This, undoubtedly, was the action to which the regimental commander had referred when he told us "he" had already "been at those bastards." No one I talked to had seen him at Porchia, nor had anyone expected to.

But I did hear many stories about praiseworthy performances. There was the gallant battalion commander, a lieutenant colonel, who seemed to be always in the forefront and who, in one version, grabbed up a rifle and led a shattered platoon forward until he, himself, was so severely wounded he had to be evacuated to the States. And he was not the only certified hero. Lieutenant Jarman and Sergeant Owens, both hospitalized with wounds but expected to rejoin the company, were also singled out for praise. Jarman with a single shot had dispatched a sniper holding up the advance; and a little later when the lieutenant went down, the irreverent and fun-loving Sergeant Owens, a company favorite, had taken over until he, too, was stopped.

But the most gratifying stories were about Captain Hall, our young battalion surgeon. He had several times led litter bearers into a minefield covered by artillery and small-arms fire to help treat and evacuate the wounded. The routine expression "above and beyond the call of duty" was never more aptly applied.

Later I got to know Captain Hall and found him all I had expected. He was a few inches under six feet and in his mid- to late twenties, just out of medical school. His brown hair was close cropped in the army style. He wore wire-rimmed glasses. He socialized easily and drank with us, although never in the way we drank, at battalion parties.

Once I heard him voice a mild, conversational complaint about his job. He was only a glorified first aid man, he told us. He patched up his patients as best he could and sent them back never to know what treatment was prescribed, how the men responded, or whether they lived or died. At the same time, he thought, doctors at the general hospitals were gaining invaluable experience.

If the captain was only a glorified first aid man as he claimed, the emphasis has to be on the glory he deserved for the way in which he did his job. He distinguished patients only on the basis of need and gave to each the best that was in him. The men I talked to after Porchia credited him with saving the lives of several people. They were comforted by the knowledge that Hall and his medics would be there if they were hurt.

But there were other stories told more cautiously, more reluctantly and privately, of something less than heroism. Apparently the actual fighting had been done by a few individuals. Most men, it would seem, simply went to ground, never fired their weapons, and moved forward only when they judged it safe. And there was much worse. Straggling was a serious problem at Porchia. An undetermined number of people simply sneaked off or took off for the rear. There were estimates that the regiment had the equivalent of a full battalion of infantry "temporarily" missing in action, men who would return to their units when the engagement was over. It had been necessary to have an equal number of combat engineers put down tools and pick up rifles.

In the fullness of my years I have learned not to be judgmental about individual cases of straggling and to realize that soldiers who bug out are not necessarily cowards, or bad men, or even weak men. But in January of 1944 I was not able to view the matter with anything like Olympian detachment. I was shocked by stories of soldiers who had, it seemed to me, deserted their friends at a crucial time. Nothing had prepared me for this. I realized that straggling, unless guarded against, would quickly become a habit endangering us all. And I saw nothing those first few days to indicate the problem was being faced let alone dealt with effectively.

But there wasn't much time to ponder this or any other problem. A week after the regiment came down from Porchia, four days after I joined it, we moved up again. There was barely time to learn the names of the enlisted replacements. The company would have to deal with the darker side of its Porchia legacy at a later date.

Chapter 5

Cassino—January 1944

The briefing which trickled down for my first combat operation was fuller than some I would receive. Our battalion was assigned to the division's CCB (Combat Command B, a mixed force of all arms and one of the two major components of the division's assault arm, the other being, you guessed it, CCA). We were to be in Second Corps Reserve behind the Thirty-sixth Division, which occupied positions along the Rapido River in front of Sant'Angelo just a few miles west of Cassino town.

On the night of January 20, we were told, the Thirty-sixth Division would force a crossing of the Rapido both above and below Sant'Angelo. When a bridgehead had been established, CCB, my outfit, would move through the Thirty-sixth, bypass Cassino town, and, as I heard it, drive all the way up the Liri Valley to Rome.

In the meantime, on January 22, Operation Shingle was to go in. Shingle was described as "a left hook." It would send the American Third Division, a veteran British division, and assorted other American and British units onto the beaches at Anzio and Nettuno, some sixty miles to the north. It was thought the earlier action on the Rapido would draw German reserves south, thereby easing the burden on Shingle, and successful landings at Shingle would then result in German abandonment of the Cassino line in favor of a defensive position north of Rome. I had little reaction to the operations described. When I briefed the platoon, some of the veterans observed that, after the breakthrough, the company would probably be outposting the tanks. I gathered it didn't sound too bad to them.

We moved out on the night of January 19 on half-tracks which took us down Highway 6 to an assembly area somewhere behind Mt. Trocchio. There we dismounted, formed up in two columns, one on either side of the road, and moved off to the northwest for our assembly area. I was at the head of the platoon, Sergeant Antonio immediately behind me. The orders were for no smoking, no talking.

We had gone a mile or so down a secondary road when suddenly there was a sharp crack and a muzzle blast from a "Long Tom" in a field just off the road to my immediate right. Without thinking, I pivoted on the balls of my feet in the direction of the ditch on the right side of the road.

"Steady," Antonio called softly. "Steady, those are ours."

There were snickers from the men immediately behind him. I felt a bit foolish as I pivoted again, this time back into the line of march. We reached our assembly area without further incident.

In the morning Antonio suggested we go on a short reconnaissance to our front. You never knew what your orders might be. Better get some idea of the lay of the land before you were activated. He and I started out.

As we moved down a narrow path, there was a loud explosion close to a house in a field to our left front. Great chunks of dirt were thrown high in the air. I started to hit the ground.

"Steady," advised Antonio. "Steady."

"What was that?" I asked. "A mine? I didn't hear anything comin' in."

"Mortar," said Antonio. "You can't hear 'um. That's why they can be worse than artillery."

I started to say something.

"Be quiet," hissed Antonio.

Another explosion threw up dirt on the other side of the house.

"Sometimes," Antonio informed me, "if you listen close enough, you can hear a little 'plop' when the round leaves the barrel; an' you kun get some idea of where it's comin' from. Did you hear a 'plop?'"

I confessed I had not.

"Neither did I, and I was listenin' for it. That one is too far off. It's a big one."

I remained silent.

"They're not shootin' at us," he concluded. "They're registerin' on that house. Even if they saw us, they don't have enough ammunition to waste on two guys behind the line."

"I don't know," I replied dubiously. "When you consider how valuable you and I are to the war effort. . . ."

He gave a snort. "Yeah," he said, "they just might make an exception for us. But I think we kun go on. As long as he keeps firin' into that plowed field, he's not gonna hurt much of anything. See how they buried themselves in the dirt? The time you really gotta worry is when you're on hard ground or pavement. Then there is nothin' but your ass to take the fragments."

"I'll try to remember that," I replied. "I'm kinda fond of my ass."

Another one-snorter. "Stick with me, Lieutenant," he said, "and you just might live through this war."

We went warily on, but I, at least, was straining my ears for the sound of a little "plop."

For the next two days, we waited, cleaned weapons, wrote letters, slept, and waited some more. On the night the Thirty-sixth Division was to attack, we heard the artillery preparation go in at the appointed time but were too far away to pick up the sounds of infantry action.

There was no word from troops at the river during all the following day and night. We witnessed a brief aerial dogfight sometime in the afternoon; speaking more precisely, we heard the sound of straining motors and the staccato bursts of gunfire. The combatants were little specks in the sky impossible to identify as friendly or hostile. When we saw one go down trailing smoke, we didn't know whether to cheer or be sorry.

After waiting through most of the morning of January 22, some of us decided to go down to the river to see if we could learn anything about the situation. The company commander gave his consent, and we moved out.

We didn't get all the way to the river but did move close enough to hear the chatter of small-arms fire and the crunch of artillery. Even I had no difficulty distinguishing the rapid rate of fire of the German automatic weapons and the slower, deeper, heavier tones of the American. It was obvious from the sounds that the Thirty-sixth Division had people across the river; it was equally apparent that things were not going well for them. Even with the field glasses we could see nothing except puffs of smoke, but as we listened, American small-arms fire seemed to dwindle while that of the enemy increased in volume. We went back to the company to report with some confidence that CCB would not be going to Rome just yet.

That proved to be an accurate assessment. Details of the disaster trickled out, but we soon learned enough to know that the Thirty-sixth had suffered much more on the Rapido than we had at Porchia. Our mission had been difficult; theirs proved to be impossible. After the war, of course, the decision to send the Thirty-sixth Division in a frontal assault against one of the strongest positions in the German line became the subject of a congressional investigation.

A night or two after the Rapido tragedy, my battalion was sent upriver to take over defensive positions near Highway 6 around Mt. Trocchio. It was here on the morning after we settled in that we got our first good look at the fabled Benedictine Abbey of Monte Cassino. In all of the literature of World War II, no battle site, I suspect, has been as frequently described as the monastery and its surrounding terrain. The best treatments I know of are Fred Majdalany, *The Battle of Cassino* (New York: Ballantine Books, 1957); David Hapgood and David Richardson, *Monte Cassino* (New York: Congdon and Weed, 1984); John Ellis, *Cassino: The Hollow Victory* (New York: McGraw-Hill, 1984); and Harold L. Bond, *Return to Cassino* (New York: Doubleday, 1964). I cite these works to give credit where credit is due, to show that I have done my homework, and to indicate that I can have little to add. If I may assume, however, that some people reading this will not have read other accounts, I must present a brief sketch.

After that buildup, it is a bit difficult to know where to begin. Since infantry troops scrutinize all terrain features relevant to their existence, Cassino town, the river to its front, and the mountain at its back crowned by the monastery were inseparably linked. There were off to the northeast snow-clad peaks higher than Mt. Cassino, but they were out of the picture as far as we were concerned. It is impossible to say what first caught the eye, but since Cassino town was the ultimate military objective, it seems appropriate to begin the sketch there.

Before the war, according to Majdalany, Cassino was a prosperous trading, tourist, and governmental center with a population of some 25,000. Its buildings were strung out for almost a mile along the base of Mt. Cassino. Highway 6 ran directly into the town from across the Rapido, made a sharp left turn to avoid the mountain, and then a sharp right turn into the Liri Valley.

The mountain which gave the town its name looked out over the Rapido and Liri valleys, and the peaks of Mt. Cairo were to the northeast. The view from its top, abbey or no abbey, must have been spectacular indeed. The only thing I can think of which, in a military sense, might be comparable was the view the Confederate army had from Lookout Mountain in 1863 of northern troops down below in Chattanooga.

But there was, of course, an abbey on top of Mt. Cassino, and that made a great difference. Or at least there was something awesome and threatening up there. It stood at the end of a switchback road leading up from the town. With its thick walls and intimidating size, it looked more like a massive medieval fortress than anything else. On its long side it extended for about twice the distance of an American football field and was four stories high. It didn't require military training to understand that control of the mountain was the key to control of Cassino town and that the abbey was as much a part of the mountain as if it had been put there by nature.

Although we had no way of knowing it, there had been unusual activity around the monastery weeks before we arrived. As Hapgood and Richardson relate in some detail, the Germans had already sent many of the abbey's art treasures and some of its monks to the north, but there had been an influx of refugees from the bombed-out valley towns to augment the monastery's population and strain its food supply. While German positions dotted the ridge and some of them were very close to the abbey, it is now firmly established, I believe, that there were no enemy troops in the abbey itself. It would have been impossible to convince us of that at the time. As we looked upward, we assumed as a matter of course that the *Tedeschi* were making full use of what seemed to be hundreds of windows on the side of the monastery facing us. In safe, cozy comfort, enemy observers could bring down destruction on us at their pleasure, or so we thought.

We cursed the abbey even though it did us no tangible harm during the seven or eight days we were under its spell. The scene was deceptively tranquil. At sunset every evening we could hear the chimes from the abbey tolling out vespers, but these usually pleasant sounds only added to our anger and frustration. We interpreted them as a callous pretense, a patent deception. From time to time we heard sounds of fighting up in the mountains to the northeast where Fifth Army troops were attacking downhill in an effort to reach the monastery from the superior heights of Mt. Cairo, but down in the valley where we were, only an occasional incoming artillery round reminded us that we, too, were still at war. We suffered no casualties.

Two-thirds of the men in my platoon were positioned in houses, barns and other structures designed for peaceful use. We had one squad on outpost duty a few hundred yards to the front, three or four men to each post, as I recall. Sergeant Antonio was still more or less leading me around by the hand. Each night I accompanied him to check our outposts. One night as we were touring our positions, there occurred an incident which illustrates how quiet our sector had become.

As we approached this post, a fuzzy-cheeked kid of about eighteen or nineteen, a recent but voluble replacement, came up to me and said with some intensity, "They've pulled out, Lieutenant."

"Who has pulled out?" I inquired.

"The Krauts, the Germans, the *Tedeschi. Tutti via,*" he replied excitedly. To demonstrate confidence in a conclusion no one else had reached, he volunteered to lead a patrol into Cassino itself.

I was incredulous and demanded to know whether he was drunk. He protested hotly that he was not.

Sergeant Antonio grabbed the intrepid warrior by the arm. "Steady, Cherry," he said, "I know damn well you've been drinkin', and if you don't shape up, I'm gonna have the lieutenant put you under arrest and send you back."

Cherry shaped up but continued to deny he was drunk. One of his buddies on the outpost, an older, more stable man said, "We'll take care of him, Lieutenant."

I told him they had damn well better and that if they allowed an enemy patrol to come through, we would all be in serious trouble. Then I asked the man whether he thought the enemy had pulled out.

He gave a short, sardonic laugh. "Naw," he said, "we bin tryin' to tell 'im they're still over thar in big, by god bunches."

After cautioning them again to keep their eyes on Cherry so the damn fool wouldn't get himself or somebody else killed, we went on our way.

"That's about all we can do," said Antonio.

There was a much more serious incident partially attributable to the deceptive calm. One day I was back at the battalion CP, which was sheltered behind the reverse slope of a hill near Mt. Trocchio, when I looked out and saw two men in a jeep driving without concern at cruising speed down Highway 6 in the direction of Cassino. In response to warning shouts from soldiers nearer the road, the driver waved a friendly hand and proceeded on his way without slackening speed. While we watched in shock, the jeep disappeared around a bend. Very shortly we heard, as we had feared, the unmistakable sounds of German schmeissers. The jeep had come within range of an enemy roadblock. I learned later that the driver was killed and his companion seriously wounded although able, with help, to make it back into our lines.

It turned out that the occupants of the jeep were two young American naval officers whose ship had docked at Naples. Having a little time on their hands and a jeep at their disposal, they decided to do some sightseeing at the front. They knew almost nothing about the fighting and had never heard of the monastery. On that fatal day which ended their journey, being uncertain as to where the front was but believing they were still safely behind it, they decided to drive into "that little town over there" and make inquiries. "That little town" was, of course, Cassino.

It is small wonder that the naval officers were confused about the location of the front. It was in the nature of the fronts which I knew to be concealed, to be fluid, indeterminate, ill defined. Stabilization was an unnatural condition from which the front sought constantly to reassert itself. The soldier could know where his squad, his platoon, and, perhaps, his company were placed; and, if he were lucky, he could know the general areas occupied by units on his flanks. Sometimes, but by no means always, he could know or pretty well guess where the main body of the enemy was. But almost all his knowledge was ephemeral and problematic. The original information might have been wrong. The friendlies might have been driven out of places which, he was told, were safely behind the front, and enemy units always had a disconcerting way of moving out. Veteran infantry could be just as disastrously wrong as the two naval officers in mistaking the front lines.

In a short time we were relieved from our not so burdensome responsibilities in front of Cassino and sent to take up positions elsewhere. I will never know what our superiors had in mind for us. On our way to wherever it was we were going, the column got lost and wandered around in the Rapido Valley almost all night. We marched, retraced our steps, rested, and marched again. It felt as if we were going around in circles.

The men bitched and moaned, mocked the army, and raised pointed questions about the intelligence of its leadership from the president on down. Some freely predicted that daylight would find us out in the bare-assed open under the enemy guns. I had not seen a foul-up of this magnitude since Louisiana maneuvers. At such times it would be nice to be a private in the ranks untainted by association with the leadership. Finally we halted for good. I suppose those leading the column despaired of ever finding their way in the dark. We bedded the platoon down behind a hillock which looked as if it might provide some protection in the daylight. At first light Bo came down the line and reported that we were going back, that we were being sent to the Shingle. I remembered from the earlier briefing that "Shingle" was the code word for the Anzio-Nettuno operation.

The men received the news, not enthusiastically, but with satisfaction. And so did I. Any time there is an opportunity to move back out of artillery range, better take it. We would be going back to Naples for a brief stay. There was almost no information about what was going on at Anzio, but you couldn't worry about "the future." Anything could happen in a few days. While we were in a "rest camp" where we were, it was too good to last. At any time someone could order us to cross the Rapido, perhaps to strike at Cassino town or the monastery above. Moving back was welcome.

Late that afternoon as we formed up on our half-tracks for the trip back to Naples, a single German fighter plane circled overhead, at first observing and then taunting us. The pilot would put his plane in a steep climb, its engine straining. Then he would level off and begin a dive which looked as if it were coming straight for us. Long before he came in range, the pilot would level off, climb, and repeat the exercise.

On his first feint, many of us jumped off the tracks, I to stand in a foxhole close at hand. On his second dive, a .50-caliber machine gun on one of the tracks opened fire and then another and another. Some of the men began to fire their M1s in the general direction of the marauder. On his third pass, an order to cease firing was shouted down the line. I noticed that the veterans had not made a move to fire in the first place, no doubt recognizing that the target was too far out of range for any weapon we had available. Most of them had not even dismounted. The pilot soon tired of the game. Perhaps mindful that the Allied forces had air superiority, he chose to head home before they had a chance to prove it.

We moved back to Naples and had a final night on the town. There was a big battalion officers' party in a hall somewhere. Several high-ranking officers, including the Fifth Army commander, put in a brief appearance. Lieutenant Ellis, the dynamic, irrepressible leader of the machine-gun platoon, added to battalion legends that evening. He and his men had somehow come into possession of a large, silver-plated loving cup, and the lieutenant had hired an Italian artisan to engrave on its sides the names of all battalion officers then in service. He told everyone who would listen that a special concoction of gin and orange juice had been prepared under his direction, then blessed by our holy men and poured into the cup. We could assure our longevity, Ellis promised, by the simple act of taking a drink of it. And it was not just simply survival in battle which was offered. I heard now for the first, but not the last, the toast for which Ellis had become known in North Africa. His brown eyes danced as he proposed in his soft, Deep South accent, "Heahs to may yew live a thousand yeahs and Ah nevah die."

Grasping one handle of the cup, Ellis assigned me the other. We sloshed across the floor from table to table, from group to group so that all might drink and assure the blessings foretold. We were the "people of the cup," Ellis said, but we would share our good fortune with our distinguished guests. When one high-ranking officer protested that he had already taken a drink from the cup, Ellis replied, "Don't make a damn, General. Take another drink and live to be two thousand yeahs old." It must have been a convincing argument. The general brought the cup gingerly to his lips.

Next day we moved on our tracks through Naples and down to the docks. Transportation to the beachhead was being provided by LSTs manned by British crews. Loading took several hours. A long column of tracks extended from the dock far back out of sight in the narrow, crooked streets of Napoli. Neapolitan vendors, coming out from the sidewalk, tried to sell vino, fruit, nuts, and God knows what else to the troops. They found willing customers, especially for their vino. As the stay in the streets lengthened, officers and noncoms became concerned with the traffic in firewater. We tried to curtail it by threatening the men and chasing off the vendors. We were not completely successful and cursed the inordinate delay. It made our jobs harder.

When my track moved up close to the front of the line, I saw what the bottleneck was. The ramp accommodated only one track at a time, and the incline was not easy for the cumbersome vehicles to negotiate. As I watched, the left front wheel of one vehicle slipped off the ramp and became so tightly wedged in it could not be moved under its own power. It had to be partially unloaded and muscled back into line.

By sundown the loading was completed, and the vehicles had been made secure. Shortly thereafter I heard the British captain ask a subordinate if the Americans were all aboard. When he received an affirmative response, the captain gave orders to prepare to get under way. At dusk we started out of the harbor.

While our enlisted men were below with the tracks, I and my fellow officers were invited into a modest lounge just off deck. Here we were served a tot of rum and treated to the unfailing British hospitality. The captain told us they had made this run several times. Not to worry. Of course, old Jerry did shell the harbor and send in air attacks from time to time, but that was all a part of the game, wasn't it? After further unhurried conversation, the captain begged our indulgence and braced himself to his duties as Churchill had exhorted all British subjects to do in a famous radio broadcast early in the war. With the departure of our host, the rest of us bedded down in the lounge for a few hours' sleep. We were up before first light and on the tracks when the ramp went down. It was much easier driving off than driving on. In a gray, overcast dawn, the tracks hit the ground at the fastest speed of which they were capable.

There had been no briefing whatsoever at my level, so I had no notion of where we were bound. The Anzio-Albano road, which we were on and with which we would soon become familiar, ran straight ahead. We could hear the sounds of outgoing artillery, but nothing much of consequence was coming in.

Just out of town a road branched off to the right. I had lost sight of the track in front and stopped to inquire of a scared-looking MP standing at the crossroads which way the First Armored had gone. He wasn't sure but thought our unit had continued on the road going to the front. The fellow didn't look any brighter than he needed to be, but I took the road indicated, praying that we would not get lost.

My prayers were answered. I soon caught sight of the dust of the halftrack ahead and was relieved to know that it was coming from our column. We moved on a very short distance and turned off into what we were to call the pine forest. It appeared on the maps as the Padiglione Woods. Whatever. In peacetime, by any name it would have been a pleasant spot. The trees were tall and straight, far enough apart to allow easy passage but thick enough to afford some concealment. The ground was strewn with pine needles. The soil was sandy enough to make for easy digging but firm enough to support the weight of our vehicles in most places. All in all it looked to be a better than average bivouac area even though the fumes from our half-tracks polluted the air and overpowered the pine scent.

There were only a few problems. The enemy held the high ground all around us. The pine forest, moreover, was the only place on the beachhead affording concealment for armor and was, as a consequence, an obvious target for artillery and air attack. Finally, all the beachhead, including the harbor, was well within the range of German guns. The men needed no urging to dig in. When individual foxholes were completed, the tracks and other vehicles were buried up to their hulls in the sandy soil. The efforts were to prove well worthwhile. This was to be home base for the next three months.

Two battalions of the regiment had preceded us to the beachhead. While we had waited down south for a breakthrough which never came, our sister battalions had been engaged in hot fighting. Casualties had been significant but not nearly as high as the regiment had taken at Porchia. From the survivors and other sources, we were brought up to date on the situation. The more I learned, the more I thought about how much better off we had been wallowing around in the dark on the Cassino front some sixty miles to the south.

Chapter 6

Anzio
The German Counterattack—February 1944

The luck of Sixth Corps troops at Anzio changed from good to bad during a single week in late January. The landings on January 22 achieved almost complete surprise and were virtually unopposed, but seven days later Sixth Corps was hemmed in on an exposed beachhead and trying desperately to fight its way out. Much had happened in a short time.

In the first couple of days after the landings, General Lucas, the Sixth Corps commander, pushed his troops inland for a distance of seven or eight miles at the deepest penetration but stopped them short of Cisterna, Campoleone, Velletri, and the Alban Hills which reached heights of three thousand feet just a few miles ahead. Up front the troops dug in on the lower ground. In the rear Sixth Corps worked desperately to land additional men, supplies, and equipment. General Lucas took the seemingly reasonable but, nonetheless, controversial position that he could not strike for the high ground until the beachhead was secure and a sufficient buildup had been completed.

The enemy reacted quickly to the successful landings but not in ways anticipated by the Allied planners. There was to be no withdrawal from the Cassino front to avoid being cut off from the rear. Instead, Field Marshal Kesselring from headquarters just north of Rome scraped together whatever units he could find close at hand and started divisions moving from as far away as southern France and Yugoslavia. As soon as they came up, these various formations were rushed forward to ring the beachhead and seal it off. When Sixth Corps did not move from its lodgment on the first day, Kesselring is reported to have said after the war, he had a feeling they had lost their opportunity. The road to Rome had been open.

By the time the buildup had been completed, the situation had changed. The road was no longer open if it ever had been. Enemy soldiers were now too numerous and well entrenched on the high ground to be pushed aside easily. They could be dislodged, if at all, only by a concerted Sixth Corps effort. General Lucas was ready for such an effort by January 29 when he launched his first major attack. On the left he sent the British First Division supported by strong elements of the American First Armored in the direction of Campoleone, a railroad station on the Cisterna-Rome line. On the right the American Third Division with three battalions of Colonel Darby's Rangers attached went for Cisterna.

After two days of heavy fighting, the British had driven a narrow wedge several miles deep into the enemy line but were unable to take Campoleone. In the course of this action, General Harmon, commanding my division, attempted to swing around the British left flank to hit Campoleone from the rear. He soon found that his tanks couldn't move far off the roads without encountering impassable obstacles or getting mired down. Once again the unsuitability of much of Italy's terrain for armored maneuver was demonstrated.

On the right the drive toward Cisterna experienced even greater difficulty. The courageous but futile effort by Darby's Rangers to infiltrate into Cisterna under cover of darkness had already become a beachhead legend when I arrived. Two battalions of Rangers were cut off at daylight still a quarter of a mile from their objective. All attempts by the other Ranger battalion and by units of the Third Division to reach them failed. Almost everyone in the entrapped force, between seven hundred and eight hundred men, was either killed or captured. The Third Division persisted in its attack on the following day but to no avail.

It was now apparent that Sixth Corps did not have the muscle to break out of the beachhead. The *Tedeschi* had been given too much time to prepare their defenses. The only question was whether Sixth Corps would be able to hold what it had. Following the bloody but unsuccessful attacks, Sixth Corps in response to Fifth Army orders, went over to the defensive on February third. That was the day my battalion was released from duty on the southern front and started on its way to Anzio. In all probability the events are related. At about the same time other forces and bits and pieces of units were being hurried to the beachhead to meet the expected German counterthrust.

The preliminaries for the major German effort were carried out between February 3 and February 12. During that time, the enemy in savage fighting pinched off the salient in front of Campoleone and in the process recaptured the "factory," a building complex constructed by the Mussolini government at Aprilia to serve as an agricultural reclamation settlement. It was from the factory that the enemy launched their main effort down the Albano Road on February 16.

I learned long after the war that Adolf Hitler himself had been prominently involved in planning for the counterattack, designed, in his words to "lance the abscess below Rome." He insisted, according to various accounts, that the main attack be made on a narrow front down the Albano Road under a rolling barrage with *Lehr* demonstration troops in the vanguard.

While the German generals on the ground may have resented Hitler's detailed interference, they apparently had little quarrel with making the major effort down the Albano Road. It was the logical way to go for at least two reasons: 1) Attacking down the only hard surface road in the area would provide opportunity for maximum use of the panzers which were held in reserve, and 2) a successful drive to the sea would cut the beachhead forces in half. This logic was not lost on the Allied high command. Enemy attempts at deception with earlier demonstrations and attacks from Cisterna were recognized for what they were, distractions to conceal the point of main effort. When the full-scale German attack was launched, the Allied forces, although outnumbered on the ground, were about as ready as they could be.

My company was alerted in the pine forest on the night of February 16 after the enemy had been attacking all day. We, of course, had no idea of the German plan and no notion we were being sent into the path of the storm. All we knew was that something big was happening all along the front. The sounds of outgoing artillery had been heavy and unceasing since dawn. Naval ships in the harbor had opened up and there were more of our planes in the skies than I had ever seen. Nothing of consequence was coming into the pines. The German gunners had little time for secondary targets that day.

We formed up and counted heads in a darkness relieved by flares hanging over the front. The muzzle flashes and the sounds of firing from an artillery battery located just outside our bivouac area were like the thunder and lightning preceding a heavy rainstorm. As we moved into line, the sudden sound of a single rifle shot and a loud scream came from the front of the column. A squad leader in another platoon had, by accident or design, shot himself through both hands. The story was that the sergeant was standing with his hands over the muzzle of his M1 when it went off.

At first there were suspicions of a self-inflicted wound. It was a bit curious. How could such an accident happen to an experienced soldier who knew how to handle weapons? But if he had acted to injure himself, had he not greatly overdone the deception? Why both hands? And wouldn't it be most difficult for a man to shoot himself in both hands? I more or less concluded that the sergeant's version was true, but I never found out. He was sent to the aid station, and none of us heard from him again.

The company did not leave the pines until several hours later. It was a classic example of "hurry to wait." We bedded down and slept in place. And when we finally did move out, it was only for a short distance. We crossed over to the west side of the Albano Road and stopped again.

Dawn of the seventeenth found us on a farm road, little better than a path, which paralleled the highway for a short distance and then meandered off to the northwest. Our forward progress was painfully slow. We would move up a few hundred yards and then halt for another two hours or so. Enemy artillery began to find us in the middle of the morning. We took casualties. After almost every bar rage the cry of "Medic! Medic!" would ring out, and as we drew closer to where the real action was, artillery and mortar fire became worse. There was nothing to do but leave our dead and wounded as we moved on.

It was Cheney's death which almost paralyzed me. The barrage had lifted. We got to our feet to move on. Looking back, I saw two or three guys at the rear of the platoon bending over a man who was still on the ground. I hurried back, knowing someone had been hurt. It was Cheney. He was lying on his back. There was a great hole where his belly should have been. It was almost completely filled with a pool of greenish tinted blood which sloshed from side to side as water in a pan will do when its container is moved. Some of his guts were strewn on the ground.

I turned away shaken, unmanned. As I stumbled on down the path, one thought kept pounding in my head: "I wish I hadn't seen that. I wish I hadn't seen that." I muttered out loud but to myself in a half sob, "I wish to God I hadn't seen that." And then I remember Kipling's advice to the "half made recruity":

When you're first under fire and wantin' to duck,
Don't look or take heed of the man who is struck,
Be thankful you're livin' and trust to your luck,
And march to your front like a soldier.

But it was too late. I had already looked.

The sun was down; darkness was coming on fast. We were getting much closer. The sound of small-arms fire had grown louder and louder, adding to all the other noise. The column stopped on the reverse slope of a hill, and the company commander came back.

"Wells," he said, "Drop off a squad and have them dig in around that old house." He pointed off to my left rear at a small farmhouse barely visible in the failing light.

"What's the situation?" I asked.

"You know as much about it as I do," he replied and walked away.

Sergeant Howard's squad was the last in line. I went back and gave him the assignment.

"What's the situation?" he asked.

"You know as much about it as I do," I replied.

There was a scared-looking kid, a recent addition to Howard's squad, standing there listening.

"Lieutenant, should I load my rifle now?" he asked.

The question startled me. "Steady, soldier," I said in a feeble imitation of Antonio. "If you're ever gonna load that rifle, now is the time to do it. But be sure the safety is on."

I told Howard to keep an eye on that boy and walked back to the head of the platoon.

After a short wait, we moved to the crest of the hill and were almost mesmerized by a scene in the valley below. Two machine guns seemed to be in a personal duel at very close quarters. The German would fire a short, rapid burst. The American would respond with a burst of his own. The German would answer; the American would fire again. There must have been at least a dozen exchanges as we watched. We couldn't see the gunners. All we could see were the fiery muzzle blasts which looked as if the barrels of the two guns were touching each other. Then I heard the plopping of hand grenades being exchanged. They sounded like giant, wet firecrackers sizzling and spewing before going off.

I was aware that the company commander had come up but had difficulty giving him my full attention. He, too, seemed drawn to the duel going on below. We stood there briefly facing each other. Both of us kept glancing down into the valley. We stopped talking. At that moment we were somewhat like two people at a social function, each of whom is bored with the other and more interested in what is going on elsewhere.

Shortly after the grenade exchange, the duel broke off. I don't know who the winner was or even if there was a winner. Perhaps I had missed something when the company commander came up. Whatever the case, he now got down to the business at hand. He told me to have my platoon dig in on the forward slope of the hill we were on. I asked him who was on the hill which we could see to my immediate right front. He didn't know but said they were friendly.

"Who's on my left?" I asked. The terrain in that direction looked flat except for a ridge to the left front.

"The British," was his terse reply.

Somewhere I had read that they were friendly too. "How far are they over there?" I persisted.

"You know as much about it as I do," he replied and once more stalked off into the dark.

Leaving the platoon at the crest of the hill, Sergeant Loman and I went down the forward slope to select positions. Flares continued to hang over the hill to our right front and the sounds of a fire fight were coming from that direction. Across the valley to our direct front we could see the dark outlines of a ridge we had to assume was occupied by the hostiles. Off to our left front was another hill which we assumed was unoccupied. Everything seemed quiet over there.

As we walked across our front after locating the place where we would establish our line, we talked about two problems. If we couldn't tie in with the British, our left flank would be up in the air, and, even if we did find the friendlies, we would be short of men. Since Howard's squad was not available, our line would have to be stretched thin.

I told Loman after he got the men started on the digging, I wanted him to take someone with him and go out on the left flank to contact the British. That was standard procedure recommended in the infantry manuals. It was also common sense. We went back for the platoon. Loman briefed the squad leaders and led the men into position. When the digging started, he and a companion took off across the field to our left while I tried to make sense out of our personnel problem.

I rather quickly jumped to one conclusion. The platoon should have more than the fourteen men I had counted a few minutes ago as they filed by. We had started out with over twice that number. Even if you added Howard's squad plus the casualties to the total, the numbers didn't come out right. Some of our people must have taken off for the rear. Exactly how many and who they were I didn't know. It would soon be time to inspect the digging and I could get some answers from the squad leaders.

But as I started to tour the line, my attention was drawn to a more immediate problem. Two men came up from the left flank and one of them began to speak in a low but urgent tone.

"Lieutenant, there are Krauts on that ridge right over there." He pointed to our immediate left front. "We heard 'um diggin'. By daylight they're gonna be lookin' right down our throat. Don't you think we oughta pull back?"

Another chill pierced my gut. Again I tried to imitate Antonio. "Steady," I said. "How do you know they're German? Maybe they're British."

They both insisted that they had heard them talking and the language wasn't English. I asked them where they were when they heard the sounds. They led me over to where they had started to dig. I got down on my belly and crawled out a little ways to listen. Hearing nothing, I quickly became impatient. I needed to be doing something, anything but waiting, to keep my anxieties under control. I crawled back and told the men to go on with their digging. If there were Germans out there, I promised them, we would call down artillery, but we wanted to be damn sure we were not shooting up our friends. I also told them I would try to get some reinforcements to help us. They seemed dubious but went back to work.

Sergeant Loman came back to report. "Shit," he said disgustedly. "Them sons of bitches gotta be at least five hundred yards over there. We went out 'bout a quarter of a mile and didn't see a fuckin' thing but Germans slippin' through the gap. They're tryin' to circle in behind us. Big, by god bunches of 'um."

He didn't think there were any Germans on the ridge to our left front. Didn't think there was anybody there but would check it out. I told him I was going back to the CP and would ask for reinforcements to plug the hole on our left flank. He said he was going to dig in over on the left and would bend the line back a little so as to have some men facing where the British were supposed to be. I approved the idea, knowing that I should have thought of it.

When I asked the sergeant about stragglers, he told me that a half dozen guys were unaccounted for but we might be better off without "them bastards." Couldn't trust them on guard. Couldn't trust them to do a goddamn thing. Anyway, he thought we still had enough men to post guard without my having to take a turn. I protested mildly and told him to put me in the rotation if he needed me.

"We'll see how she goes," was his parting shot. "All of us may be up—or down."

He walked over toward the left flank and I started for company headquarters.

The CP was in a large hole about twenty-five yards down the reverse slope of the hill and about an equal distance off to the east of the road. Two men were still busy enlarging the shelter which was to serve the company commander, Lieutenant Jarman, who had returned from the hospital, and a communications man or two. A telephone line was already in. Fast work by our battalion communications section. They had followed behind us, stringing wire along the way. The rest of company headquarters was dug in nearby. From what I heard and saw, I surmised that the other two platoons were strung out in a kind of semicircle on my right facing the Albano Road. I never knew their exact location.

The other platoon leaders were coming in when I arrived. We made our reports. All of us had problems, but, of course, mine loomed largest in my mind. I tried to remain cool and keep the hysteria out of my voice as I told the company commander about the big gap in our left which Loman had reported. I made sure to stress that Loman with his very own eyes had seen Germans moving through the gap. I knew his report would be respected. I also mentioned that we might have enemy on the knoll to my left front but played that low key for fear of being thought too alarmist and destroying whatever credibility I might have. All of us agreed we needed help.

The company commander heard us out. Then in his slow, methodical way he called battalion and asked for "Big Six," the code word for the battalion commander. On the Cassino front we had joked about how devilishly clever our code was. "Let me speak to your six," was a request to speak to the company commander or the platoon leader, but no listening enemy could possibly guess that. We had speculated that to reach the division commander, you would have to call for "Big, Big, Big Six" and to get in touch with the commander in chief, you would ask for, "Six to the Maximum Power." On that night there was no six, big or otherwise, at the battalion CP. "They" would tell him of our troubles when he came in. "They" would see what "they" could do about our request for help. In other words, don't call us, we'll call you. When the company commander relayed the discouraging news, we platoon leaders dispersed to go back to our units.

I had dropped my pack at the spot where I planned to dig my foxhole. A small shell crater had already broken the ground which was rocky and hard. There was some comfort in the thought that lightning never strikes twice in the same place. I borrowed a pick and set to work. In less than an hour I had scratched out a place long enough to lie down in and deep enough to afford some cover. My digging was interrupted by the sound of M1s firing off to the left. There was no answering fire. I went over and contacted Sergeant Loman. They had challenged somebody to their front and heard a voice cry out, "Kamerad! Kamerad! Germans!" The enemy out there may have wanted to surrender, but Loman was afraid to let them come closer. Knowing how thin we were on the ground and fearing a trick, he and his partners blasted away at the sound. We never learned anything further.

All of us were up most of the night. I dug a bit more on my foxhole and toured the perimeter again. The two men who had heard the digging on the knoll in front of them had nothing further to report but insisted they had heard what they had heard. Loman gave their report no credence whatsoever. Still no sign of the British. Gradually the front quieted down. The flares died out. After about 0300 there was no more small-arms fire in our area and the sounds of artillery had diminished. I stretched out in my foxhole and immediately went to sleep.

At first light I awoke, feeling considerably refreshed, and got my first good look at the Moleta River Valley, which the British and the men of my division called "the wadi country." The term "wadi" had come into their vocabulary in North Africa. It referred to a deep gully or a dry streambed. While I could not tell the extent of it, the terrain directly ahead and especially the area to the west was crisscrossed with a maze of frequently intersecting wadis, most of them partially concealed by vegetation, brush and brambles. Some of them had steep sides extending as high as thirty or forty feet. This was the area over which General Harmon, deceived by aerial photographs which failed to reveal the number and depth of the wadis, had tried to bring tanks for the earlier attack on Campoleone.

The Albano Road was off to my right, although I couldn't see it. Across the valley to the front of my platoon was the grossly misnamed Buonriposo Ridge, now occupied by the enemy. To the left or west, the wadis ran all the way to the coast in the sector of the British Fifty-sixth Division. There was a small wadi at the forward base of the hill on which we had dug in. It appeared to contain a small stream. There was a path leading through our positions down to it. It was still very early in the morning. Everything was quiet. There was fog and mist hanging over the valley. I moved down the forward slope in front of our positions to relieve myself. As I squatted there behind some brush, I kept looking at the hill to our immediate right front where I was sure our nearest friends were. I walked back to my foxhole and was eating out of a can of cold C ration when Sergeant Loman came over. I told him I was going over to the hill on our right front to see if I could find out anything. He made no comment. I think he would have remained silent if I had said that I, personally, intended to make a frontal assault on Buonriposo Ridge. He might have grunted and prepared to go with me.

Leaving Loman in charge, I made my way down the gently sloping path to the wadi. When I got down there, I saw the bodies of at least a dozen enemy soldiers most of whom seemed to have been stopped by artillery fire. Some of them may have died of heart failure, for all I know. I didn't try to find out. There was a trickle of water, perhaps two or three inches deep in the stream. Looking to my immediate right from the streambed, I saw that the walls of the wadi on both sides rose sharply to heights which made them next to impossible to climb. I couldn't tell much about the wadi to my left, the part which ran in front of my platoon. There were no high walls as far as I could see. We would have to assume that the little stream was readily negotiable all along the platoon front. I crossed the stream and immediately started climbing the hill which was my destination, fully shielded now from observation on Buonriposo Ridge. There were even more German bodies on the slope. Soon I was challenged by a sentry guarding the path. After warning me to keep down because there were snipers on the hill, he showed me to a small natural cave which served as his company's headquarters.

I had entered the domain of the Second Battalion of the 157th Regimental Combat Team of the Forty-fifth Division, a unit which was to receive a well-deserved Distinguished Unit Citation for the defense of the positions it now occupied. The men of the 157th had stood astride the Albano Road on the morning of the sixteenth of February and had taken the full force of the initial German drive for the sea. Not surprisingly, the 157th was overwhelmed. The survivors of the Second Battalion moved off the road, drifted west, and took refuge in the caves which marked the beginning of the wadi country. At the same time, the 179th Regimental Combat Team of the Forty-fifth on the right flank of its sister regiment had been broken and driven to the east. Thus the enemy, with sledgehammer blows, had chipped a big hole in the line.

The initial wedge extended to a depth of two or three miles down the Albano Road but it didn't have sufficient width for the enemy's purpose. As long as the 157th on the west and the 179th on the east held the shoulders, Kesselring's troops would have to attack down a narrow corridor in the face of concentrated artillery fire, the fire of naval guns offshore, and air bombardment from the skies. The Germans had a numerical superiority of infantry but were greatly outgunned in artillery and air power. To avoid excessive casualties, they had to widen the shoulders of the bulge to allow for greater dispersal of their infantry. That is why, although we didn't know it, they were coming at the Second Battalion of the 157th with such ferocity.

There were a half dozen enlisted men in the cave I entered. The company commander, a young captain, was on the telephone to his battalion. He interrupted his conversation to report my arrival. Then, telling his CO that he would get back to him, he put down the phone and turned to me. His eyes were red-rimmed. The stubble of a red beard showed on his face. He looked tired but calm and in good spirits.

The first thing he said was, "How did you get here?" When I told him, he warned me about snipers and said they had uncovered two of them the day before hiding in a haystack within his company area. Then he wanted to know who we were, exactly where we were and in what numbers, whether anyone else was coming up, whether we had brought any medical supplies or ammunition. I am sure my answers were disappointing to him. He said his greatest need at the moment was for medical supplies. They had been able to scrounge ammunition, but, he said, "We can't even get these people out," indicating three or four recumbent figures at our feet. I had assumed these men were a part of company headquarters sleeping in after a hard night, but then I noticed that one was curled up in a fetal position and another had blood on his uniform. I don't know how long they had been unable to get proper attention for their injuries or how serious the wounds were.

After promising to relay any messages, I asked him some questions. Where was the rest of his regiment? Did he expect reinforcements? What were his orders? Where were the British who were supposed to be on my left? It was his turn to disappoint me, although, I am happy to report, he did not tell me that I knew as much about the situation as he did. His only orders from battalion were to hold on; and, he reported proudly, they had been doing just that for the last twenty-four hours. He suggested that I could see from the number of German bodies how his company had been "stacking them up." I expressed my admiration. We shook hands, wished each other luck. I went back the way I had come, although fainter of heart now that I knew about the snipers.

Shortly after I got back, a runner came down to report that the company commander wanted me to send Sergeant Loman and five other men to the CP for an important mission. During the night the Germans had, indeed, infiltrated through the gap on our left and had cut the company off. They had run over Howard's squad, killing or capturing all of them, before moving on to entrench themselves on a hill to our rear. A scratch force under lieutenants Jarman and Lebec consisting of men from company headquarters and reinforcements from the three platoons was going after them. Loman was notified and took his detail back to the company CP. Soon I heard a flurry of small-arms fire, mostly ours, and the crunch of .60-MM mortars. The fight didn't last long. I don't know how they did it, but our people took about forty prisoners off our rear with little harm to themselves. Loman and the others came back unscathed.

Shortly, to my very considerable surprise, First Sergeant Antonio and a driver came up to the crest of the hill in a truck with rations and supplies. I moved back to the CP to investigate this minor miracle. The prisoners were still huddled in a little dip in the ground on the reverse slope of the hill under guard. We stared at each other. I noted that all of them had thrown their steel helmets aside. They, as well as we, cringed as the heavy stuff whooshed overhead and exploded to our rear. Another fight was shaping up back there as the enemy drove down the Albano Road toward what Sixth Corps called "the final beachhead defense line." I never found out how Antonio made it through.

I went over to say hello.

"Goddamn it, Sergeant, I thought you were gonna take care of me," I said reproachfully. "And I'm up here getting my ass shot off."

He laughed. "I am takin' care of you, lieutenant. I've got a motorboat stashed in a cove out there. It's all gassed up, supplied, and ready to go. Get's too hot up here, say the word. We'll take off."

I told him he had better keep the motor running.

When they found out how fluid the situation was, Antonio and his driver hurriedly unloaded and scampered for home. They didn't come up to see us again and we didn't want them to.

There had been movement all over our hill during the morning. We paid for it that afternoon when enemy mortars and artillery turned their attention to us. It started out with a long range exchange of small-arms fire. First we heard the sound of bullets zipping overhead and a machine gun firing from some place over on Buonriposo Ridge. One of our guys thought he had located the machine-gun position. We opened up with our rifles and directed artillery fire on the suspected location. The enemy increased his small-arms fire. And so it went for thirty minutes or so. Then the big stuff started to come in. We tried to burrow deeper into the ground.

They pounded us without let up until after dark. I cursed myself for not having dug deeper. Several rounds came so close they threw up great clouds of dust and rained down rocks on my unprotected back. I was so terrified I barely felt the pain. I remember urinating in an empty C ration can and waiting for a lull before daring to raise my hand and pour it over the side. A rifleman who had his M1 on top of the parapet in the approved manner to repel an attack, saw its stock shattered and its trigger housing bent by a round which barely missed being a direct hit.

It was only by the grace of God that we suffered no casualties. We were fortunate in another way as well. There was no infantry attack coming in under the barrage. The real objective of the enemy was the position held by the Second Battalion of the 157th. They saved their infantry for that. Apparently the *Tedeschi* were simply trying to neutralize us while they went for the big stakes. If that was their purpose, I would have to count their efforts a success. They neutralized the hell out of me.

After the first twenty-four hours in the wadi country, I pretty well lost track of time. The sequence of events remains unclear. I have never been able to give a coherent account of everything that happened. For a time afterwards there were vivid flashbacks. In some cases I didn't know whether the scenes had really happened or had taken place only in my nightmares. But some of the things that happened are clear enough.

I remember alternately praying and cursing through long, lonely, indistinguishable days under fire in a kind of numb, half-crazed, immobility. In the daytime I prayed for dark and in the dark I prayed for the morning light. Daytime brought the artillery, the mortars, the direct fire which kept us cowering helplessly in our holes; but darkness meant enemy patrols which prowled around our front, threw grenades in on us and tried to infiltrate or run over our positions. And day and night there were the tensions of waiting for a major attack which never came.

Along with the nightly patrols there were the intimidating sounds of guttural voices ringing through the dark. Almost every morning near daylight we could hear a German noncom from behind Buonriposo Ridge waking his men with deep roars, the equivalent, I am sure, of "drop your cocks and grab your socks" as he moved from one point of his line to another. And one night down in the valley I heard the deep voice of an enemy unit leader as he directed, steadied, and cajoled his troops forward in an attack on the hill to our right front. He seemed to be counting cadence. German soldiers frequently called out to each other in situations where our troops would have remained silent. I often thought it might be a calculated tactic, a product of their training.

Our tactical officers at Benning were right about one thing: we did have a lot to learn from the enemy. The *Tedeschi* didn't look with favor on manning daytime defensive positions on the forward slope of a hill as we had been taught to do. Instead, they usually kept a light screen forward and dug in on the reverse slope where they were shielded from direct observation and had the option of contesting the crest of the hill or of launching a counterattack to dislodge adverse possession.

That lesson was made clear to me in front of Buonriposo Ridge. Near daylight on about the fourth or fifth or some day, Sergeant Voss, one of my squad leaders, suggested that we move the platoon forward down into the wadi at the base of the hill we were on. That way we could escape direct observation and still be able to carry out our mission of protecting the hill. We could move back to the forward slope after dark.

It was an obvious move. I hadn't thought of it. My reactions had been too sluggish, too rigid, too closely tied to the book. I felt somewhat as a punch-drunk fighter must feel after taking too many blows on the head.

Just before daylight we moved down to the wadi and set up so that we could bring enfilade fire across the valley at the base of the hill against anyone trying to cross the stream. We dug vertical holes in the walls of the wadi to our back so that the bulk of the platoon would have places to shelter during heavy bombardments.

It was somewhat more comfortable in the wadi. Several short rounds fell into the stream, one right next to me, but in accordance with Antonio's earlier teaching, this one brought up only mud, water, gravel and sodden vegetation. Reflecting on the experience later, I vowed never again to leave a platoon on an exposed forward slope in the daytime if there was any alternative.

We moved back up the forward slope at dark. One night an enemy soldier either intentionally lagged behind or was accidentally separated from his patrol and came in to surrender. We took him back to the CP where Lieutenant Jarman grabbed him, called him a "wise ass" and shook him severely. I felt rather sorry for the prisoner. I could appreciate what he was going through.

I didn't have the heroic mentality which makes surrender unthinkable. During long, lonely days in the foxhole with debris from near misses showering down, I had seriously considered it. Why not give up? The answer which came to me was cast in pragmatic terms. There was too much risk in throwing away your weapons in a situation where blood lust might be running high. Adrenalized men, theirs or ours, were quite capable of the summary execution of prisoners. The German who had given himself up that night had taken a desperate chance and knew it.

In the daytime isolation of the foxhole, there was no social corrective to moderate exaggerated fears. The nighttime conferences at the company CP provided an indispensable opportunity to move around, to resume human contact, to discuss alternatives. The possibility of surrender was never mentioned but moving back from our exposed position was. We weren't sure that the road back was open, but the massive infiltrations around our left flank seemed to have stopped after the first night. In any case, we were prepared to fight our way back if necessary.

All of us were taking punishment. The company commander, huddled in the big foxhole usually with a blanket around his shoulders, relayed our increasingly urgent requests to move us back or send us help. When battalion told us to hold what we had, we became more specific, asking—almost demandingly now—that Lieutenant Ellis and his machine-gun platoon be sent forward. One night they came.

Ellis was a fabulous character, always smiling, laughing, joking, always ready for a fight or a frolic. As Loman put it, he would "fight you, fuck you, or shoot marbles with you." Ellis, at five feet eleven inches, commanded a platoon made up largely of men who had "screwed up" in the battalion and were regarded as chronic disciplinary problems. He led them, dominated them, partied with them, fought his superiors on their behalf and forged them into what was generally conceded to be an elite unit. The men were proud of their reputation, proud of their leader. They might swagger a bit and cause trouble in the rear, but they were much in demand at the front.

The arrival of Ellis in our front lines served as a remarkable tonic. My spirits began to revive the moment I heard the sound of his voice. At the front or in the rear he was the same old Ellis. When he reminded me that we were "the people of the cup," our situation seemed to improve immediately. I was sure to live a thousand "yeahs" and he would "nevah" die.

After brief preliminaries, we got down to the question of placing the automatic weapons. There was some difference of opinion on that. Each platoon leader put in a claim to have some or all of the guns in his sector. The company commander wearied of the debate and simply said, "Well, do somethin' with them." With that he stretched back out to his full length in the hole and pulled his blanket over his head.

"May Ah make a suggestion?" Ellis asked softly. "Let's divide 'um up, an' Ol' L will hep you spot 'um."

The manual warned against splitting up sections of .30-caliber machine guns, but whoever wrote the manual had never been in front of Buonriposo Ridge with a determined enemy prowling around. We agreed that "Ol' L" had found a sensible solution.

The next night, or perhaps it was the same night, we were quite unexpectedly relieved by the British. The record shows it was the night of February 21–22. While we had no way of knowing it and certainly had not felt it, the main force of the German offensive had been shattered on the beachhead final defense line two days earlier. That was the day on which Sixth Corps gave rifles to the cooks, clerks, drivers, and all other "rear echelon" personnel and sent them up the Albano Road to meet the enemy assault. It was also the day on which a powerful counterattack led by General Harmon and the First Armored, minus my battalion, had slammed into the enemy flank east of the Albano Road.

West of the road the counterattack by the British was a little slower in getting started. It was designed, among other things, to relieve the Second Battalion of the American 157th, still holding out in the caves. The unit chosen for the relief effort was 2/7 Queens Royal Regiment.

Of the several accounts I have read of this action, some are vague and all are incomplete. One report informs us that the Queens got lost. I can't confirm that. Another says that they ran into difficulty from the start and were met by a hail of artillery, mortar, tank and machine-gun fire. Probably true, but I have no firsthand knowledge of that either. All reports agree that 2/7 Queens was in very bad shape when they reached the caves. I do know something about that because I saw them sustain major damage as they neared the end of their journey.

I was at the company CP with other junior officers. We first saw the Queens in the fitful light of the flares as an almost ghostly manifestation in a column of twos coming up the road from our rear. We had no idea of who they were but assumed they were friendly. Hostile forces usually don't try to enter your positions from the rear at route step with rifles slung.

We shouted at them. They strode stolidly on, coming up the reverse slope until they were abreast of our CP. The head of their column was approaching the crest of the hill. We challenged again and shouted warnings, but in all the noise coming from the hill to our right front, the Queens paid us no attention. Someone at the CP fired rifle shots into the air. It was a dangerous thing to do but it produced the desired effect. The column stopped in place. Their leaders turned off the path in our direction.

Before they could reach us, a single German plane coming from the rear of their column swooped low and shoveled out antipersonnel bombs which flashed and exploded pop, pop, pop, pop, down the middle of the road like a long string of firecrackers. At the sounds, I dived with other junior officers on top of the company commander who occupied the only shelter immediately available. The plane was gone in a split second and the sound of firecrackers was replaced by the cries and moans of the wounded. We quickly untangled ourselves and moved out to the road.

There were wounded British soldiers all over the place. I came upon one man who was standing, apparently unscathed, and asked him where his officers were. He led me over to the other side of the road where a man was sitting quietly under the only tree in our area. Not recognizing his condition, I informed him that there was a wadi below the hill where he could shelter his people in case another plane came over. He thanked me politely but said I would have to tell someone else. And then he reported, "I'm hit, you know."

Our hill now began to receive an unusually heavy volume of machine-gun fire. We went to ground until we found that it was coming from long distance. The aim was high; the bullets zipped harmlessly overhead.

It took some time to get things sorted out, the wounded started back and the able-bodied reorganized. The remaining British officers moved with cool efficiency to get the job done. They left a very few men on our hill. The main body, what there was left of it, moved on to the caves which had been their destination. I have no difficulty crediting reports which conclude that 2/7 Queens was itself in need of relief when it got there.

I led them down to the wadi at the foot of the hill and showed them the path which led up to the caves. On the way down the forward slope, the British lieutenant colonel—whether the original commander or a replacement, I don't know—stopped to observe an enemy tank firing from partial defilade behind Buonriposo Ridge. He asked an assistant to make a note of that fact and gave him the map coordinates to the tank's position.

I was surprised to see anyone with a map of the area. To my knowledge no one in my company had one. Nor did we know that, according to Howe's *Battle History,* our battalion had been attached to the Forty-fifth Division since February 17.

I have never known where the rest of the battalion was positioned. Apparently one company, maybe more, had plugged the gap between us and the British. Part of our difficulty in getting reinforcements may have been due to the fact that our battalion commander had to get clearance through an unfamiliar headquarters.

In all the confusion of that blessed night, one thing was clear. We were going back! But careful now, Wells. You're not out of it yet. This is no time to let your guard down. No one wants to be the last man killed in a battle or in a war, not when hopes are running high and deliverance seems at hand. You have to hang on a little bit longer.

Finally after what seemed an almost unbearable delay, we started back down the road we had come. Down in the valley, we had to move around a jeep whose dead driver still sat behind the wheel, his head lolled back, his throat cut and most of his face shot away. Thank God he was not one of my friends. I thought about Antonio and his truck coming up that road earlier.

After we got back a short distance, a reaction set in. It had been only a few days but it seemed forever and we were tired, oh so tired. We began to stagger all over that road as if we were drunk. I fell asleep on my feet several times and was jarred awake as I drifted off the road or when my knees began to buckle and I instinctively sought to right myself.

The column took a break every fifteen minutes. We went to sleep immediately upon hitting the ground and it was difficult to arouse us. More than once the man behind me gave me a nudge and reported, "Lieutenant, the column has moved out." Then we would try to catch up.

After several short breaks, the people at the head of the column let us sleep for an hour or so. There were no complaints when our rest was interrupted. All of us wanted to put as much distance between ourselves and the front as possible. But we needed someone to goad us into action.

We crossed the Albano Road and saw some of the human wreckage, the flotsam and jetsam left when the German offensive reached its high tide and then receded. Once an enemy plane flew overhead and dropped flares which illuminated the column for what seemed hours. Someone yelled, "Freeze!" and we tried to stop in place, suspending all movement as we had been taught to do.

At last we were home in the pines. My modest dugout had, in my absence, suffered a direct hit. No matter. I flopped on the ground beside the wreckage and went to sleep.

Late next morning I woke up and went down to the mess tent for a cup of coffee. I felt depressed, weak, shaky, numb, sad. The chill in my guts hadn't gone away. Would my luck hold out the next time and the time after that and the time after that? I didn't see how it could.

As I sat there sipping my coffee and trying to regain some semblance of normality, the company commander came over and gave me news which might have brought despair to a career officer. It meant considerably less to me. Regimental headquarters had already been on the telephone that morning wanting to know who the company mess officer was. The company commander had given them my name. It seems the regimental commander had made an inspection of our kitchen area and had found it in a most deplorable, most unsanitary condition with slop and unburied refuse on top of the ground in plain view. The mess officer was to be relieved of his duties, a mess officer only, of course, and in addition was to receive a written notice of reprimand for his impossibly low standards of sanitation. He was also to be notified that he had no chance of promotion as long as the colonel had anything to say about it.

I don't know the exact date of the inspection, whether it came on, before, or after the day on which our kitchen crew had been given rifles and sent up the Albano Road to meet the enemy. As a matter of fact, I didn't even know I was mess officer at the time, but it wouldn't have made any difference if the assignment had been made clear to me. It didn't matter. Nothing really mattered. I accepted the blame, incapable of comment, contemptuous of my superiors in the chain of command, mad at the world, bitter against everybody who had not been up there with me. And why shouldn't I be? There were not more than a dozen people in the whole fucked-up world who really gave a good goddamn whether I lived or died.

Some of the bitterness was irrational and soon disappeared. The contempt and resentment at what I saw as an injustice lingered. But later in the war I was to receive an equally undeserved citation for heroic achievement in action. In the army I knew these kinds of things had a way of balancing themselves out.

Around noon that first day back from the front we were transported in relays for hot showers at a portable unit near Nettuno. It was a very efficient system. You dropped your grimy uniform, underwear, socks, etc. in a great pile as you went into the shower and picked up a new, or at least a clean allotment, on the other side. Even a brief period with hot soapy water was a great luxury. I felt better on the way home.

Late that afternoon our battalion commander showed up at company headquarters. He was a friendly, cheerful man whose manner reminded me of a jovial pastor visiting members of his flock to console them in a period of distress. He said the company had done "a good job" up there, that he had heard "good things" about the new platoon leaders, that he had wanted to come up front to visit us but problems demanding his personal attention kept cropping up, etc., etc., etc.

None of us said anything. We just looked at him.

There were two items of good news that day. The best was that General Truscott had assumed command of Sixth Corps, replacing General Lucas. I never thought a change in command at that high level would mean anything to the men in the line. Generals were all alike. The more things change, the more they remained the same. I was, of course, not entirely wrong in that assessment, but somehow this change was different. I shared the view of everyone around me. It was about time.

And yet it was a bit strange. None of us, as far as I know, had ever seen or had any personal contact whatsoever with either Truscott or Lucas. We knew them only by the images we had acquired. At the time General Lucas was seen by the troops I encountered, both American and British, as the numbskull who had put us down on the beachhead in the bare-assed open at the mercy of an enemy which held the high ground. Truscott was viewed, on the other hand, as the brilliant, aggressive, commander of the Third Division, undoubtedly one of the very best in the entire army.

Truscott's division had a song, "Dog Face Soldier," which rang out to the exuberant cheers of his men in every watering hole in southern Italy where entertainers were capable of making music. If the musicians didn't know the song, Third Division men were available to teach it to them. While still assigned to the repple depple in Naples, I was required to stand or fight when the song was played late one evening in an officers' club. I stood.

General Lucas had neither a song nor an enthusiastic following. He was a cautious man and a convenient scapegoat for the failure of an operation which must have been seriously flawed in the planning stage. Lucas probably did the best he could with what he had, but we sensed in Truscott a commander of superior talent and imagination. He didn't disappoint us either as Sixth Corps or later as Fifth Army commander.

Our second item of good news was that the Allied air force had pulverized the Abbey of Monte Cassino on the day before we had begun moving up for our ordeal in the wadi country. The bombing turned out badly, of course, but at the time it symbolized to us the belated willingness of the high command to take common sense precautions to protect the lives of the troops and to punish the enemy. The destruction of the monastery along with the appointment of Truscott were indications that serious mistakes had at last been corrected.

On a more mundane level, I received additional comfort. Learning of the destruction of my dugout, someone invited me to move into the company CP where, it was said, there was plenty of room. My benefactor was probably Sergeant Antonio. I don't believe it was the company commander who extended the invitation. Whoever it was I was glad to accept the hospitality. It relieved me of the necessity of constructing another shelter and provided me with companionship during the nighttime bombing raids which were directed at our portion of the pine forest with considerable frequency.

The pines seemed more and more like home as we renewed our acquaintance with hot meals and were delighted at how much better field rations tasted when prepared by the kitchen. No one would say so, of course. There seemed to be a tacit understanding in the infantry that it was bad form to praise the kitchen crew.

About thirty-six hours after we came back to the pines, Sergeant Howard showed up. We were surprised but very happy to see him. He was the only survivor of the squad which had been detached to guard the company's rear.

It never occurred to me to doubt the story he told, although I was suspicious of some of the others who showed up late. The sergeant had earned his stripes, and everything I learned subsequently squared with the account which he gave of his actions. There were curious features of his story, but almost anything could have happened up there in the confusion.

At the time the squad was hit by the enemy, the Germans had managed to push a self-propelled assault gun, or, Howard called it a tank, through the gap on our left flank. This enabled them to bring direct fire on the house in and around which Howard had positioned his squad. The area was illuminated by flares when the *Tedeschi* struck.

When the flares went up, Howard had his last glimpse of the kid I told him to keep an eye on. The boy had his raincoat on and was walking up and down in front of the house at sling arms despite the shelling. His body was not found. Howard thought he must have been taken prisoner.

In combination with the flares and a hail of machine-gun bullets, a few rounds of direct fire from the tank or assault gun was enough to take the heart out of the defenders. The squad members still on their feet came out with their hands up, all, that is, except Sergeant Howard.

The sergeant played dead out in the barnyard near a pigsty or some such thing until the enemy had passed on by. When he was sure they were gone, Howard said he took off in the opposite direction and eventually made contact with the British on our left. He attached himself to a unit of 2/7 Queens and served with them for several days.

He didn't know where his company was. When the Queens began their counterattack, he was told that "the Americans" were in the caves. He assumed they were "his" Americans. Even the British officers were surprised to find our company in the positions we occupied. Everybody seemed to have forgotten about us.

Howard may have been confused by the bombing that night. He knew there were Americans on the hill but didn't seem to recognize, or recognized too late, that he had made contact with his company. When he finally "looked around," Howard said, we had gone back. He was left with the British and moved into the caves with them.

Consistent with Howard's story are the historical accounts which reveal that the Second Battalion of the 157th didn't come out on the night we did. They stayed over for another twenty-four hours, because the British battalion had arrived short of everything, men, ammunition, support weapons, etc. It was Howard who first gave us that information. We had assumed the Americans in the caves had come out behind us.

All next day, Howard said, the *Tedeschi* threw themselves at the caves but were again beaten off, this time by the combined British and American force. On the night of February 22, the Americans were ordered to split up into small groups and break out to the rear.

Sergeant Howard came out with them. He told of crawling on his belly for the better part of two or three miles before reaching safety. Many of the other Americans didn't make it. According to Wynford Vaughan-Thomas in his excellent account, the Second Battalion of the 157th had gone into battle on February 16 with eight hundred men. Only two hundred succeeded in getting back and half of those were wounded. (*Anzio*, New York: Holt, Rinehart and Winston, 1961)

A few days after Howard's return, we learned that the Queens had suffered a similar fate. Units of a sister battalion tried to reach them but failed. On the night of February 23, the Queens were ordered to move back, using the same tactics the Americans had used. They did so and with the same kind of result.

The enemy was left in possession of the caves but the defenders had served their purpose and, perhaps, saved the beachhead. By the time 2/7 Queens came out, the main German counterattack had been turned back. Widening the shoulders of the salient didn't do them any good.

The last serious enemy attack against the beachhead was in the Cisterna sector against the Third Division. It ended on March 2 when a massive Allied air strike went in. We came out of the pines to watch and cheer as an impressive swarm of perhaps five hundred planes passed overhead to bomb the German positions. It was a great boost for morale. At about this time, I found confidence enough to write home that the Germans were not going anywhere at Anzio.

Later we were to witness and cheer an even larger armada of bombers which passed overhead bound, we surmised, on a mission to the enemy heartland. I speculated that the planes must have gone a bit out of their way to cheer us up. If so, the operation was a success from our perspective.

We rested. Replacements came up. They were assigned to the depleted platoons on the basis of need. Training was limited mostly to brief orientation lectures and simple inspections. We tried to get to know the replacements. At a minimum, I wanted to be sure that all of mine knew how and when to load their rifles.

Lost and damaged equipment was replaced. We were issued for the first time warm combat jackets and combat pants. Although winter weather was almost over, the new gear would still prove useful on our next trip to the front. And that time would not be long in coming.

Chapter 7

Anzio

Stalemate—March–April 1944

After about three weeks in reserve we were sent back to the front, but this time things were different. It was the middle of March. The front had stabilized with neither side capable of supporting a major offensive. We knew where we were going this time and it was not, thank God, back to the wadi country.

Instead, we relieved elements of the Forty-fifth Division in a sector just east of the Albano Road. There was even time for a limited daylight reconnaissance before taking the troops up. On the morning before the relief, I went forward with the other platoon leaders in a jeep. We turned off on a track running behind the Forty-fifth Division's positions. After traveling a short distance, we got out, went forward on foot, and then crawled on our bellies to a vantage point from which we could sweep the area with our glasses.

From a distance the terrain to the front looked deceptively flat except for the hills on the far horizon. There were only a few trees and splotches of color. New, dark green vegetation had begun to appear causing the scattering of white, stone farmhouses which could be seen in the distance short of the high ground to stand out more prominently. It was ten to one those farmhouses were occupied by the hostiles.

We had a few minutes to get oriented before a German 88 brought us under direct fire. It took only a couple of rounds for us to get the message. We tried to sneak back to the partially concealed jeep, but the 88 tracked us with another round. That settled it. There could be no doubt we were a very specific target. We hunkered down and sped from the danger area as a final round from the German gun fell behind us. But at least we had seen from a distance where our friends would be on both flanks and we knew our rear was secure. That was a vast improvement over our last time up.

That night we hiked silently up the Albano Road, no smoking, no talking, and were guided into trenches similar to those of World War I. What had once been individual foxholes were now linked in a continuous line protected by sandbags. Except in a few places, you could walk all the way down the platoon front without bending over. Dugouts, some capable of holding three or four men but most designed for just two, provided some overhead protection from the weather. They were not intended to be bombproof. There was even a shallow ditch coming in at right angles to serve as a connecting trench between the front and a support line located a few hundred yards to the rear.

Both front and support lines were out in the open with almost no natural concealment. Brush had been used for camouflage. The company CP was in an isolated stone house just back of the support line. It was an obvious target for artillery and tank fire. From most of our positions you could see off to the left front the factory from which Kesselring's troops had erupted in their attacks of the previous month. It was still in German hands and had become, for American and British troops alike, one of the most familiar landmarks on the beachhead.

The company had two platoons up and a third platoon on the support line. In keeping with our usual practice, the platoons were rotated from time to time, but there was no clear advantage to being held back in "company reserve." Artillery, mortar, and tank fire struck all positions including the company CP with about equal frequency and violence. There were, of course, some differences and trade-offs. In the front line you had to be a bit more concerned with enemy patrol activity and our own patrols were usually drawn from the front line platoons. On the other hand men in the support line were required to serve as stevedores, lugging forward crates of ammunition, rations, marmite cans when we had hot food, and other supplies. This became rather onerous duty. We were in the process of placing barbed wire in front of our positions and the rolls of wire were heavy and clumsy to carry.

Initially my platoon was on the support line where I had an opportunity to do something I and the other platoon leaders thought had to be done as soon as possible.

Mention had been made of the problem of straggling, a serious matter at Porchia before I joined the company, a serious problem in the wadi country after I arrived. On the hill in front of Buonriposo Ridge I was too preoccupied with saving my own skin to think about anything else. On this less dangerous, less volatile front, I had more time.

There was a man in the company we had been watching rather closely. He was said to have boasted that he had come overseas with the First Armored Division and had never made an attack with them. He always "got lost," he was reported as saying, and drifted back to the kitchen where the goodies were. He was a big man with an engaging sense of humor, a bold man who challenged authority with a lighthearted familiarity bordering at times on insolence. In many ways he was a likeable man and had a following in the company. That was the nub of the problem. He was also, as we saw it, a dangerous man. His example invited imitation.

This individual was not in my platoon but he and a friend were assigned to the work detail I was in charge of that night. Our task was to carry rolls of barbed wire to a designated point in front of our first line trenches.

About halfway across the field between the support line and the front line, flares went up and we were plastered with artillery and mortar fire. There was nothing to do, of course, but to drop our burdens, hit the ground and pray. After what seemed an eternity, the flares burned off and the enemy gunners stood down. It was time to reassemble the work detail.

I now discovered that two men were missing including, not surprisingly, the man I had my eyes on. I made a big to-do about the absences because of the need for witnesses. Knowing that a military court would ask if I had "caused a search to be made," I did just that. Why, it might interest the court to know, I participated in the search myself. We called the names of the absentees in voices loud enough to be heard as we circled around rather aimlessly in the dark. I really didn't want to find them.

When we got back from the front, I brought charges, testified, and secured a conviction. The sentence was twenty years at hard labor and a dishonorable discharge, a very stiff penalty on its face. I had no interest in causing the man to serve time; I just wanted him out of the company. But I didn't waste sympathy on disciplinary cases of this kind, partly because I never believed that those convicted would actually serve the sentence originally imposed. On the only other occasion when I had to perform this unpleasant task again, the convicted man made his way quietly over to where I was standing. He informed me that he would be back in the States before I was and that never in the world would he serve all that time. He even promised to look me up, if by some freakish chance, I should survive the war. I believed most of what he said except for that promise. He never kept it, and I can't say that I am one bit sorry.

The living in the front line trenches was easy only when compared to the life in the wild confusion of those hellish wadis. The heavy shelling from the artillery, the *nebelwerfers,* and the 88's was more than enough to keep us immobilized during the daytime and to interrupt our movement after dark. Knowing exactly where we were, the enemy plastered us at will even though we took pains not to show ourselves. But we soon got the feel of this front and adapted quickly to the demands of trench warfare.

Despite the heavy shelling, our casualties were light. One of the platoon's dugouts received a direct hit, but the men were out at the time and only their equipment was destroyed. Almost every day one of our dugouts would cave in after a near miss, but we were always able to dig out and to repair the damage.

One night soon after moving into the front line trenches, I was called to a platoon outpost where the men had picked up two prisoners. Looking at their captives in the dim light of the flares, I sensed something unusual in the situation. The prisoners were about the same size and were not nearly as muddy and dirty as we were. Somehow their battle dress didn't have that long, lived-in look. Most curious of all, they stood there with rather new looking steel helmets on.

Other German prisoners we had captured seemed to perform a little ritual when they surrendered. Their hands would go up, the steel helmet would be tipped to the ground, and then, on command of their captors or when it was safe to do so, their hands would be partially lowered and their fingers laced behind their heads.

My snap judgment was that the men in our custody were poorly trained replacement troops new to front line duty. We had no capacity to interrogate them since no one in the platoon spoke enough German. The few questions we asked in English were met with shrugs and mumbled German expressions indicating they didn't understand. We searched them again and sent them to the rear under guard.

The next morning I talked with Captain Yount, battalion intelligence officer, on the telephone. There seemed to be a sneering undertone in his voice. He thought I might like to know that the "prisoners" we had sent back were American. They were OSS (Office of Strategic Services) men who had come out from Rome with the intention of coming through our lines. Concealed on their persons were all kinds of documents, maps, and sketches of enemy positions in and around Rome.

In our searches we had been looking for the hard stuff, pistols, trench knives, grenades or other lethal weapons. I was glad our outpost had been cool enough to challenge before shooting, I ignored the captain's insinuations that we didn't know how to identify or search prisoners.

A curious feature of this sector of the front was the fact that enemy patrols were relatively inactive. As a general rule, it is probably fair to say, German patrolling was more aggressive than ours. Knowing exactly where we were would usually impel the *Tedeschi* to send over a combat patrol to knock out an exposed position and keep us off balance. That didn't happen here. We wondered why.

They may have been dissuaded because their front lines were thinly held with their main line of resistance positioned further back in the hills. There were many things we didn't know about the enemy, things which higher headquarters thought we should try to find out. I would have been quite content to let sleeping Germans lie. But I was not running the show.

Most of our excursions into no-man's-land were limited to reconnaissance patrols on which we merely tried to find out whether a particular house, ditch, or other terrain feature was occupied by the enemy and, if so, in what strength and in what ways. The company sent out only one combat patrol during the three weeks or so we were up there and I was fortunate enough not to be directly involved in that.

My patrol responsibilities involved the much easier task of acquiring information. The ordinary reconnaissance patrol, as I had been taught, requires a force small enough to move quickly and silently but large enough to provide mutual protection. We usually took five or six men, but some patrols were larger and some smaller depending on the specific mission. The more difficult tasks such as bringing back prisoners for interrogation were, in my experience, always relegated to the division's excellent reconnaissance battalion.

On my first and most complicated reconnaissance patrol, I went to sleep between the lines and brought back only a minimal amount of information. Our mission was to find out what we could about a particular stone house which lay perhaps a mile and a half across the field. At a minimum we were to find out if the house was occupied.

All of us assumed it was. The enemy was not likely to deny himself the use of any substantial shelter. To help find the place in the dark, our artillery was to fire a single round of white phosphorus on the objective at a certain time. The patrol was supposed to be in position to take advantage of the marker when it impacted.

I selected five or six men to go with me. We started off on a compass reading calculated to take us directly to the target, realizing that we would have to adjust our route to the terrain. There were surprises. We encountered more obstacles, more wadis, more mud than I had expected for one thing. For another, it soon became obvious that a part of the German counterattack had come through here. Abandoned equipment, mostly American, empty ammunition boxes, rations cans and other litter told the story. At one point I thought we had stumbled into an abandoned mine field. We detoured again and picked our way carefully.

I didn't want to get too close to the target and was prepared to err on the side of caution. In addition to the continuing worry about mines and about enemy patrols circling in behind us, I had additional fears. We didn't want to get hit by our own artillery and, more importantly, I feared a violent reaction from the house when the white phosphorus landed. When the *Tedeschi* felt themselves threatened in situations of this kind, they usually sent up flares in preparation for bringing down mortar fire.

As we moved forward, I consulted my watch and compass. Despite the zigging and zagging, I was reasonably sure we were still on the right track. When my watch showed ten minutes to impact, we stopped and went to ground with different guys facing right, left, front and rear.

Ten minutes is a long time to lie on soft, springy, even if damp, ground when you have been short of sleep. At least it was too long for me. I dropped off and was awakened as an artillery round whooshed overhead, struck the ground and threw off white sparks about two hundred yards to my front. We were much too far back to get a good view, but, no harm done, I thought. At least we were going toward the right house.

True to form, the *Tedeschi* sent up flares shortly after our marker hit. Their light didn't help us. We were so far back I could have benefited from my field glasses, but whoever thought of taking field glasses on a night patrol?

We waited for the flare to burn out. Then with pounding heart and trembling hand, I moved forward, trying to count off one hundred paces. When I thought we had moved that far, we stopped and listened for a while before moving forward more slowly to count off fifty more steps. We stopped, listened again, and then moved forward even more slowly and reluctantly. At about the time we got a good look at the house, a voice which seemed to come from the front yard, roared out a challenge. We hit the ground. A burp gun opened up. Before the flares went off, we began scrambling to the rear on all fours making enough noise for a whole platoon of men.

Apparently the enemy didn't see us. They probably were looking closer to the house, thinking we were coming in when we were moving in the opposite direction. After scrambling and crawling for a while, we straightened up and moved back faster. Glancing over my shoulder, I could see flares hanging over the place we had just left.

I felt a sense of failure after that patrol. When I reported to the intelligence people at battalion, I didn't tell Captain Yount or anybody else about going to sleep or about being much too far back when the marker landed. Nor could I provide much information. I could only tell them about the route I had taken and that the house was damn sure occupied by people of unfriendly disposition.

It was the next night we sent out the combat patrol from another platoon to knock out the position. They reached their objective and became involved in a brisk fire fight. The German position proved too strong and our patrol was beaten off. They returned without getting anyone killed but with a few men nursing minor injuries.

I felt partially responsible. I knew failure to provide the combat patrol with more information had been due to my mistakes and timidity. But I didn't tell anybody about that either.

In thinking about it later, I also wondered about the white phosphorus markers used both nights. Perhaps they had done more harm than good, simply alerting the enemy to the probability that something was up. The *Tedeschi* had played this game before.

After those two patrols, I tried to do more napping in the daytime. It wasn't exactly easy. An incoming artillery or mortar barrage almost always compelled attention and the flat trajectory of direct fire was an immediate eye opener. Even when the stuff was falling safely behind us, we frequently received calls from battalion asking whether we could tell anything about the location of the enemy pieces from where we were. During a long barrage, we tried to keep the distant terrain under continuous scrutiny. Sometimes when a German mortar or tank opened up from a new position, we were able to register artillery fire on the suspected location.

There were, nonetheless, long periods in which the enemy gunners were relatively inactive. Sometimes four or five hours would pass with only desultory firing. I could nap by the telephone during these periods.

I gradually came to realize that the trenches were providing us with more than shelter. They also eliminated the great loneliness which comes from isolated confinement in an individual foxhole over a long period of time. In the trenches we could talk to each other, bolster each other, keep up appearances for each other, joke with each other, quarrel with each other during lulls in the action.

Throughout all our training the undeniably sound principle of keeping "spread out" had been iterated and reiterated again and again. The emphasis was necessary. Men in great danger tend naturally to huddle together and for good reason. Their very sanity may be at stake. There are obvious dangers of bunching up but there are subtle dangers in excessive isolation. Maybe we ought to think more in terms of two-man foxholes, teams, partners, etc.

In the nature of things my closest partner in the platoon was, of course, Sergeant Loman. He contributed much to my understanding. One day discussion turned to the capacity of the enemy to make himself comfortable at the front with far less than we had at our disposal.

Loman was a great admirer of the German soldier. On this occasion he expressed the view that we did too much "pussy footin' around" on the line. He made an invidious comparison.

"Take a wet night," he selected as an example. "01 *Tedeschi*'ll build hisself up a big fahr to git warm and dry out. You come in on 'im, he'll grab 'is gun and shoot your ass off. Then he'll go back to his fahr. We jest set around shiverin' and frostin' our balls."

He had a point, I told him, adding that they also scare the livin' shit out of you with their noise.

But one day in the trenches was pretty much like all others. Once again the calendar lost significance. None of us knew whether it was Sunday or Wednesday or some other day. We couldn't even keep accurate count of how many days we had been in the line.

The weather was in transition, no longer winter but not yet spring. The sunshine was intermittent. Clouds brought brief periods of cold drizzle. The ground was cold, soggy and damp.

Much of our time was taken up with primitive concerns; survival, sweating out the artillery, maintaining concealment, keeping our weapons clean, keeping dry, keeping warm, repairing our shelters. Even relieving ourselves required thought.

Food and water, except for the problems of transportation and distribution, were not of major concern. There was no shortage of drinking water. As for food, we ate little. Exposure to the front did something to the stomach muscles which took away hunger, and the sameness of the field rations added to our disinterest in eating. For me, hot coffee was almost as much appreciated as hot food.

The way we lived undoubtedly had something to do with our minor ailments. A number of the men had colds. Exposure to the elements didn't improve Loman's lung condition, but neither he nor anyone else had to be sent back for medical attention. Most of us were constipated. All of us were stiff from the dampness and the unnatural confinement.

Nerves became frayed. The few abrasive personalities in the platoon seemed to become more abrasive. Some of the men became edgy and snappish. But most of the guys bore up well. We were grateful that our difficulties did not compare with the hardships experienced by others we had heard about, or with conditions we had experienced in the wadi country.

Eventually we were relieved by elements of the Irish Guards, and a very proper relief it was too. They sent an advance party forward twenty-four hours ahead of time and left guides, not as hostages against their return, but in order to facilitate the transition.

I spent most of the day prior to the relief with the guide assigned to my platoon. He was an enlisted man of about my age, very polite, respectful of authority but by no means overawed by it. We got along well as we toured our line, studied enemy positions through the glasses, lounged with our backs to the front wall of the deepest part of the trench, and talked.

He was proud of his unit, scornful of General Lucas and respectful of the German soldiery. I gathered from listening to him that a recent incident in which a Guardsman "got lost" had scandalized his unit. I didn't tell him about our problems, and he may very well have understated the problem in his. He studied the factory for a long time, remarking that it was a "bloody shame" it had been lost. The Guards Brigade had named the factory and had lost a lot of good men taking it. He had been beyond the factory on patrol in the first couple of days, he said. In reading much later, I was not surprised to find what he told me was true. The Guards had been there all right.

When we got back to our bivouac, the promise of spring was beginning to be fulfilled. The weather was warmer, the sunshine more consistent. The earth was beginning to dry out. The grass was greening and here and there flowers had begun to appear. I missed hearing or seeing birds at Anzio. People said there had been owls in the pines when the troops first arrived. They were long gone and nothing had replaced them. Another thing detracting from full enjoyment of the spring breezes was the sweet sickly smell of death which sometimes wafted back to assault our nostrils. It was especially bad over behind the Cisterna front where, we were told, the corpses of some of the Rangers killed in the earlier attack still lay unburied between the lines. Up close the smell would have been gagging and gut-wrenching. I much preferred the acrid whiff of cordite.

Once we had settled into the pines again, many of the men turned their attentions to spring housecleaning with a display of pride and diligence which would have done credit to middle-class home owners. There was much cleaning and repair to be done. Company vehicles, available to squads and platoons, resumed their foraging trips to Anzio and Nettuno to secure additional building materials and furnishings for our shelters.

As our stay on the beachhead lengthened, the underground shelters became more spacious and elaborately furnished. Some men took great pride in showing people around their homes, and, I must say, these showplaces were sights worth seeing. There were rugs on the floor of the best of them, blackout curtains over the entry way, mirrors and pictures on the walls, chairs, tables, sometimes glass tumblers and a jealously guarded supply of candles.

Once a company officer had accepted an invitation to visit one shelter, he felt obliged, of course, to accept invitations from the people next door and the neighbors across the street. And so it went. Not everyone participated in this form of keeping up with the Jones's but enough did to raise delicate questions of etiquette.

The social calendar of a platoon leader could be managed easily as long as he accepted invitations from only the "right people." If he became too democratic and started to move in companywide circles, he would at least triple his social obligations and might need an appointment secretary to keep track of them. And how does one go about complimenting one's hosts without seeming to take sides on what might be burning issues? Not only was there rivalry and a certain coolness between neighbors; sometimes there were long festering disagreements between roommates on abstruse questions of décor, taste and the desirability of discarding or of acquiring this item or that.

We had lots of time on our hands and other recreational interests were not neglected. Many of the men had been brought up on what was then called "hillbilly music." One young fellow with a respectable repertoire of country songs had acquired a guitar. He was a rather shy person but would occasionally appear in concert after supper and before darkness in a small but appreciative circle of friends. If the audience got too large or too critical, he would cut his performance short.

Hillbilly music did not enjoy the wide following it was to acquire later. Some members of the company, the sophisticates and city boys, would have none of it here. As an Ozark Mountains boy, I enjoyed it, but I listened unobtrusively from the sidelines to avoid being too closely tied to the hillbilly faction.

The song most frequently requested at these entertainments had a verse which rings in my ears as I write:

"In the pines, in the pines, where the sun never shines,
And you shiver when the cold wind blows,
Little girl, little girl, what have I done,
To make you treat me so?"

It was a mournful tune, one well suited to the mood of homesick men who had been ill used, or wanted to feel ill used, or feared they might be ill used by their women at home.

There was a fair amount of recreational gambling in the pines that April. Among the troops it took the conventional forms of playing cards and shooting dice—there was a song about that too. With the officers it mostly involved betting on the timing of anticipated events.

The center piece of our speculation was "Operation Overlord," the cross-channel invasion of what Hitler called *"Festung Europa."* We had, of course, neither the code word nor any details of the planned operation, but we, along with everybody else, knew the invasion was imminent. While some of my friends made side bets on such things as when the breakout from the beachhead would occur, the date for victory in Europe, the date for total victory, etc., most of us contented ourselves with participation in a pool organized by someone at battalion headquarters in which the pot would go to that battalion officer who came closest to picking the exact date for the cross-channel effort.

I chose May 10 because, I reasoned, on that date exactly four years earlier the Germans had begun their brilliantly successful moves into France and the Low Countries. I was wrong, of course, by about a month and didn't win the prize. I still think it was a good theory. It just didn't take into account such little things as the weather, the tides, the moon, the availability of shipping, etc.

But gambling was very much a part-time entertainment. For the more actively inclined, there was volleyball. Over in the British sector they could have their beetle races. The Special Service Forces along the Mussolini Canal could amuse themselves by playing little jokes on the *Tedeschi* in nightly raids far behind enemy lines. We preferred the less alien, less dangerous sport of volleyball.

A volleyball and a net were thoughtfully provided by the rear echelon. We organized ourselves raggedly and informally into teams. Games would sometimes be interrupted by enemy action for brief periods of time. On one occasion I walked back to the service line with the ball in my hand and turned around to face the court only to find that the men on both teams had completely disappeared. They had heard something I had paid insufficient attention to, namely, an artillery round coming in too close for comfort. Realizing immediately what had happened, I also dived for cover.

There were nightly bull sessions at the company CP. Home, girls, and current events other than domestic politics were recurring items of interest. It is a bit difficult, after all, to carry on a political discussion with someone who observes at the outset that all politicians ought to be strung up by the balls unless, that is, you are prepared to argue for a more severe punishment.

There was some talk, but very little interest, in soldier voting in the presidential election of 1944. The latent sentiment seemed to favor a continuation of the present governmental leadership. Some of these citizen soldiers thought it was sheer folly to hold elections in wartime, while I expressed the view that elections should be held but that people in the service should not be allowed to vote. Reasoning with the literal and uncompromising mind of the young, I thought the logic of civil supremacy led inevitably to that conclusion. At that time, in that place and on that issue, I had become more military than the military. But neither I nor anyone else cared enough about voting to pursue the issue.

Nor was reading a favorite pastime. I had just about given up reading books as a frivolous pursuit, unbecoming a man of action such as I. Apparently most of the others had not acquired that pernicious habit. Issues of *Stars and Stripes* were passed around unless someone needed them for toilet paper. Informative articles on the progress of the war were read and discussed. Ernie Pyle's dispatches were a favorite, partly because he had spent time with the division in North Africa and his reports could be trusted. But mostly we just looked at the pictures in the publications which came our way. Bill Mauldin's cartoons were applauded; *Yank* magazine was valued for its chaste pieces of "cheesecake." The fevered imagination of sex-starved men could work wonders on pictures of fully clad ladies with oversized breasts, shapely legs, and attractive rear ends.

The major exception to the widespread lack of interest in the printed word was mail, any kind of mail, from home. Mail call was always an eagerly awaited event and never more so than at Anzio. Almost always I received artistically decorated envelopes containing loving, tender letters from my talented sweetheart and affectionate, informative letters from my mother who took care of correspondence in my family. All the letters I received were upbeat, optimistic, and positive. I tried to answer in the same vein. On those rare occasions when, for one reason or another, I didn't hear my name at mail call, I felt much as a little boy must feel when Santa Claus has forgotten him while all around others are receiving presents.

Company officers were supposed to censor outgoing mail from their units, but I and most others I knew had long since stopped taking that function seriously. Faced with a stack of outgoing letters, we usually signed and sealed the envelopes automatically without looking at what was inside.

Censorship struck me as a waste of time as well as an invasion of privacy. Military secrecy could not provide a justification since the people at home seemed to know more about the situation than we did. What other justifications for censorship were there? Well, bad letters home might have an adverse effect on civilian morale and lessen domestic support for the war effort. But that was not a legitimate governmental concern as far as I could see.

There were two kinds of situations in which I did read outgoing mail. One of these was legitimate; the other was not. I thought I was justified in reading a man's outgoing letters when we were concerned with his emotional state, especially after an action in which he had experienced more than ordinary trauma or when he appeared to be under great stress for unknown reasons. The other situation in which I stuck my nose into the private affairs of other people was reprehensible. That was when I had absolutely nothing else to do and sought amusement or titillation.

Apart from one Lothario who wrote passionate and sexually explicit love letters to each of three or four different girls, these pleasures were rarely forthcoming. Most of what I read confirmed and deepened my sympathy and respect for the men in the platoon. Some of the letters were barely literate, sad and depressing. I couldn't help feeling sympathy for people separated from home by long distance, facing grave danger, and unable to express their feelings.

There was no boasting of heroic exploits in any of the letters I read. Most men adopted the strategy of minimizing the danger they were in, sometimes claiming to be in safe jobs which they didn't have. Strong religious beliefs were evident in some of the letters where men admitted to the dangers and sometimes to the great guilt they felt at having killed a fellow human being. But these men usually expressed faith in a God who would forgive them and see them through.

I never saw anything in my small sample of outgoing mail to compromise security or lower home front morale. Perhaps realizing that their letters were subject to scrutiny, the men never complained about company officers although they sometimes expressed veiled criticism of higher authority and wondered why they were where they were. It was obvious many were homesick and almost all said they looked forward to seeing their loved ones soon.

But there were frequent reminders that death was an ever present possibility and some of us would never see our homeland again. One of the most sensational of these was an incident which all who were there could not help but remember.

Just outside the company area, there was a clearing in the Padiglione Woods, and in that clearing a landing strip had been scrapped off to accommodate piper clubs engaged in spotting for an artillery battery located in the same area. Late one afternoon as the men were lining up for chow, there was a rending crash overhead. I hugged the trunk of a tree as a rain of debris began to fall in the company area. Others also took defensive action.

It turned out to be a freakish accident, or perhaps, a not so freakish accident given the crowded conditions on the beachhead at the time. An observer plane with two men aboard had been directly in the trajectory of an outgoing artillery round with the inevitable result. That was the explosion we heard. It was bits and pieces of the men, the plane and their equipment which had fallen on us.

One of our replacements hurried up with a look of ghoulish fascination and horror on his face.

"Look, Lieutenant," he said in a tone suggesting he needed to share his information with anyone else who would look and listen, "A piece of real meat fell in my meat can."

He held out his bloody mess kit which held chunks of flesh, bone, and gristle. I strongly advised him to throw the residue away and to wash his meat can in hot, soapy water. He continued to look at me, seeming at first not to comprehend. A friend of his came up and took him gently by the arm. They walked away together.

Our maintenance people broke out their shovels and used them to scoop up bits and pieces of what had been human beings. They deposited their loads in the shredded parachutes which the unfortunate victims had no chance whatsoever of using. The rest of the company stood around watching. Supper would be a little late.

The accident created considerable commotion, but the beachhead was always a very active, a very noisy place. A company of First Armored Division tanks located near us, might, at any hour of the night, start their motors, wheel out of their entrenchments and roar out of the area to prepared positions up front for firing missions. In a few hours they would come clanking back, but we became so accustomed to this activity that we ceased to pay attention.

That was even more true of outgoing artillery. Our guns were seldom silent for more than ten minutes at a stretch. We became habituated to their sounds. They seemed natural, even comforting. An infrequent interruption of routine firing would raise comment or an unexpectedly heavy barrage might give rise to the gleeful speculation that one of our observers might have sighted some lone German going out to take a shit. By this time we had artillery capacity to spare.

But enemy gunners didn't seem to be in short supply either. We gave them respectful attention. All of us developed a degree of expertise in distinguishing the sounds of different artillery pieces. Some of it was easy to learn. Having once heard the sound, only subsequent deafness or serious memory loss could prevent anyone from identifying the overhead rush of "Anzio Annie," the giant 279 MM railroad gun which the enemy kept up in the mountains. Actually, as it turned out, they had two such guns but we weren't keen enough to realize that. In daylight both of them found shelter in railroad tunnels; in darkness or in periods when Allied air power was immobilized by low visibility, one or the other of the two would venture forth, fire a few rounds and then lumber back into shelter.

No matter what we were doing, we could not help but note the times when the big gun was active. A round passing overhead sounded a bit like a giant locomotive moving through the sky. It was the noise which fascinated. Barring a short round, there was little for us to fear from the impact. We all knew that Annie was seeking to mate with ships in the harbor or with other targets more promising than armored infantry troops well dispersed and well dug in. The unmistakable sounds of the *nebelwerfers* would sometimes come in on the back of the night wind, but we knew they were aimed at targets nearer the front.

Initially, the night time air raids gave us greater concern than the artillery. Every night about 2200 hours with a regularity which caused the troops to refer to him as "Bed Check Charley," an enemy observation plane circled over the pines. Frequently flares would be dropped to mark the target. Then additional planes would come over to broadcast antipersonnel bombs much as farmers might broadcast seed on fertile ground. Heavier stuff from either the air or the ground fell around us every day or so and we learned to be especially wary of tree bursts. But the deeper we dug and the more overhead protection we added to our shelters, the safer we felt.

By the middle of April a constant cascade of men and material added to the noise level and threatened to inundate the already congested beachhead. New divisions, parts of divisions and assorted other units flowed in to prepare for the breakout. The remainder of our division which had been kept on the southern front until late in the game rejoined us at this time.

Space for the lodgment of these new units and for stockpiling munitions and supplies was hard to come by. That was no problem of ours. We would let our brilliant planners worry about it. The already dense cluster of confusing signs pointing to this and that headquarters was augmented by additional signs directing the possibly bewildered traveler to units recently arrived, installations recently established. And on the roads in the American sector larger signs appeared to warn drivers, "SLOW! DUST BRINGS SHELL FIRE."

But it didn't take dust to bring shell fire. More and more the degree of congestion invited it. As the buildup proceeded, enemy action on the ground and in the air increased. Almost every night you could hear explosions as an ammunition dump, a supply depot or some other installation went up somewhere behind the front. Sometimes fires and secondary explosions would continue for hours. Sometimes a fire would seem to die down only to flare up again as the flames reached additional combustible material. As a number of people remarked at the time, enemy bombers and gunners had a high probability of hitting something even if they fired blindfolded.

Despite the increasing sound and fury, my company suffered relatively light casualties that April in the pines. Occasionally fragments from a bomb or shell would strike the unlucky or the temporarily unwary. The combined effects of continual harassment by land and air, the high decibel level, and, perhaps, the realization that no place on the beachhead was beyond the reach of enemy guns so unnerved a few men they were sent back to Naples with a diagnosis of "combat fatigue." There were also accidents and more conventional illnesses. This had been a malaria-infested area and we took large quantities of atabrine tablets. The food was boring and the water in the Lyster bags had a funny taste. Still, all in all, Anzio was a much better place in April than it had been in either February or March. And a much better place than it would be in late May when we would try to implement plans for the breakout.

Chapter 8

Anzio
Breakout and Holiday

By the first of May plans for the breakout were far advanced. The briefings were extensive and detailed with much of the information reaching down to the individual soldier. Very near our company area a sandbox replica of the terrain around the perimeter of the beachhead was constructed and, when destroyed by enemy action, reconstructed. Company officers and noncoms filed by the sandbox with at least time for a quick look. Maps and aerial photographs were made available to junior officers and were perused intently.

We knew in broad outline what was supposed to happen. The outward thrust from the beachhead was to be preceded by a full-scale attack on the Cassino front. At a propitious moment to be determined by Fifth Army, or perhaps by General Alexander's Fifteenth Army Group, it mattered little to us, the beachhead forces would sally forth to complete the second part of a one-two punch. Higher headquarters would also decide later which of several plans Sixth Corps would implement.

The alternatives were named and outlined. From what we were told, higher headquarters would choose between operations Turtle, Grasshopper, Crawdad, and Buffalo. All but one failed to gain our approval. One plan, for example, called for a major effort up the Albano Road in the direction of Campoleone. It was the most direct route to Rome, but who in his right mind would want to attack near those wadis? Another involved a concentrated thrust to the south for a quick link-up with forces coming up from the Cassino front. But why should we try that? Why not let the Cassino front come up to us? Only Operation Buffalo made sense to company officers. We were so sure it would be adopted we focused almost all of our attention on it.

Buffalo called for a major attack through Cisterna and the Velletri-Valmontone Gap with the ultimate object being Valmontone itself. A glance at the map revealed that possession of Valmontone would put us directly astride the primary escape route of the German Tenth Army which had done such a professionally admirable job of holding Cassino throughout the winter. If we got to Valmontone in time, the German army under General von Vietinghoff would be smashed one way or another. It could not live to fight another day. The war would be shortened. Buffalo was only common sense to us, and, with unusual charity, we generously credited our high command with having sufficient intelligence to see the obvious.

At some point General Harmon and his staff came into the pines to speak to us. I can't specify the exact audience but since I was there, it couldn't have been an exclusive gathering. This was my first and only glimpse of our division commander and I remember only he told us he would have, I thought he said, five hundred tanks, to throw at "those bastards."

He would need them. Operation Buffalo placed the Third Division and the First Armored in the first wave of the assault. After diversionary attacks in the British sector and elsewhere around the beachhead perimeter, the Third Division would take Cisterna, while the First Armored Division on its left would drive toward and across the railroad embankment on the Cisterna-Rome line, and proceed in the general direction of Valmontone.

The first few days threatened to be the most difficult. The initial task of my division would involve breaking through the extensive mine fields and wired in strong points which barred the way. There was much discussion of these problems and the related problem of getting the tanks across the railroad embankment.

Our briefings included information on how the division proposed to deal with the mines and the wire whichever plan was adopted. In the tank regiments there had been experimentation with improvised weapons and new techniques. Someone had developed a grappling hook which could be propelled by an 81 MM mortar mounted on a tank. Once the hook had landed on the other side of the wire, it could be reeled in, clearing out in the process a path through which tanks and infantry could advance. Another device was a chain flail which enabled tanks to beat the ground in front of them detonating the mines before they could do major damage. Finally, we were told about the "snakes," and these proved to be the most effective weapons of all. The snakes were long metal rods containing high explosives, giant bangalore torpedoes. The tanks could push them under the wire and then detonate them, cleaning out both wire and mines at the same time.

The adoption of new techniques required additional training. For a couple of weeks in late April and early May we moved out of the pines for rather intensive fieldwork on tank-infantry cooperation. Both day and night exercises were carried out.

The training sites were over by the Mussolini Canal behind a front which had been occupied by General Frederick's First Special Service Force from the beginning. It was an elite formation of volunteers, American and Canadian, which made up for its lack of numbers by technical proficiency, dash, and daring. Numbering perhaps twelve hundred men the Special Service Force held a very long front but one where the terrain strongly militated against a major thrust by either friend or foe. The canal fronted the Pontine Marshes, an area inhospitable to large-scale troop movements.

While all of us respected the First Special Service Force, we were considerably less than enthusiastic about carrying out maneuvers behind their front in plain view of the enemy. We scoffed at the idea we would be completely shielded from enemy observation by artificial fog. But, miracle of miracles, something protected us! According to one explanation, the Germans were so dumbfounded at our stupidity, they held their fire. Whatever the case, going back into the pines seemed hazardous by comparison.

Sometime about the middle of May we got word that Operation Buffalo would be implemented. After that, I had no doubt the attack would ultimately carry us in triumph to Rome. My only question, a not insignificant one, was whether I would make it.

The attack on the Cassino front was opened on May 11. We assumed that in a day or so we would be called upon to do our part. A week passed. Somehow we got reports of the fighting down south. We knew that the French Moroccan *Goumiers* were running through the mountains to the west of the Liri Valley. We heard that the Polish Corps had at long last taken the monastery and that Cassino town had fallen. Somehow we learned that the American Eighty-eighth and Eighty-fifth Divisions, coming up the coast road, had reached Gaeta and then Terracina. We felt an impatience, stemming from a wish to get the dread over with and a belief that if we waited too long, the German Tenth Army would escape through Valmontone. When, finally, on May 22, we moved out of our bivouac to our assembly area, I feared we had already waited too long.

At our last briefing we received what was probably lifesaving news for some of us. At least it was a reprieve. In the initial assault my battalion was to be in division reserve. CCA and CCB were to go in abreast with CCA on the left next to the Forty-fifth Division and CCB on the right next to the third. The division's assault units would be the ones to test the snakes under battle conditions, and even if they didn't achieve an early breakthrough, they might at least delineate and soften up the enemy's main line of resistance. We would be perhaps a mile to the rear of the start line in comparative safety.

After trudging through the dark to our assembly area, we found the place crowded with tanks and other units of the reserve. That was bad news. Being positioned around this armored might greatly complicated the problem of concealment. Besides, we were "bunched up" and would have to live in military sin until a breakthrough brought room to spread out.

There was another complication. Our training and experience had taught the importance of "digging in," but we couldn't dig here because of the danger of creating obstacles for our own tanks. Our sins were compounded, our sense of unease was increased. We were told to do the best we could.

My platoon found a ready-made drainage ditch, not big enough to stop tanks but deep enough to afford a small amount of protection. To hearten myself and the noncoms, I told them the enemy gunners would, in all probability, concentrate on targets closer to the front when the balloon went up. I surely hoped that was true. It was our only chance.

Around midnight we were treated to the most fantastic, the most remarkable display of fireworks I had ever seen or hope to see. At the height of the display the entire sky to our left and rear was lighted up with different colored flares, red tracer bullets, green tracers, air bursts from artillery, bombs bursting in air from antiaircraft fire around the harbor. Back toward Anzio and over in the British sector you could see fires burning out of control and hear muffled explosions. Had it really been this way every night? Or was this something extraordinary, something to be concerned about? In the sheltering pines we had seen and heard only a part of the show. Now all of the show came to us unbidden and an awesome, beautiful spectacle it was.

There was little sleep that night before 0400 hours. Units of the reserve were still coming in. There seemed to be a good many people just milling around. It was going to be even more congested than we had first thought. I cursed the master minds in charge of this operation.

Toward dawn the big guns, after firing intermittently all night, opened up with full force. In a sense this was nothing new. In order to keep the enemy guessing as to the time and place of a move which they had to be expecting, Allied artillery in the last couple of weeks had greeted each dawn with an intense barrage directed at different sectors of the front. It was hoped that the Germans had become so habituated to the practice they would regard this bombardment as just another exercise. We, of course, knew this one was for real and our friends would be going in when it lifted.

After about thirty minutes, the barrage slackened for a time only to start up again with renewed fury. We knew the guns had shifted to targets further back. The attack was under way. Our friends were at risk. When the rhythm of the firing was again disrupted and became more irregular, we knew that our artillery was responding to specific requests from forward observers pinpointing their targets.

I had guessed right about the enemy artillery. Only a few rounds came our way. If our friends kept moving, the enemy would have little time to turn on us. To our great relief, some of the tanks moved out of the assembly area to go forward. Our prospects were brightening.

Later in the morning a few prisoners filtered back through our positions. We interpreted the smallness of the catch as an ominous sign, an indication that there would be no quick breakthrough. We had, of course, hoped for but had not expected easy success. The German, as General Lucas is reported to have remarked to the press on an earlier occasion, was a very tough fighter.

But the attack was going better than we had thought. By dark I heard a report that the division had crossed the railroad embankment and a seemingly conflicting report that we had elements up to the railroad embankment. From historical accounts I later learned that both reports were correct. There was no contradiction. CCA, using the snakes, had crossed the embankment and moved a quarter of a mile beyond. CCB, which for some reason, had not adopted the experiment, made slower progress and suffered greater losses in both men and machines. Even at that CCB was in a position to cross the embankment the following morning.

In the earlier afternoon of the next day, my battalion moved up a couple of miles nearer to the sound of small-arms fire. More artillery was falling on us now. We took casualties. When we crossed the railroad embankment, I at first didn't recognize it for what it was. It didn't fit the image built up in my mind from listening to the briefings and looking at the aerial photos. The excavation had been completed so long ago it seemed a natural part of the terrain. The slopes of its sides were not nearly as steep as I had expected. There were no signs of railroad tracks and ties. In all probability the enemy had taken them up to strengthen the elaborate shelters which had been tunneled into both walls of the embankment.

In some of the dugouts the men found lingerie and other evidence of the recent presence of females. Talk about the enemy knowing how to live well at the front! He was either demonstrating that here or else he had some rather kinky *soldaten* on his roster.

At first light the next morning, we started to move up again. Cisterna was off to my right rear. All seemed quiet over there. I could see smoke curling up from the town but couldn't tell whether it had fallen to the Third Division or remained in enemy hands as a possible threat to our right flank.

We were moving up a rather narrow path which had been cleared through a mine field. White tape clearly marked the path's boundaries. Suddenly I felt something slap into my side and a great blast struck the upper part of my body. There was a loud explosion. An antitank mine had been detonated in the field to my immediate right. The concussion threw me back on a scout car which was moving forward, trying to negotiate the path we were on. I fell, and the right front wheel of the vehicle rolled over my left foot before coming to a halt.

The next thing I remember is being in an aid station. Someone was cutting off my boot. My ears were still ringing. I had trouble understanding what was being said. Blood had seeped through my uniform from a superficial wound in the side. They patched me up and took me back to an airstrip where a plane was loading to take the wounded back to Naples. I saw what I assumed were newsreel cameras grinding as I was carried up the ramp.

It was my first plane ride. The involuntary flight was on a C-47. There was no welcome aboard, no seats, no solicitous hostess to anticipate our needs. There must have been medical personnel aboard but I don't know. I slept all the way on a very short flight and didn't need attention.

When they took me to a clean bed in the Naples hospital, I was a bit hesitant about crawling between white sheets with all the dirt and grime on my body. It was the kind of situation which mothers are supposed to warn their children about. The pretty, young nurse, a perfect stranger, could see very well that I had not kept myself clean. I should have paid more attention to what Momma said.

After the doctors had put my foot in a cast and taken care of my less serious injuries, I found myself back in bed in a long ward filled with other platoon leaders. Ward attendants were installing additional beds in the corridor. Apparently the influx of new patients had not subsided. And these were only the American wounded. I don't know who took care of the British, the Poles, the *Goumiers,* etc. But from what we had heard, the *Goumiers* probably didn't even know about hospitalization. Maybe they just cut off an injured arm, leg, hand or whatever and went back to killing Germans.

After lights out that first evening, the ward was more raucous and unrestrained than any military barracks I have ever slept in. A couple of guys were in pretty bad shape, but most of us had less serious injuries. I, for one, felt exhilarated at having escaped from Anzio with my life.

The anesthetic which had been administered to most of us gave a boost to our sense of well-being. I was told later it was something called Sodium Pentothal. Whatever. Its aftereffects made us feel tipsy and talkative. We laughed a lot; we engaged in scintillating repartee with unseen companions in beds distant from our own.

One man, more out of it than most, kept reporting that he "couldn't see a fuckin' thing." He was encouraged to restore his eyesight by calling the nurse and asking her to get in bed with him. To our only partially smothered laughter, he did just that, explaining in plain words what he proposed to do and why. She was not amused.

The staff had considerable difficulty keeping us quiet until the anesthetic wore off. Pleas and threats produced only temporary results. We were like exuberant little boys who delight in testing the limits of adult authority. Following one stern rebuke, there was much shushing and the ward became quiet for a few minutes. Then someone farted. After the first round of laugher had subsided, someone else began witty commentary on this hilarious occurrence. Another guy who specialized in impersonating the head nurse used a falsetto voice to proclaim, "Now, I will not tolerate farting, fucking, or fighting on this ward. We have to have rules. I just will not stand for this noise." And then, when the situation threatened to get completely out of hand, we were warned officially. We quieted down for a little while.

Next morning I heard one patient making abashed apology for his behavior of the night before. I decided to brazen it out.

"What was wrong with those rowdies in here last night?" I asked the nurse. "I had trouble getting my sleep."

She gave me a sour look. I don't think she was deceived.

After breakfast I decided to contact my parents. I wanted them to learn where I was from me rather than from the War Department. Through the Red Cross I was able to send a routine telegram:

"Slightly injured. Safe in hospital. Not to worry. Will write," or words to that effect. The Red Cross lady seemed to know the appropriate words by heart.

As it turned out, I didn't need to be in such a hurry to get a message off. Even my follow-up letter reached home before the War Department notice. Unfortunately there were many similar and much worse messages to be processed.

When Saturday morning inspection came, the hospital staff was again thrown into a state of agitation. Every patient who could get out of bed was to stand at attention by its side when the inspecting officer made his way down the aisle. Upon receiving this information, a number of patients began to show alarming symptoms of extreme weakness bordering on total debility. They had to be coaxed and then bullied into cooperation.

Those who couldn't possibly get out of bed were instructed to *lie* at attention. At first I thought that was a joke. Not so; it was standard operating procedure. One of the bedridden patients, perhaps realizing that the staff was simply carrying out orders, was very cooperative indeed. He offered not only to lie at attention but, if it would be of any help, to salute the inspecting officer with a rousing fart when the great man approached his bed. I think the nurse in charge was half fearful that something such as that would happen. She seemed more than a little relieved when the inspection was over.

In the first few days I tried to learn what I could about the progress of the First Armored Division. I read every paper I could get my hands on and made inquiries from people on the staff. Whenever possible, I tried to talk with visitors and new patients coming down from the front.

The news which I eagerly waited for, that we had taken Valmontone, that the German Tenth Army was trapped, never came. Instead, I became aware that the major thrust had shifted toward Campoleone and that Fifth Army units were engaged in a "race for Rome." Valmontone was eventually captured but by then it was too late. Most of the German Tenth Army had escaped to the north. The Fifth Army's triumphal entry into Rome on June 4 was celebrated with great fanfare in the *Stars and Stripes.* Valmontone, which had never been a household word, ceased to have any military significance whatsoever. My attention shifted away from the front to focus more sharply on my immediate surroundings.

Most of the general hospitals serving Fifth Army that spring seemed to be clustered in one great medical complex at Bagnoli, just outside Naples. The buildings were modern, constructed by the Mussolini government, it was reported, in anticipation of hosting a World's Fair. Whatever the original intention, the structures and their concentration served our purposes very well and brought unanticipated benefits to the patients.

After a big offensive everybody who was anybody among the surviving junior officers of Fifth Army was likely sooner or later to show up in Naples with a temporary address in the Bagnoli complex. It was a place to see and to inquire about old friends.

In a short period I was ambulatory. My foot was in a walking cast and I was able to throw my crutches away. I acquired a new set of O.D.'s and applied for a pass to go into Naples. I got the pass but it was so restrictive and obtained with so much bureaucratic difficulty that in future I avoided going out through the main gate and, following the lead of others, gave myself a pass by the simple expedient of climbing over the chain link fence which surrounded the compound. With a little boost from my friends I had no difficulty climbing out and in. I missed a lot of bedchecks that way and further annoyed the nursing staff, but I never missed doctors' rounds in the morning.

Transportation to and from Naples was no problem. The military provided a dependable shuttle service, no questions asked. In addition, a more or less continuous stream of military traffic made hitchhiking easy, especially for a guy with a cast on his leg.

The road from the medical complex led through the Bagnoli tunnel where, it was said, Neapolitans had sheltered during the worst Allied air raids. It was a relatively short, dimly lit, poorly ventilated place when I first saw it, but it was a place, a shelter which soldiers of the line could appreciate. The physical scars above the entrances to the tunnel and the slag heaps of concrete, dirt, rock and rubble which had been pushed off to one side were easy to read. In leaving the city, German demolition teams had sought to delay Allied military traffic at this point. When Fifth Army earth moving equipment came up, as it must have done shortly, the tunnel was cleared. How much time had the enemy bought? A day, perhaps? A week?

A few miles of coast road through manmade squalor on one side and the natural beauty of the Bay on the other separated the tunnel from the lower end of Via Roma, the main street I had first seen from the harbor back in December. Viewed up close, the street was a bit more irregular than I had imagined. It inclined downhill at a somewhat steeper angle and there were, slanting off in different directions, numerous alleys which I hadn't detected. Most of these were posted as off limits to military personnel. Each of them gave forth a distinctive mix of odors, mostly unpleasant. The pungent smell of piss provided a common denominator.

Some of the Neapolitans still called their main street "the Toledo" for such it had been named earlier. Mussolini, presumably after he got the trains running on time, had changed that. It was now officially Via Roma and the street signs proclaimed the great reform.

The war, of course, had brought much more devastating change to the Toledo. Its once fashionable shops and department stores were now boarded up or bombed out, replaced by hordes of open-air merchants, black market entrepreneurs, shoeshine stands, sellers of souvenirs, trinkets, sex. The most visible of the purveyors of goods and services were the *scrugnizzi,* Italian street boys between the ages, let us say, of six and sixteen, who roamed the streets waging hundreds of little private wars for survival. And a desperate struggle it must have been. I heard more than one kid of less than teenage years calling out to passing soldiers variations on "Hey, Joe! You sleep, my sister? Good, clean stuff. Only fourteen years old."

The smaller children, especially little girls five or six years old, made more timid, more conventional requests for *caramelle,* chocolate, and chewing gum.

Usually, except during afternoon siesta and after curfew, Via Roma was crowded with a broad sample of the Neapolitan population: clerics, housewives, students, doctors, civil servants, the *carabinieri,* small shopkeepers, derelicts, unknowns, prostitutes, working men and women, and men and women who looked as if they had never done a day's work in their lives. There were well-chaperoned young ladies and children with shoes. And, of course, as a temporary part of the populations, soldiers, soldiers and sailors everywhere.

A favorite promenade for soldiers and civilians alike was the Galleria Umberto, a large arcade featuring shops which sold cameos, bracelets, art work souvenirs, army insignia, etc. It also had small bars offering white wine, vermouth, espresso, etc. The Galleria cut diagonally from Via Roma across the block to Via Verdi, making connections at its terminus with the San Carlo Opera House and, across the street, with an army prophylactic station. Lines for the opera formed late in the afternoon; business at the pro station didn't become brisk until well after dark.

A few blocks up the street on the Via Roma side of the arcade, a Peninsular Base Section officers' club served, although that was not its intended purpose, as a forward assembly area for infantry officers whether on leave from the hospitals or attached to units temporarily close at hand. Before the Fifth Army took over, the multistoried building had housed the Bank of Naples. The structure had an impressive grayish façade and massive wooden and brass doors suitable to an establishment seeking to give the impression of power and permanence.

Unlike most of the other large buildings in the area, this one showed no war damage. Most surprisingly, even its glass was intact. Since the Galleria just down the street had lost its great skylight to near misses, we were puzzled. What was going on here? Was God on the side of the bankers? That taxed credulity. Had damage been inflicted but quickly repaired by good old American know how? Entirely possible. It was well known that the American "can do" spirit could accomplish miracles undreamed of by less favored people in the rest of the world.

But the explanation current in the circles in which I moved was that the farsighted brass of the Allied high command, anticipating their early possession of the city and having already assigned uses to the bank building, had given the bombers strict orders to leave it alone. At first I had doubts about conspiratorial explanations and assumed they were offered jokingly. As I saw more and more of the rear echelon, however, I realized that such speculation was not necessarily presented in jest and began to put more credence in it. In my outfit the acronym "PBS" was almost always linked with "son of a bitch."

I was also told, and this I could believe without question, that the Peninsular Base Section had originally sought to maintain its club on Via Roma for members only as a way of keeping out undesirables. Apparently the policy, if it had ever come to that, was rather quickly abandoned. It would have been difficult to enforce. The club was large and prominently located. While transient officers might well have been willing to settle for "separate but equal," there was no equal, or separate either for that matter. And by no means all the combat officers passing through Naples were ambulatory patients from the hospital. Many of them were physically healthy and had ready access to firearms. Men "armed and presumed dangerous" is, I believe, the way police reports sometimes phrase it. My memory is that PBS sold us temporary memberships in the club for a fee, but I can't be sure of that. Whatever the case, our right to use the facilities was firmly established in the late spring of 1944.

We didn't exactly overrun the entire place. There was no reason, for example, to explore the first floor which provided entrance to the club. A wide, circular staircase of the kind beloved of Hollywood when it wants to depict the elegant lifestyle of the very rich, led to the second floor where the action was. There were several large rooms up there with high ceilings and arched windows. Several bars operated simultaneously. They served gin and juice, cognac, pastry, and sandwiches of ham or cheese. There was a dance floor and a small Italian band.

The establishment was, in the words of the economist, "labor intensive." Substantial teams of appropriately uniformed Italian bartenders, waiters and busboys were in place to serve our needs. We complained only about the lack of cocktail waitresses. There were few women, Italian or otherwise, working in the club and the Italian girls who did have jobs functioned mostly as cashiers selling chits from inside little teller cages.

We made little use of the dance floor. Finding a dance partner or, indeed, acquiring female companionship for any purposes was a problem for us in Naples. The American women, nurses, Wacs, Red Cross workers, and other female service personnel, were out of our league. We could not hope to compete with the multitude of more or less permanently assigned higher ranking officers whose statuses entitled them to jeeps, apartments, and other privileges. I and many other line officers reacted to the situation with a haughty pride to ignore even the best looking of the girls from home. It was not entirely sour grapes. In most cases, the Italian women were prettier and more desirable.

But there were other kinds of problems in going out with Italian women. We had little opportunity for meeting respectable girls and were afraid of those who walked the streets .

That reduced our alternatives to a nearby whorehouse licensed and inspected by the British military. I went there one time and stood in line to wait my turn. Apart from the waiting, the service was excellent, but I didn't go back. You may think me unduly demanding, but I had discovered there is something just a tad unromantic about queuing up for sex. Masturbation may not be very romantic either, but as one of our number reminded us, it is safe, economical, and not at all unpleasant.

In the club we refugees from the hospital congregated at tables, preferably close to a bar and as far removed as possible from the dance floor and the band. It was here we assembled to compare notes and celebrate our good fortunes. The only other part of the club we had occasion to use frequently was the large, spotlessly clean men's room. If it is of interest, I can report that the plumbing was working perfectly.

When I went to the club the first time, I ran into Ellis, the platoon leader's platoon leader. We settled in to drink and to exchange information. He couldn't tell me much about the outfit because he had been hit about the time I was.

Before long I got around to telling him how much he had boosted my morale in front of Buonriposo Ridge. I told him I had been scared shitless up there, that I had frozen and couldn't think straight. I said I wouldn't have made it if he hadn't come up when he did. I told him I didn't think I was going to make it through the war anyway. I don't know what all I didn't tell him that night.

Ellis was kind, but I could tell he was a bit embarrassed and put out with me. I had talked too much about the wrong things. It was bad form. I would never do that again.

He said I had done a good job up there. What else could he say? Although I knew my monologue had invited such a response, it was comforting where similar words from our jovial battalion commander didn't mean a damn thing. Ellis said he didn't know whether I would make it. Didn't know whether he would make it. Hell, we couldn't know about things like that. Better stop thinking about them. If our luck held out, we would make it. If not, then not. And "Heahs to may yew live a thousand yeahs and Ah nevah die."

Other people came to the table. The conversation had been all wrong anyway.

I saw Ellis for the last time a week or two later. It was late in the evening. We were coming out of the men's room to return to a table of boisterous celebrants. He reached into his pocket and brought out $45 or $50 in occupation currency, all that he had. He counted out a few dollars for himself and gave me the rest, explaining that he was going back up the next day. I would need the money, he said. He wouldn't. I protested mildly, then thanked him and promised to pay him back.

I never got the chance. When I returned to the battalion, I was told that Ellis had been killed. I couldn't imagine him dead.

I felt the loss more than I should have. Ellis and I were not close friends. I looked up to him, recognizing that he had qualities which I could never acquire. I never knew what he thought of me. When I asked about next of kin to whom I could repay my debt, I was told by someone who knew him better than I that Ellis was most unhappily married and would want me to keep the money. After all it was only money, something which Ellis treated very casually. So that was that. There was nothing I could do. I would never even have the chance to buy him a gin and orange or a cognac and water.

In the meantime, while luck was running out for Ellis, it was holding fast for me. My holiday in Naples continued. If we had no X-rays, other tests or therapy sessions prescribed during doctors' rounds, many of us on the ward considered our duties at the hospital over for the day and took off. The nursing staff threatened repeatedly to put us on report, but nothing ever came of it.

One afternoon as I was boosted into a truck bound for Via Roma, I heard a good-natured voice cry out, "Don't let that man on! He's A-Wall. Don't let him on!"

More than a little startled, I looked up to find Lieutenant Dono, an old friend from Camp Breckenridge days. He was in another hospital at Bagnoli but was following a course of action parallel to my own. A platoon leader in the Thirty-fourth Division, he had also been hit on the breakout. We spent considerable time together.

There was more to our holiday than drinking and carousing. We found time for sightseeing and window shopping in the Galleria. To give the folks back home visual evidence that each of us was physically intact, we had our pictures made singly and together. While Vesuvius had erupted earlier that spring and was still smoking and grumbling from time to time, I hobbled around with Dono for the better part of one day in the ruins of Pompeii. It was fascinating. We planned a return trip but there were so many other things to see and do I didn't get back to Pompeii until long after the war.

We had discovered a funicular railroad still in operation and made several trips up to Vomero, a much more prosperous part of the city. The Germans had maintained important headquarters installations on these heights and the Allies, knowing a good thing when they saw one, followed the example. But Dono and I didn't go to Vomero on official business. Nor did we, except on one occasion, go up there for hospitality.

One night as the guest of a major somebody or other, we were taken to an exclusive field grade officers' club. It was an uncomfortable experience for everybody concerned. I felt much as a day laborer in working clothes might feel after stumbling into a bankers' convention by mistake. The members of the club were dressed in blouses and pinks. They wore ties, of course, ribbons, and low-cut shoes with a high shine. After the first shock of our entry wore off, most of the members ignored us as we wanted them to. Some continued to stare, and the few who tried to be genuinely friendly overdid it, treating us as if we were Congressional Medal winners. We left early and had no desire to return.

It was the view from Vomero which attracted us. From tables in a pleasant outdoor café, you could sip wine and look out over the Bay to Sorrento, Capri, Vesuvius, and the entire Naples Harbor which was already beginning to fill up with more ships than I had ever seen in one place at one time. It was no secret that a great armada was being assembled for an invasion of southern France later in the summer.

We talked about the problem of achieving surprise in an operation of this kind. How could the enemy fail to know what everyone else seemed to know? Could the assumed destination be a deception? Was that large fleet really going to the Balkans or some other place? But, no, as it turned out, they really did go into southern France.

Even with our various sightseeing excursions, we found time for what are generally deemed to be culturally uplifting activities. In the Naples of the day that meant, most notably, an evening at the San Carlo Opera House, said to be one of the largest in Europe.

Dono and I went to the San Carlo just to be able to say we had gone and to see what opera was like. *La Bohème* was being presented. Lacking the cultural background to appreciate the performance, we focused on nonessentials. The opera company featured an ample-bosomed "Mimi" who, the libretto informed us, was wasting away from consumption. Maybe so, but I had seen line backers who didn't look as healthy as she did in her death scene. At least we could criticize what we took to be miscasting.

The audience on the main floor commanded our attention almost as much as the stage. It was more colorfully costumed than the cast. There was a profusion of dress uniforms in what could have been mistaken for a meeting of the General Assembly of the United Nations if that organization had been in existence at the time. The Fifth Army was surely one of the most cosmopolitan ever assembled, and all the nations seemed represented that evening; the Americans, of course, but also the British, the Scots, the Indians, the New Zealanders, the French, the Australians and others impossible for me to identify. To this colorful melange were added the dress uniforms of American and British naval officers and the simple but attractive attire of a few service women.

We foot soldiers with tickets obtained from the Red Cross, occupied seats higher up. No problem. Our uniforms were nothing to brag about and would have looked out of place on the main floor. There were very few civilians in attendance but we were told one day a week, or, perhaps, it was a month, was set aside for the Italians. In the future, Dono and I agreed, we would be happy to relinquish our seats to the natives.

One evening just before I left Naples, I accompanied my friend to dinner at a black market restaurant which had benefited from word of mouth advertising. There was nothing secret about its outward operation. It was located on a main street close to the officers' club and was frequented by a substantial clientele, mostly American army officers. The place was expensive, perhaps $5 for a full course dinner, but it was said to be worth it.

The establishment featured horse meat, or, if you preferred to believe the waiters, *bistecca.* It had good pasta, a green salad, a choice between *vino blanco* and *vino rosso* and gelati for dessert. There were white tablecloths on the table and attentive waiters at our side. There was only one problem.

Outside the restaurant as we went in, a small group of Italian kids had assembled. Some of them had their noses pressed against the glass window of the store front. They were watching the diners inside.

After we had been seated and given our order, we again became aware of the children. The waiters were having trouble keeping them out of the restaurant and away from the tables. We saw them chase one small kid who had sneaked in and moved forward with the obvious intention of grabbing something to eat off the table, perhaps thrusting it in his mouth and bolting for the door before his prize could be taken from him.

A little bit of this was entirely too much. Dono and I rescued another kid who had been stopped and instructed the waiter to let the boy be seated with us. He might have been seven or nine or one hundred and nine if you looked only at his eyes. We ordered the *bistecca* dinner for him. When the waiter asked if we wanted to include wine, we paused to confer with each other and to consult the boy. He indicated he did want wine, and we concluded we were within the bounds of the customs of the country in ordering it for him.

The hungry kid went after the horse meat, the pasta and all the rest with a gusto which both gratified and saddened us. I revised downward my original estimate of his age when I saw him grasp his wine glass in both hands as smaller children do. He soon cleaned his plate, finished his wine and gelati. Then he got up, bowed, said, "Grazie. Grazie," and hurried out the door with wary glances directed at the waiters.

After splitting the bill, my companion and I also left the premises, but leisurely and without fear of being cuffed or reviled. Outside the children must have observed the whole thing. They crowded around us, some clutching at our uniforms. One little boy with big brown eyes, a thin face and an emaciated body pointed a finger to his mouth and said, "Fame, Joe, fame." Other little voices echoed in doleful, pitiful tones, "Fame. Fame." Whenever I hear the phrase "a chorus in a Greek tragedy," I think of those little people.

To hide my feelings, I roughly tore myself away and walked rapidly from the scene. Jesus Good Christ and Holy Mary, Mother of God, I couldn't produce loaves and fishes to feed this hungry multitude. So they were *scugnizzi,* masters of deceit and play acting, thieves, pickpockets, pimps, rollers of drunken GIs and all the rest. My God! So what! They were kids; they were hungry.

As far as I was and am concerned the plight of the Italian children ranks very high among the real horrors of war. The men who had been blown to bits over the pine forest were soldiers, after all, and in war soldiers are sometimes mutilated and killed. It goes with the territory. But the children? How could anyone ever be the same after getting even a glimpse of the slower, more subtle, but infinitely more cruel destruction of the children?

When the hospital certified that I was again fit for duty, I was not particularly sorry. The pleasures of Naples had begun to pall. The pretensions, the unmitigated arrogance of so much of the rear echelon, the willingness of so many Americans to profit from the black market while lording it over a desperate and conquered people left an increasingly bitter taste in my mouth. Perhaps I felt a bit guilty for lingering in this exciting but tragic and corrupted city while my friends were God knows where experiencing God knows what.

On the other hand, I was not overjoyed at the thought of going back either. Getting wounded the first time is a bit like getting hurt in your first car accident. In both instances the fact that you and not just other people can be killed is brought home forcefully. Just as a motorist ventures into the crowded highways on a Fourth of July weekend knowing that a certain number of people will be maimed, I guess I had gone into the attack, despite my great fears, unable, really, to envisage my own death or injury. I would be careful. It would not happen to me. I would not become a statistic.

Now a part of that feeling was gone. Now I knew it was the lucky and not necessarily the careful who survived. Did I want to go back and try my luck again? No, not really, but I didn't want to desert the only friends I had either. In any case there was no choice to be made. My orders said go and I would go.

The next thing was to locate my outfit. I knew only that the division was somewhere north of Rome and south of the Arno River. More precise information came from a Lieutenant Gentry of the Eighty-first Reconnaissance Squadron, who was also being returned to duty. Since he and I were in the same division, our first stop would be the same. We teamed up.

The military had arranged our transportation on a ship heading north, apparently at a leisurely pace, for the port of Civitavecchia. We didn't know where Civitavecchia was, but we did know we were not expected in Rome for three or four days.

Gentry and I made our own way down to the harbor and boarded the ship to which we had been assigned. It was a small cargo ship flying the American flag. There were very few other passengers. I don't know what cargo had been or was being carried, but the deck was not exactly clean and something from below smelled, if not to high heaven, at least high enough to reach the off deck cabin we occupied along with three or four other junior officers.

Somehow we got the idea, quite possibly mistaken, that the ship had been carrying livestock for the French Colonial *Goumiers.* I don't even know whether the *Goumier* tribesmen actually carried their families, their goats, sheep, chickens and other possessions along with them, but that was the common gossip and we had no reason to doubt it.

As we sat there pondering the dismal prospects of a slow voyage up the coast in this decrepit old tub, we were joined by another junior officer also on his way back to the division. We deplored our common fate and began musing aloud about alternatives.

Soon a consensus emerged. We would jump ship and hitch a ride to Rome with the army air corps. That way we would surely beat the possibly unseaworthy scow we were on, have a little time in the Eternal City, and still check in with our outfits on schedule.

The decision made, we grabbed our gear and hastened on deck. The glorified raft to which we had been condemned was in the last stages of getting under way. The gangplank was up and members of the crew were throwing off the lines which tied us to the dock. Seeing all this, I hesitated momentarily. Gentry of the Eighty-first, a leader of men if there ever was one, climbed over the side.

"Come on! Hurry up!" he called urgently.

I dropped my gear over and scampered down. The third member of our party, a kindred soul, did likewise. There were cries from what must have been a rather surprised officer on the bridge. We paid no attention.

Within a few minutes, we got a ride in a military vehicle going to the airport. Upon arrival, we checked in with a dispatcher and showed him our orders. He said he would have a C-47 going to Rome in about an hour. We could take that if we wanted to. We took it.

When we got to Rome, the third man in our party told us goodbye and good luck. He had his own plans. Gentry and I pooled our resources and sublet a room in a small but modern apartment for a couple of days. It was a barter transaction. In return for a few bars of soap and two or three other little items purchased at the army PX, our host and hostess, a middle-aged Italian couple, made us welcome.

I visited the Forum by moonlight and some of the other ancient sights in the daytime. I dallied dangerously with a darling of the streets and worried about it for several days thereafter. The Fifth Army officers' club became our headquarters. There I met friends from the battalion and arranged a ride home. Our modest plan for seeing Rome had worked out perfectly.

1945: Fifth Army, Montepastore area, Italy. Vehicles moving over the dusty roads near Montepastore, Italy. Cloud hindering heavy traffic moving toward the Po Valley.

March 22, 1944: Fifth Army, Anzio area, Italy. A mechanical smoke generator of the 179th Chemical Smoke Co. is shown in a defilade at the beach-head where a constant smoke screen is maintained during daylight hours to screen Fifth Army operations from German observation.

March 27, 1944: Fifth Army, Nettuno area, Italy. Men of the First Armored Regiment, First Armored Division, unload used shell casings, used in breaking up one of the many German counterattacks on the beachhead. These shell cases are gathered from all artillery units for salvage.

January 31, 1944: Anzio area, Italy. Walking wounded leave lot and go aboard hospital ship.

March 22, 1944: Mussolini Canal. Men of the 463rd Para Field Artillery. Firing the .75-MM Pack Howitzer on enemy positions.

October 27, 1944: Fifth Army, Gabbiano area, Italy. Men of the Thirty-ninth Engineers of the First Armored Division removing the old treadway bridge, which is no longer safe due to heavy rains, in the Gothic Line in the Apennines.

March 17, 1944: Fifth Army, Anzio area, Italy. German prisoners being evacuated to rear from the Anzio beachhead. Note camouflage uniforms in center.

January 30, 1944: Anzio area, Italy. Grave registration assistants place body of dead ranger on litter for carrying to grave. Unburied bodies form double line in background.

June 15, 1944: Fifth Army, Anzio area, Italy. Reserve battalion moving up ditches to the front during attack of May 23. Photo made near Highway 7 to the left of the Mussolini Canal.

1945: Four soldiers on hill, looking down into valley.

May 24, 1944: Fifth Army, Anzio area, Italy. Tank retriever with runways for lifting up damaged tanks seen on road ("Purple Path") on way to bring back knocked out tanks.

April 27, 1944: Italy. These tanks of an armored regiment, debarking from an LST in Anzio Harbor, added strength to the U.S. Fifth Army on the beachhead. First Armored Division, Thirteenth Armored Regiment, CCB.

January 13, 1944: Prata, Italy. Seated on the front bumper of his jeep "Rough Rider" is Brig. Gen. Theodore Roosevelt, Jr., Director of [Liaison to] Canadian Expeditionary Force.

September 7, 1944: Fifth Army, First Armored Division, Italy. First Armored MP Det. Guarding the north approach of a Stanley bridge across the Arno.

April 18, 1945: Fifth Army, Marzabotto area, Italy. Infantryman of the Sixth Armored Infantry, First Armored Division, crosses a feeder stream of the Reno River with a bicycle he found. This is just south of Marzabotto, Italy, which is the furthermost point of advance on Highway 64 and 23 kilometers from Bologna.

May 7, 1943: An infantry battalion advances up a hill about ten miles from Bizerte, N.A. (Tunisia). This was about 2:30 p.m., May 7, 1943, just prior to the entering of Bizerte.

September 7, 1944: Fifth Army, Italy. Civilians waiting for men of the First Armored Division to finish their meal so they can gather the leftovers in containers.

September 7, 1944: Fifth Army, Italy. A cook with the First Armored Division feeding a half-starved youngster.

Chapter 9

Pontedera
Close Encounters of a Dangerous Kind

When I got back to the company, I found my erstwhile friend and one time social equal, Frank Lebec sporting the brand new "railroad tracks" of a captain. We greeted each other with obscene epithets and other soldierly signs of affection. He had become company commander after the breakout but thought we could still be friends if I would remember my place.

I had been gone about eight weeks, so long in fact that the company officers thought I had died of my injuries or had been shipped back to the States. At least that is the excuse they gave for having divided up my meager personal belongings. I told them they were a bunch of goddamn grave robbing ghouls on their own admission and asked if they had cast lots for my garments. They said they were hurt and saddened by my attitude.

With a little detective work I was able to reclaim a trench coat here, a pair of boots there, etc. I had special need for that trench coat with its zip out liner. It was a most versatile item, serving as rain gear, an overcoat, a blanket or a pillow on the line and, with a little cleaning, as part of my dress attire in the rear.

Somewhat inconsistently, I thought, Frank claimed he had saved a job for me as company executive officer. Why had he saved me a job if he thought I was dead? Well, he told me with what we used to call a shit eatin' grin, he knew I would surface sooner or later because it is well known that only the good die young.

In the company we followed the practice of assigning platoon leaders recently returned from the hospital to company headquarters without definite responsibilities for a time. An assignment as company exec meant that I would not be excess baggage and would have duties I more or less understood. I welcomed the change.

The exec was second in command. In theory he had responsibilities for supervising paperwork but with good clerks and noncoms this was no burden. In addition the exec acted as an extension of the commander's personality as one of the manuals put it. In practical terms this meant he took on tasks delegated to him by the company commander. Frank would be a good man to work for.

There were other changes in the company. A sizeable contingent of enlisted replacements had been added. Some of the old noncoms were gone. Former squad leaders had become platoon sergeants and some privates had become squad leaders.

Company headquarters had taken on a new communications corporal with whom I would have frequent contact. He was Chris Fielding, a husky, bright, bespectacled soldier of about my age. We were *simpatico* from the beginning. Through long nights sitting by the radio and telephone we would learn more about each other than either of us needed to know.

We had also acquired three new platoon leaders. The first of these was Lieutenant Sandosky, a man of contradictions, tall, well built and handsome but clumsy and painfully shy until he got several drinks in his belly. I would soon learn that at the front with Sandosky on your flank, there was nothing to worry about from that quarter. In the rear when he had drunk his fill, it could be a different matter. He might sight enemies you had not seen and provide you with flank, front and rear protection you had not requested.

Lieutenant Norman had taken over my old platoon. He was short, gregarious, comical and courageous. A convivial companion in the rear, he was a dependable man at the front. After a few days in the line, the whites of his big eyes always showed prominently out of a bewhiskered and begrimed face. His appearance alone was sometimes enough to bring a laugh.

Rounding out the triumvirate was Lieutenant Olson, the only married man among the company officers. He was in his middle twenties, blond, good looking, gentle, and very much in love. When he talked about home and his wife, his face would light up, the crinkles around his eyes would deepen. She was a beautiful girl and he had pictures to prove it. He hinted very, very delicately that she was incomparable in the bedroom.

But it was not simply the company which had changed. The division itself was in the throes of a reorganization postponed since the end of the campaign in North Africa. It was being streamlined, I was told, to conform to the table of organization already implemented in other armored divisions. In practical terms again, this meant a reduction in personnel of approximately 3,500 men, from an authorized strength of some 14,500 to about 11,000. In part the reduction was to be accomplished by abolishing regimental headquarters for the two tank and one infantry regiments. In other words there would no longer be a Sixth Armored Infantry Regiment. Instead, we would be organized into three armored infantry battalions reporting directly to the division commander. There would also be three tank battalions and three battalions of artillery along with the usual specialized and support units.

Surplus personnel were to be disposed of in a variety of ways. Men with lengthy overseas service, and that meant the old North Africa hands, were to be rotated back to the States. Unneeded personnel not eligible for rotation might be transferred to other units in the division where their services were needed or sent back to repple depples, a fate which most regarded with considerable distaste. I was glad Frank had "saved" a job for me.

I don't know how the junior officers in the tank regiments felt about the changes, but the reaction in our company was generally favorable. There were costs. We lost some very good men to rotation. Sergeants Antonio and Loman went home at this time along with Pfc. Jerry Bozart. I hated to see them go, but all of us approved without question the justice of the policy. Our losses, moreover, were compensated for by the disbanding of regimental headquarters.

Never in my experience had we operated as a regiment. Nor did we socialize with the regimental staff. Thus we had little feel for "the regiment" except possibly the negative impression that it sheltered far too many comfort loving time servers who made a niche for themselves by making trouble for us. Exceptions were always made, of course, for any personal friends one might have in this segment of the rear echelon.

The battalion was different. It was the largest cohesive unit to which we felt personal attachment. Battalion headquarters was not rear echelon except in banter or when we were forced to implement distasteful orders. With but few exceptions the battalion commander was considered one of us. As the war progressed, the "old man" was likely to be a lieutenant colonel in his late twenties who was a familiar figure to the troops and readily accessible to company officers.

Relationships between battalion staff and company officers, both on and off the line, were close. The battalion cup, a central part of the Ellis legacy, was preserved, polished, and displayed on appropriate occasions. He would have been pleased although fewer people wanted to drink from it after he was killed. Since turnover in officer personnel was somewhat greater at company level, the battalion commander and his staff provided a necessary degree of stability and continuity to our organizational life.

This was a matter of no little significance in a violent world where larger organizations were in a state of continual flux. The battalion was the basic building block with which the combat commands and task forces were constantly being formed, disbanded and reconstituted in different configurations depending on the mission involved. The battalion was now with CCA, now with CCB, now in division reserve. Not infrequently we would be detached for temporary service with some other regiment or division, and while we might not know at any given time exactly who was directing us from on high, we always knew we belonged to the battalion. Reorganization would leave the battalion intact and relieve us from responsibility to a headquarters which, as far as I was concerned, was worse than redundant. I had my own special bias stemming from the Anzio experience.

While implementing the reorganization, the division was located at Bolgheri when I rejoined them. Gradually I learned in bits and pieces a part of what had happened while I was gone.

Immediately after the capture of Rome, my outfit had pursued the disorganized foe, at first against light resistance. There was brief action at Civitavecchia but the port was taken on June 7 before the battalion moved with most of the rest of the division back to Lake Braccino, about thirty miles north of Rome. Having been in the forefront of the breakout and the pursuit, division vehicles were in urgent need of maintenance and the men were exhausted.

Rest, maintenance, and resupply continued for a couple of weeks. Some members of the company got back to Rome at this point. In the latter part of June they were sent back to fronts where resistance had stiffened and "rapid pursuit" could no longer describe what was happening.

By the beginning of July the Germans had reestablished for the first time since the breakout a continuous line extending all the way across the peninsula. It was intended only to delay the Allied advance while the enemy strengthened the Gothic Line further north, but the terrain favored the defensive and resistance was strong enough to inflict significant casualties. Kesselring's last defensive position south of the Gothic Line was the Arno River. There had been many short stops along the way.

It was the same old story. Kesselring was pursuing a course which he had employed previously in withdrawal to the Cassino Line and with similar purpose. In the fall of 1943, he had sought to deny Allied access to the Liri Valley prior to the spring of the following year. He had succeeded. Now in early summer of 1944, he was trying, against possibly greater odds, to prevent access to the Po Valley until the spring of 1945. He would be successful in that too.

There can be little doubt that Allied decisions made at the highest level facilitated Kesselring's success in this later endeavor. Following the capture of Rome, our friends in the Third, the Thirty-sixth and the Forty-fifth divisions were pulled back for the invasion of southern France along with General Truscott and several divisions of French and French colonial troops. While additional divisions were being added to Fifth Army, Kesselring's command was augmented by forces closer at hand. The shift of substantial resources from Fifth to Eighth armies may have shortened the war, but, of course, we doubted it.

My battalion had been involved in the hard fighting which took place around the first of July. They took a number of towns, removed a larger number of road blocks and pushed north to the Cecina River. Sometime around July 12 the battalion moved back but without Ellis and without other men most difficult to replace.

That much was history. Now there was more action ahead. Toward the end of July we mounted half-tracks and began to move back north. I don't recall any briefing whatsoever this time. All I knew was that we were moving up. When we got within range of enemy artillery, we dismounted and said goodbye to the tracks. Our further movement would be in darkness.

Initially the company was placed in battalion reserve behind the rather sizeable town of Pontedera on the Arno River. Most of the enemy had withdrawn behind the river line and from the foothills of the Apennines just to the north had excellent observation over the sector we occupied. In that respect it was somewhat similar to Cassino and Anzio. I wondered if we would ever have the advantage of holding the higher ground.

In our reserve position, we found partial concealment in vineyards and more protection in scattered stone farmhouses. Daylight movement was inadvisable. Enemy artillery was active. The hot summer sun had baked out the countryside and the dust kept most vehicular traffic off the roads in the daytime.

By this time I had become somewhat habituated to hostile artillery and had lost some of my inordinate fear of it. I knew we were reasonably safe in the stone houses as long as the enemy didn't bring up tanks or assault guns for direct fire. I also knew that we had little to fear from enemy bombers at this stage of the war. Nonetheless, cold fear and feelings of helplessness and frustration would always accompany a prolonged artillery or mortar barrage.

By comparison, small-arms fire, except in close encounters, was of decidedly secondary importance. Some men had trouble taking it seriously enough. I had seen people cower and tremble under artillery but move forward all but ignoring rifle and machine-gun fire which clipped tree branches over their heads or kicked up dust near their feet. It was strange. That was not at all the way I had thought it would be.

It was not just that small-arms fire makes a less intimidating sound. That, surely, was part of it, but there was more. A head shot or a gut shot or a heart shot from a rifle could kill but was likely to kill cleanly and quickly. Artillery, mortars, mines and bombs could not only kill but mangle, mutilate and leave people better off dead.

By this reasoning, I suppose, a warrior should welcome the opportunity to close with the enemy where heavy weaponry wouldn't decide the outcome. That might be OK for a warrior, but if you are a fraction of an inch under five feet nine and not very brave or warlike, it won't work out. Besides, hand-to-hand combat is too personal. I have known citizen soldiers who were shattered by having to witness the death throes of men they had killed. No, the best place to be at the front was in reserve several hundred yards behind the line with good, thick walls for protection.

Unfortunately front line soldiers are not consulted about their preferences. After a short time in reserve, we moved up to front line positions in Pontedera itself.

The Arno River at this point flowed through the town between rather steep embankments and levees on each side. We were positioned in a residential area of rather substantial houses. The buildings we occupied fronted on the street to our rear with their backyards running down toward the levee. There was a retaining wall at the rear of the properties. Many of the backyards had grape arbors and fruit trees. A few were enclosed by stone walls. At ground level the levee provided us with a measure of concealment from direct enemy observation from the flat, marshy land just on the other side of the river.

While the *Tedeschi* sometimes came up to the levee on their side of the river at night and opened up with machine-gun fire, their main line of resistance was in buildings further back.

Our line way thinly held and there were gaps on both flanks. Apparently the high command didn't expect a major enemy attack through this position. Many of the houses on our side of the river had been mined and booby trapped, but since we were not the first American occupants of this position, we found enough places which had been cleared out to afford shelter. Most of the civilians had been evacuated. I learned later that our Forty-seventh Medical Battalion had spent several days evacuating elderly and infirm patients from a hospital in the town.

From an upstairs window in the house where the company CP was located, I could see plainly through the field glasses the leaning tower of Pisa off to my left front. I studied it carefully, not for possible military advantage, but because I thought it might be the only view I would ever get. Pisa was on the north side of the river, and I assumed it was still held by the enemy. There was no movement whatsoever in the vicinity of the tower.

Active patrolling on both sides was a characteristic feature of the Pontedera front. Sometimes patrols collided in the dark between the lines and sharp fire fights would ensue. To help us carry the battle to the enemy, we had with us for the first time what apparently troops in Viet Nam called a "Kit Carson." Lacking their imagination, we simply called ours a guide.

He was a sturdy young Italian of average height who had been in the Italian army until the Allied invasion. When Italy took herself out of the war, our guide walked out of his barracks and went north to his home. Following the fall of Rome and while the front was still fluid, he came back south and offered his services to the Americans. Since he spoke a passable English, made a good impression and claimed to know the country around the Arno, he was given a job. At least that is the way I sized it up.

There was skepticism within all ranks when he first came to the company. Attitudes changed at Pontedera. Our man really did know the area, the best places to ford the river and the safest ways of getting to where we wanted to go on the other side. He served as a guide on every patrol the company sent out. Once when he found a patrol had left a wounded man on the other side of the river, he went back under fire and brought him out.

That feat alone was enough to qualify him for a medal, but I doubt if he ever got one. At our level we didn't set much store by citations. A glance at the ribbons on the chests of generals and other high-ranking rear echelon officers was enough to suggest that most decorations had been cheapened. Off the line a combat officer was set apart by the lack of ribbons and the simplicity of dress.

Among ourselves we pretty well knew who could be counted on to do their jobs, and, as we told the troops, doing your job in obedience to orders is what soldiering is all about. Don't take unnecessary chances. Don't get yourself killed. Don't try to be a hero and pray to God heroism is not thrust upon you. A hero very frequently is an average guy trying to do his job in a desperate situation where he has little choice but to fight as wild animals will fight when cornered.

Our guide at Pontedera did more than his job. I, as company exec, should have taken responsibility for writing him up. His situation was different from ours. He might have been able to use an American medal to advantage. But I didn't even think of those things at the time although I liked and admired the man.

I also wondered what motivated him to outperform all the rest of us. Perhaps he thought he had something to prove. Many Italian men of military age I had observed on Via Roma seemed dispirited, lost and uncertain. And for good reasons. Their pride had suffered. They must have felt their manhood called into question every day. The soldiers of the victorious army, swaggering through the streets, served as a constant reminder to the Italian men of their helplessness, their inability to protect their families, their inability, in the case of many single men, to compete for the available supply of native women. They had seen, I am sure, Italian girls from good families turn in desperation to the victors.

The Americans as well as the Germans held the Italian soldier in contempt. There floated around in the circles in which I moved, a riddle which asked: "What is the shortest book ever written?" The answer: *Italian War Heroes.* After Pontedera, I knew the joke was grossly unfair. It was the cause, the leadership, and the sorry equipment foisted off on the troops which was at fault.

From our guide I learned a little about partisan activity in Italy. The *Partigiani* were much more numerous and better organized in the north, he told me. He planned to join them later. He was somewhat contemptuous of the character of his countrymen around Naples. The real Italy ended just south of Rome as far as he was concerned. And Rome was infested with *Fascisti.* In central Italy, where his home was, the situation was some better, but we couldn't expect major support until we got closer to the big cities in the Po Valley.

It was a question of how long it would take to get up there. We were aware that a Fifth Army buildup for crossing the Arno was under way all along the line to our rear. A part of our job was to keep the enemy guessing as to where and when it would come.

One night the company was ordered to fake a river crossing by helping put on a demonstration upstream. Lieutenant Sandosky's platoon reinforced with additional automatic weapons and supported by mortars, artillery and the battalion assault guns was to open up with everything they had at a scheduled time. Frank asked me if I wanted to go down to the river and watch the show. I told him I did. His wish was my command. Later, he decided to go too.

Shortly after dark we moved upstream for a few miles and came to a place to ford the river. There were no steep banks and no levees here. From what we could see, it looked as if the water was shallow. It was such an obvious ford that I thought immediately of a probable enemy strong point on the other side. We couldn't tell because visibility was poor and the area just in back of the river was covered with tall, spindly trees. There was some, but considerably less, concealment on our side.

Sandosky deployed his platoon and all weapons including those of the support elements, opened up at the appointed time. There was a terrible racket. It sounded most realistic to me.

For a short period there was little reaction from the enemy side of the river. Then we heard the "plop" of the mortars. Frank and I dived for a small culvert which spanned a shallow drainage ditch. Flares went up. The mortars were joined by small-arms fire and artillery. The *Tedeschi* had this crossing registered as we should have known they would. If this had been a real attack with men going forward, we would have taken casualties. As it was, we hunkered down to sweat it out. The barrage lasted for about twenty minutes. It seemed longer. When we walked back home that night, I asked Frank if he was ever going to develop enough smarts to avoid sightseeing at the front. He said he would have been all right if I hadn't tried to push him out of his shelter under the culvert.

A day or two later the enemy, not to be outdone, put on his own demonstration. Suddenly in broad daylight the heaviest artillery and mortar barrage we were to experience at Pontedera began to fall on our front line positions. Machine-gun fire played on an empty C ration can, making it skip down the street in erratic little bounces. Worst of all an 88 opened up across the way and threw in several rounds of direct fire. There was no mistaking that sound. The "whoosh" as the round passed overhead, the "wham" as it smacked its target, and the loud crack of the gun seemed to come almost simultaneously. We experienced a few anxious moments until the *Tedeschi* apparently felt their point had been made. Two could play at the demonstration game.

On the fateful morning of Friday August 13 an unarmed young soldier in the battle dress of the Third Reich walked into the kitchen of the house in which the CP was located. Frank and I were drinking coffee and heating up something for breakfast. There was quite a little commotion. I wondered how the intruder had managed to get through the CP guards until I saw one of them standing unobtrusively at port arms by the open door. We sent someone to rouse our interpreter.

Even before the interpreter arrived, our unexpected guest wanted us to understand that he was Romanian, not German, and most assuredly not Nazi. That message was repeated several times. He had been forced to serve in the German army and didn't believe in the cause. This was his first chance to defect.

The night before, he told our interpreter, he and four other men had crossed the river for the purpose of pinpointing artillery targets and reporting on our movements. They had a radio with them and were under orders to remain in hiding on our side of the river until relieved. The prisoner seemed eager to prove his good faith by betraying his comrades. He offered several times to lead us to them.

We mulled over the story he told. We asked more questions. Our trust in a prisoner so willing to sacrifice men with whom presumably he had shared danger and hardship was not high. This might be a trap, but we couldn't just ignore what the man had said. We finally made the common sense decision to follow him but with great caution. If there were Germans on our side of the river. Frank didn't think the enemy would bring down artillery in our sector even if they saw us prowling around outside the houses.

Using the telephone to alert and brief the platoons, he directed Lieutenant Norman, who was nearest at hand, to send a squad to the company CP and directed the rest of the outfit to stay put until we checked out the prisoner's story. If we found anything, any or all of the platoons might be called upon.

We organized headquarters personnel as reinforced into two small groups, Frank leading one and I the other. Both groups were to move through the backyards to our left with the prisoner leading the way. My column was to proceed along the back property line marked by the retaining wall with a watchful eye on the levee to prevent a surprise assault from across the river. Frank and his people would be just a short distance on my left next to the houses.

Guided by our prisoner, we moved through the backyards toward a large stone wall which separated the property of two adjacent houses about a city block away. As we got closer to the wall, our Romanian, if that is what he was, urged greater caution. This, he indicated, is where he had left his patrol. Slowly we moved forward and could see that the troops who had previously occupied this position had blasted a big hole in the wall presumably to facilitate lateral movement up and down the line.

Guns and grenades at the ready, both columns converged on the opening in the wall. There was nothing unusual on the other side, just more houses, more backyards, a few grape arbors and fruit trees. It was another false alarm.

Our skepticism of the prisoner now reached its height. Frank threatened him with fatal consequences if he led us into a trap. The prisoner insisted that he had no such intention with such obvious fear, desperation and sincerity I began to believe him. Logic was on his side. His patrol had moved, we concluded. You wouldn't expect them to remain in place after one of their number had disappeared. But where had they gone? Under the circumstances it would have been logical for them to move forward and completely out of the area, but they couldn't hope to move far in daylight without detection. That meant they must be close at hand.

Frank stayed back with the prisoner who was no longer of any use to us as a guide and might be a threat. The rest of us moved forward as before. My column was still over by the retaining wall.

We didn't have to move far. I glanced over toward the levee on my right and back toward the men who were now searching the houses. Suddenly I got a silent signal from Sparky Fahrenkopf, a company jeep driver and a friend of mine. Sparky was standing on an open landing before an open rear door of one of the houses. The landing was not small but not large enough to be called a deck. There were wooden banisters around it and perhaps a dozen wooden steps leading up to it.

Sparky beckoned me over, pointing eloquently to the open door before which he stood. There was no mistaking his meaning. He had found something, or thought he had, and wanted help.

There is an important element of unreality in many combat situations. For every sudden, deadly encounter there are literally hundreds of dry runs in training and false alarms on the battle field. If I had known for a certainty there was real danger on that landing, I probably wouldn't have gone up there. But I didn't know and I guess I didn't believe there was. I reacted automatically in accordance with my training. Without thought, I crossed the yard and mounted the steps. I felt no particular fear.

When I looked inside the open door, I saw immediately what had excited Sparky's attention. It was a table, empty except for a bottle of ink and a cluster of freshly picked grapes. Under the table was a pair of German boots. The men had waded the river and one of them was allowing his boots to dry. He or someone else was having grapes for breakfast. Our approach had not given them time to remove the telltale signs of their presence. That much was apparent at a glance.

Sure now there was at least one man in the room, I held my rifle in one hand and reached down to my belt for a hand grenade. As I did so, I heard Sparky moving off the landing and down the steps.

My hand touched the grenade but that was all. Before I could pull it from my belt, a German soldier, flattened against the wall by the inside of the door and apparently watching, stuck the barrel of his weapon around the corner at me. I reacted without thinking. My free hand must have come back to the rifle. My M1 came up and its barrel clanked against the barrel of the enemy's weapon. He got off a burst but it went high in the air.

Now everything seemed to be taking place in very slow motion. I tried desperately to pin his weapon against the outside wall to prevent his firing again. He came out of hiding to extricate himself. His eyes bulged and glittered insanely. The rest of him was a blur. We stood there in the doorway for what seemed the longest time, straining and pushing our weapons against each other. When we disengaged, he jumped back behind the wall from which he had come. I pulled off three of four shots, firing blindly into the room.

Something struck me on the forehead and began to trickle into my eyes. I thought I was hit. Very, very slowly, or so it seemed to me, I started to wipe off the blood. My hand came back blue, not red. I stared at it. How very curious! How very interesting! One of my shots had exploded the bottle of ink. That was ink running into my eyes. Then I became aware of shouts from below. Chris was yelling, "Get down! Get down!" Others yelled, "We'll cover you."

I scrambled down off the landing and, fearful of exposing myself to machine-gun fire, flattened myself against the base of the house. I moved to my right looking for another entrance to the building. I found one but it was covered from above. I had neglected to note that there were upstairs windows looking down from the room I had approached from the landing.

From one of these windows someone began throwing "potato mashers" down on me. There was more concussion than fragmentation. The ground seemed to rock with each explosion. I tried to move further back the way I had come, but on the fourth or fifth toss, grenade fragments peppered me. One entered my right forearm raising a lump about the size of a large marble before making its exit. There was quite a bit of blood but almost no pain. Nonetheless, I left the base of the house and ran for a tree in the side yard, half expecting at any second to feel slugs from a schmeisser stitching a pattern across my back. I didn't need to be afraid of that. Whoever was at the window couldn't throw grenades and fire his weapon at the same time.

Company reinforcements were now at hand. A platoon had moved quickly to the sounds of the firing. The German patrol found itself surrounded. Rather than surrender as I would have done, they made a desperate run for it, clambering down the steps with guns blazing. Except for the battle dress, the automatic weapons, and the real blood, it might have been a scene from an old western movie.

Some of the good guys were pinned down, but one of our squad leaders standing behind a tree, his M1 cradled against his side, acted with deadly coolness. He fired once, rocked back and fired again. The first two Germans out of the door lay dead at the bottom of the steps. The other two, wounded as they crossed the yard, managed to get out into the river. Their comrades came out to get them under a red cross flag. We respected the red cross this time as we usually did unless we thought it was being abused. There was no question their men needed help, and I don't think anyone on our side really wanted to kill them. I didn't. For some reason, I was glad to see them get away.

Somewhat paradoxically, after my brief encounter around the houses, the action seemed to speed up to a normal pace. A medic came up and told me to lie down so that he could take a look at me and stop the flow of blood from my forearm. Chris and Sparky came over to see how I was. Frank tousled my hair.

"You blue blooded son of a bitch," he said, "We can't keep you out of the hospital."

"I'll be back," I replied, "and don't let anyone go through my barracks bag this time. I was just beginning to like it around here."

That last was a bald face lie, but in the excitement of the moment the words came unbidden to my lips. I had said it just as Ellis would have.

The fear came in as the adrenalin died out. It is curious I hadn't felt it on the landing. Momentarily I had been out of touch with reality. Now I began to shake.

At the aid station, I was sedated and prepared for evacuation by air. This time I was flown to Rome. Soon after arriving at the hospital, I was wheeled into a large operating room, containing, it seemed to me, dozens of operating tables at each of which a surgical team was working. I was still alert enough to hear when someone came over to my surgeon and asked whether he wanted to see "what one of our grenades could do to a man's leg." He was working on a German prisoner and had the wound exposed. Apparently my surgeon wanted to further his education. He left my side briefly to have a look. I lay there reflecting how lucky I was not to have been hit by one of our "pineapples." Someone told me to count slowly up to ten just before they put a mask over my face. I made it to about three.

When I regained consciousness, I was back in bed feeling drunk and groggy but experiencing no pain. Sodium Pentothal again. A side door leading out onto a balcony was open. There was the sound of music coming in. Sitting quietly at my bedside was my former platoon sergeant from Camp Breckenridge. He now wore the emblem of a paratrooper. I thought at first I might be hallucinating, but he was real. I recorded nothing of what was said and remember nothing. I surmised that he, tiring of repple depple confinement, had volunteered for paratroop training. I have an image of his standing up to his full height of six feet, six inches when we said goodbye and wished each other good luck.

I was left alone. Still feeling drunk and haunted by the music coming from a radio outside the room, I got out of bed and walked out onto the little balcony. There was a gorgeous sunset. The lyrics of a popular song came to me more clearly. It had a line which went, "The curtain descends, everything ends, too soon, too soon." For some reason I thought it was the saddest, most beautiful song I had ever heard.

Grateful for the *beau geste* of my former platoon sergeant, still half drunk, overcome by the sunset and the music, I began to cry.

Leaning against the balcony rail, I stood there crying until a nurse or someone in authority insisted I go back to bed. Would those medics never leave you alone? All I needed, all I wanted was to be left alone, to stand on that balcony to watch the sunset, listen to the music and cry. Was there anything so terrible about that? But I lost the argument.

Chapter 10

Bombiana and Porretta Terme

If I had to judge the progress of the war by the forward movement of my outfit, I would have to conclude that we had been spinning our wheels the last four weeks. The battalion had not moved far. I found my friends in a farming area a few miles north of the Arno in division reserve.

It was the middle of September. The countryside had the tawny, brown burned-out look of late summer but the temperature had moderated, giving some relief to the splotchy patches of green vegetation which had stubbornly resisted the onslaught of the sun. It was harvest time and not even the war could prevent Italian farmers from sowing and reaping in season. Earlier, I had watched through the glasses as a man placidly plowed his fields between the lines with occasional shells from both sides passing overhead.

The war did, of course, require all touched by it to modify their behavior in greater or lesser degree. Despite the fact that they were behind the lines, the farmers in our area worked under grave difficulties. There were shortages of almost everything, labor, draft animals, transportation, threshing equipment. In addition there were special problems of storage. Mounds of portable grain, for example, would be an inviting target for military or civil authorities as well as for freelance expropriators. For these reasons, the farmers would leave their wheat shocked in the field, threshing only enough grain for their own personal use. Everything else they produced had to be concealed. Even the bunches of onions I had seen suspended from the rafters in a barn were not safe. We had found out long ago that a few onions carried around in our pockets could be used to flavor the field rations.

There were fewer changes in the company this time. Frank was still the CO. I resumed my job as exec. Fielding was still minding the radio at company headquarters. He and I resumed our discussions. When we were not reminiscing about the good old days in high school, we most frequently talked football, baseball, boxing, or the 1936 Olympics where Jesse Owens took away all the gold he could carry while Glenn Cunningham and Archie San Romani, American 1500 Meter hopefuls, lost out to Jack Lovelock of New Zealand in the stretch.

Olson had been shipped back to the States after receiving a tree-burst which took off his right arm at the shoulder. We hoped his beautiful wife would help him recover. His replacement was a man some of us called "the Pathfinder" because he proved to have an uncanny sense of direction and a special feel for terrain. These talents were a bit unexpected because Pathfinder was a rather pale, sophisticated city man. He was of average height, thin, with a hooked nose, a "fellow of infinite jest" and a very capable, technically proficient soldier.

Lieutenant Norman, still in command of the second platoon, was showing signs of emotional stress although I didn't recognize the symptoms at the time. The first night I was back he and I stretched out our sleeping bags on the floor of a shed which had an open side facing the yard. I was tired. There were the soothing night sounds of "jar flies" as I had known them at home, along with faintly pleasant harvest smells to lull me to sleep even though I didn't need them.

The sounds and the smells didn't affect Norm the same way. He woke me shortly after I had fallen asleep and asked in a tense whisper, "Did you hear that?"

I roused up momentarily. We had guards posted. It is true we were within artillery range and the front was somewhat fluid. Still, I assumed we were a safe distance back. I listened a bit but could hear nothing unusual. I went back to sleep.

In a few minutes he woke me again to report that there was "something moving around out there."

I sleepily suggested it was probably one of the guards and turned over.

When he woke me the third time, I told him sharply for Christ's sake, and Mark Clark's sake, and my sake, to try to get some sleep. I suggested that he check with the guards if he thought something was up. When he got up to go out, I told him not to wake me until the battle was over.

I thought no more about the incident until later. All of us at one time or another had seen things which just weren't there and heard things we misinterpreted. I had been living it up off the line while Norm had not had that opportunity. Small wonder he was a little jumpy.

At company headquarters there was talk of a cadre of officers and noncoms attached to the battalion since late August. They were what polite society then called "Negro" troops from the 370th Regimental Combat Team of the Ninety-second Infantry Division, an all black outfit. It was a recent addition to Fifth Army and some of its leaders had been sent to us for combat seasoning because we were located on a relatively quiet sector of the front.

Frank told us that, prior to the assignment of the cadre, our battalion commander, knowing that Frank was an old Louisiana man, had broached the race question in an embarrassed and roundabout way. Stripped of all the preliminaries and circumlocutions, "Big Six" had wanted to know how "Little Six" and his company would react to providing hospitality and instruction on terms of equality to black people. Would we be able to cooperate with them as equals?

Our company commander was an educated man and no bigot. He told the old man there would be no problem, that we would cooperate fully and welcome the man of the Ninety-second because we needed all the help we could get.

There was no "problem" I was aware of. We did cooperate but, of course, there were from time to time little racist jokes and comments exchanged within the family of white men smug in the sense of their own superiority. All of us, I think, took a patronizing attitude toward our guests, and our condescension went beyond that which veterans might display in dealing with unseasoned white troops. Even Frank recounted an incident in which a smoke shell came over and the officers and noncoms of the Ninety-second donned their gas masks in unseemly haste. Our troops had not carried gas masks since I had been with the company, and the story seemed to imply, not only that Negro troops were woefully inexperienced, but that they had excessive fears. At least that is the way I interpreted it.

On the race question I was no better than others in my circle. I hope I was no worse. In my hometown which had a population of about 60,000 at the outbreak of the war, there was a surprisingly small black population. Facilities such as schools, hotels, restaurants, swimming pools, and theaters were segregated by law. I had little contact with black people and had absorbed the dominant stereotype of them. In the army I gave the matter no thought. It seemed "natural" to see black soldiers in menial roles. I had never thought of them as combat troops.

When I began to reflect on my attitudes, it didn't take long to see the obvious. I was already acutely aware of great gaps between the ideals set forth in the Declaration of Independence and the realities of daily life in my native land. Our treatment of blacks was another striking example. It doesn't take a degree in moral philosophy to understand that fair is fair. That comes on the playground. Everybody deserves a chance. But why did it take me so long to make the application in this case?

The appearance of the Ninety-second Division on our front was not the only and not the major topic of conversation around company headquarters. It couldn't compete with such topics as the wonders of Florence, Rome, Naples, home, the women we had known in every sense of the term and women we would like to know in a biblical way. Beyond all that there was frequent mention of Bologna and the Po Valley. Just as Cassino and the Liri Valley had been much in our thoughts earlier, Bologna now became the magnet to which we would be attracted for the next seven months.

Bologna was the center of the Gothic Line which we knew had been under construction for a long time. It was widely reported that a specialized engineering and construction firm, the *Todt* organization, had been called in to do for the Apennine defenses what they had earlier done for the Cassino Line. It was also no secret that the *Tedeschi,* in order to provide the hewers of wood and the drawers of water for such an elaborate project, had assembled a considerable labor force by simply pressing into service all able-bodied Italian men they could lay their hands on. We had met civilians who reported personal involvement in this work along with others who feared involvement for their sons, brothers or husbands if the Germans could find them. The prospects for a quick breakthrough of a line on which so much energy had been expended seemed remote to say the least. Better not dwell on that when brighter hopes were possible.

By far the most cheerful news to reach us concerned the success of Allied armies in France. We referred back to that as new reports came in. In the early fall of 1944 for the first time, I think, we began to see the possibility of an end to the war in Europe, not from our efforts but from the powerful thrusts of the friendlies to the north. The fact that we were in a backwater of the war suited us just fine. Let the men from Omaha Beach, St. Lo, Caen, etc. get the glory. They deserved it. They might get to Berlin before we had to go up against Bologna. We wished them God speed.

From somewhere we picked up the slogan "Stay alive 'til Forty Five" but on a more cautionary note there was added "Golden Gate in Forty Eight," an unneeded reminder that when it was all over over here, the Japanese would have to be dealt with over there. Finally, there was a bitter and pessimistic sentiment expressed as "Bread Line in Forty Nine."

We didn't dwell on forty-eight or forty-nine. They were light years away. Stay alive 'til forty-five seemed an excellent idea. The way to live to be a hundred, as my first love was to write, is to get to ninety-nine and then be very, very careful. Well, "Heahs to may yew live a thousand yeahs and Ah nevah die."

Actually, the situation in our sector was much more favorable to the company and the battalion than we knew. The major efforts to crack the Gothic Line were already under way and we were only indirectly involved. I have never known why we were not briefed on the situation. There was time enough and it would have made for a considerable boost in morale. As it was, I had to wait several years after the war for historical accounts to reveal what had been going on.

The British Eighth Army, now under command of General Leese, had launched the initial attack during the last part of August while I was still in the hospital. Mark Clark's Fifth Army, as he wanted war correspondents to designate it, would have major responsibilities a bit later. My division, assigned to the Fourth Corps was given a secondary role. A secondary role in a secondary operation in a backwater of the war. Not bad.

Thus far there has been little occasion to refer to the British Eighth Army. We were aware of their presence in Italy under General Montgomery, but they were so far across the mountains on the Adriatic coast that, insofar as we were concerned, they were fighting another war and a not very successful one at that. While we had worked closely with the British units assigned to Fifth Army and had great respect for them, the British Eighth never loomed either large or small in our conversations.

In the drive on the Gothic Line the British Eighth Army, as I have said, was in the forefront. In what must have been some of the hardest fighting in the Italian campaign they advanced some thirty miles in the direction of Rimini and, according to all accounts, drew in *Wehrmacht* reserves before the Fifth Army attack got under way. As a result of British operations, the enemy withdrew from the Arno River without a fight. When my outfit crossed on September 1, they encountered mine fields and artillery fire but no enemy foot soldiers to speak of. Nor were the benefits of the British effort limited to the river crossing. The entire Fifth Army attack north of the Arno was facilitated by the Eighth Army drive up the Adriatic coast.

This is not to say that the Fifth Army continued to play a minor role. The center of the Gothic Line was on the right flank of the Fifth Army sector, and it was here, where two important mountain passes led to Bologna, that the Allies came closest to a breakthrough. From where we were, a motorist looking at a map in peacetime and wanting to go to

Bologna would have chosen Highway 65 leading through the Futa Pass as the obvious route. His second choice might well have been the Giogo Pass which lay approximately seven miles to the west.

In its efforts to get to Bologna, Fifth Army reversed the order. Believing correctly that the more obvious route would be the more heavily defended, General Clark elected to make his main effort through the Giogo corridor. The American Second Corps, which had under command the Thirty-fourth, Eighty-fifth, Eighty-eighth, and Ninety-first divisions, bore the brunt of the hard fighting and suffered the highest casualties. They ultimately succeeded at Giogo but, while the issue was still in doubt, my battalion was committed further over to the left in the Fourth Corps area.

When our orders to move came down, I was taking care of administrative duties. Our men had been in action on the first of the month and hadn't been paid. A supplementary pay period was called for, and I was the company paymaster.

The task was more difficult than usual. Company units were scattered rather widely about the countryside. We had a squad here, an outpost there, and a platoon headquarters some place else. Without a careful study of the map overlay, all units could not be visited.

I studied the overlay and took it along with me, strapping on a .45, which few officers in my outfit ever carried with realistic expectations of serious use. The .45 was supposed to be symbolic or something. I was given a sack of money and the appropriate records. A jeep and driver were at my disposal. We took off.

It proved to be an all-day job. In the middle of the afternoon when I had made most of my appointed rounds, I got orders to report back to company headquarters. We were moving out.

What to do with the remaining money and the records? I contacted battalion. They didn't want them and suggested I call the division finance people. I couldn't contact anyone back there, wherever back there was, so I acted on my own initiative. All my responsibilities were thrust on my jeep driver, Sparky Fahrenkopf, he of the Pontedera landing. I instructed Sparky to locate division finance and return the bundle to them.

That may have been sloppy administration, but this was a sloppy war. I moved out with the company and neither thought of nor heard about the incident again. After the war I remembered it, but since no one had come around to arrest me for embezzlement or whatever, I concluded that everything was in order.

When we got to the front, we were committed to a reconnaissance in force up the Serchio Valley. For the most part this meant, for my battalion, sweeping the heights above the river.

We received small-arms fire, sometimes mortars, sometimes artillery.

Not infrequently the company was forced to halt and sometimes to deploy. We took casualties, but resistance was nothing like that experienced by Second Corps over on the right.

Frank went back to Fifth Army rest camp in Florence. I took over the company. We plunged deeper into the mountains where there were no roads and frequently no paths. A few days after the Eighty-fifth and Ninety-first broke through at Giogo, the enemy abandoned the Futa Pass and began a slow withdrawal along the entire front. We simply followed them up. Enemy resistance lessened, but the terrain alone prevented anything like rapid advance. We relied on pack mules to supply us if that tells anything.

Late one afternoon at sundown, we came under small-arms fire somewhat heavier than usual from a ridge to our front. We deployed and returned the fire to feel them out. Their fire increased but its volume was still not heavy enough to indicate a large force. A platoon, I thought, or a company at most. Still, they might be holding back something.

I was in no great hurry to move against them, whoever and whatever they might be, and thought it prudent to stop for the night. We dug in and reported to battalion. I tried to make a reconnaissance of the area on our flanks but couldn't see much in the growing darkness. The next morning, I thought, we could send one platoon around to the right on a flanking mission while the other two platoons maintained a fire base on the hill we occupied.

During the night the German artillery started up and kept at it intermittently for several hours. There was little of it coming our way and the sounds were comforting rather than disturbing. Enemy activity of this kind was frequently intended to mask a withdrawal. The platoon or whatever it was to our front might be gone in the morning.

It was gone. Our patrols climbed the ridge from which the enemy fire had come and signaled an all clear. Moving to the top of the hill, I marveled at the strength of enemy dugouts in such a remote area. There was no wire. There were no concrete emplacements, nothing to indicate that the *Todt* organization had ever seen this place, but the enemy had dug deeply, using logs, dirt and brush to provide overhead shelter and camouflage. We did little exploring for fear of booby traps, but I saw enough to give me greater understanding of how the *Tedeschi* were managing to survive American artillery.

The next day the company was given a blocking mission. We were directed to move a mile or so to our right, descend the heights, and dig in so as to deny the enemy access to a little valley running between our positions and those of the company on the next ridge over.

I put Pathfinder and his platoon at the head of the column with me. I didn't want to get lost in this God forsaken country. We stopped a couple of times to compare the map with the terrain. When Pathfinder found what looked to be a rough fit between where we were and where we were supposed to go, we began to pick our way down grade.

The valley was not over three hundred yards wide at this point. I decided it would be sheer folly to string the company out from one hill base to the other. Instead, we dug in a bit higher up on the hill we had come down so that we could bring fire across the valley floor. We had flares with us and could put outposts in the valley at night to prevent enemy patrols from sneaking through. Since we didn't know where all the other units of the battalion might be, we didn't try to register artillery fire. That wouldn't be necessary unless we became involved with a strong enemy force coming down through the valley.

Our blocking positions were not tested. We stayed there the rest of the day and through the night. It turned out that a group of our engineers was sweeping mines from the path leading to the rear. The following day we were directed to move back to the ridge and continue our own sweep.

For another day or so we moved forward slowly, encountering only occasional sniper fire. And then we came down the hill to the now mine-free road we had outposted for a rendezvous with a truck column. The trucks were to take us further down, out of the mountains, and, we hoped, to a place of greater safety and comfort.

It was very dark that night. There was fog and then rain. The switchback mountain road was narrow, muddy and slick. There were steep, unguarded drop-offs on one side. We would be driving with only the dim blackout lights showing, and there was always the possibility of being on the receiving end of enemy artillery. Somewhat surprisingly the "lorries" were British. Not surprisingly in view of that fact, so were the drivers.

When the company loaded, I climbed into the cab with one of them. The windshield wipers were working furiously. We had lost pack mules on these trails and in better weather. I would have felt better with Sparky Fahrenkopf or one of the other First Armored drivers at the wheel. They had been in the business a long time and I had the utmost confidence in their expertise. The competence of this British unit was completely unknown.

Before I went to sleep, I made an effort to allay my anxieties.

"I suppose," I said casually to the driver as if to make conversation, "You have been driving a long time?"

"Not bloody likely," he snorted. "Joined this bloody outfit a fortnight ago. Don't know why they sent me 'ere."

At this point I more or less gave myself up for dead and began to doze.

Several times I was jerked awake as my head snapped back when the driver, to avoid ramming the truck in front, slammed on his brakes. I might have been more alarmed. As it was, I dozed off again while the driver cursed and said that nobody had told him "fookin' aught" about this part of the job.

It was not the driver's fault. Visibility was so very poor he had to follow closely to keep in view the blackout lights of the vehicle ahead. They provided his only assurance he was not about to drive over the edge. With all their experience the First Armored drivers would have been sorely taxed by the conditions. But we got down without serious mishap. When Frank got back from rest camp to resume command, I told him he hadn't missed "fookin' aught."

The battalion was down from the heights, but instead of being sent back with the rest of the outfit, we were detached for special service with the Sixth South African Armored Division. They used us on Highway 64, a hard-surface road running roughly parallel to Highway 65 on the other side of a substantial mountain ridge, as protection for their left flank. We moved east and, after a day's rest, started down the road in the direction of Vergato and Bologna.

The weather, which had been bad, grew worse. It rained almost constantly for over a week. On Highway 64 we were sometimes on the road, sometimes on the heights above it. The rain didn't seem to discriminate. On the road we were held up by blown bridges and by enemy roadblocks most frequently the result of rock slides induced by the German demolition experts. One time we were held up for the better part of a day by a flood which washed away the bridges so carefully constructed by our engineers.

In the hills to our west we encountered slick trails, hard climbing, and snipers. I remember entering one primitive, almost medieval village which, nonetheless, had electrical power. Since rural electrification had barely touched Missouri when I went away to war, I was impressed. Someone in this tiny village must have had good connections with Mussolini's Fascist Party. Not many other mountain towns I saw had such trappings of modernity.

Further up in the mountains we encountered an old couple who didn't have electricity or much of anything else. They occupied a very modest shelter and seemed to be subsisting primarily on potatoes baked in their fireplace. A few of us from company headquarters took advantage of their hospitality overnight to protect ourselves from the rain and to keep our radio dry. They said the Germans had been to their *casa* and had behaved "*come animali.*" The earthy old lady demonstrated how the enemy soldiers had squatted around the back of her house to relieve themselves. The *Tedeschi* were "*tutti cativi*," she said, "*tutti mali*." But now, "*Tedeschi tutti via, tutti via*," and they were glad to be rid of them.

When I asked about family, I understood them to say that one of their sons had been taken away by the *Tedeschi* and the others had run off to join the "*Partigiani*." They had two or three daughters in Bologna where he had a "*sorella*." There was no one else, they said. Their extended family had been broken up by the war.

We shared our rations with them and gave them most of what was left. It required no great sacrifice on our part. We could always get more C and K rations; they wouldn't find it easy to get anything. They might starve to death; that wouldn't happen to us whatever our fate might be.

Back on the highway we were most frequently in an approach march formation, a column of twos, one on each side of the road. Temporarily out of contact with the main force of the enemy, we occupied Silla and slogged on down to Porretta Terme, a fairly large town and an attractive one.

"Terme," I found out, means "spa" or "hot spring." The scenic setting reminded me more of a prosperous mountain town in the States where people go on vacation to fish for trout. I didn't see any springs, hot or otherwise. I didn't see any trout either, for that matter. We stayed on the road. On the northwest side of town it curved sharply to the right to avoid a hill mass and followed the Reno River up to Vergato which was still fifteen miles short of Bologna.

It was at this bend in the road we once again established contact with the enemy. They were entrenched on a ridge to our front at a place called Bombiana. From the volume of fire coming from the hill, it was readily apparent that Bombiana would have to be cleared before we could move on.

The company got off the road and into the big houses in the outskirts of Porretta. I set up the company CP in one of them. We waited for the rest of that day and all of the next one.

The town seemed deserted, the houses unoccupied. The wooden shutters on most of the windows were closed. There was nobody on the streets. We did encounter one vigorous, mustachioed Italian gentleman of about sixty who, during an enemy mortar bombardment, entered the CP with a cheerful "Gilornooo," drawling out the word in a most comical and distinctive manner. After that in entering a shelter under similar circumstances we tried to imitate him.

After an uneventful night, Frank was called to battalion headquarters. He returned with orders. The battalion would go up to Bombiana the next day. There was one company on the road ahead of us. They would make the initial assault and we would move up as needed. It didn't sound too bad. We were temporarily in battalion reserve.

The weather had cleared. The sun was shining. That afternoon we went out into the backyard to dry out and take advantage while we could of "sunny Italy." The sounds of American artillery reverberated down the Reno Valley, bouncing from one hill mass to another. After several days of being grounded by the weather, the air force was out.

Two P-47s, both with five hundred pound bombs strapped under each wing, approached our position from the rear. This was a cause for at least mild rejoicing. The general belief was that they were on their way to plaster Bombiana and soften it up before the attack next day.

While the planes were still over Porretta, the first one peeled off and began a dive which seemed headed straight for us. An optical illusion, I thought, they are aiming at Bombiana. Within seconds I was disabused of that notion. The planes were indeed coming for us. We scattered for cover. I dashed back into the house.

There was a short whistle and then a mighty crunch as the first bomb struck. The house shook; there was the sound of breaking glass and crockery. Another bomb impacted with similar results. We heard the planes climb in preparation for another bombing run.

By this time everybody in the CP had lighted cigarettes as they usually did when we knew we had to settle down and take it. I was still a nonsmoker, but now I bummed a cigarette from somebody to the grim amusement of all who witnessed the transaction.

"What's the matter, Lieutenant," someone asked, "getting a little nervous in the service?"

I had no snappy comeback. The jokester had diagnosed the symptoms accurately enough.

Their bombing runs completed, the first plane came back to strafe. This surely was not to be tolerated. At least some of the men thought that way. Somebody opened up with a .50-caliber machine gun, and when the second plane came in, there was an additional fusillade of rifle fire.

There were shouts of, "Don't shoot! They're ours!" But there was an answering cry of, "I don't give a country fuck who they are! We've gotta drive the bastards off."

After the planes had completed their strafing, they headed for home to be credited, no doubt, someone observed bitterly, with another combat mission. Fielding had long ago contacted battalion to demand sarcastically that they get our air force off our backs. Battalion had already sent the message. Since headquarters was not far away, they seemed to share our sense of urgency.

When we were reasonably sure the ordeal was over, we came out. Thank God I had heard no cries for the medics either during or after the operation. The company was shaken but had taken no casualties of significance. We had found, nonetheless, something worse than direct fire. A five hundred pound bomb would have gone all the way through any of the houses, probably exploding on the main floor and killing all of the occupants. Worst of all was the fact that our own people had tried to do us in.

That night I joined Chris who was tending the radio. Over a period of time we had gradually confided more and more of our hopes and fears to each other. On this occasion the conversation was almost entirely personal.

Chris told me of his plans for the future. He would go back to school, get his degree, and study war no more. My sentiments exactly. He would marry the girl he was engaged to, perhaps immediately, or he might wait awhile. It depended on whether he went into his father's hardware business, something Chris had reservations about.

His parents, I had gathered, were sympathetic, comparatively well-off middle-class people who would help out financially. I had already seen pictures of everybody he talked about including one of a twelve- or thirteen-year-old brother. And I had shown him pictures of my parents, my younger brother, now in the Pacific, and my shapely sweetheart who had taken a job in Washington, D.C.

It was a bit different with me, I told him. He was lucky to have a family business to go into. My parents were hardworking people who would be willing but unable to help out financially. I would go back to school but didn't know when I would ever be able to provide for a wife and family.

Both of us had been scarred by the Great Depression. Both of us felt, I, perhaps, a bit stronger than he, that the role of "husband-provider" carried awesome responsibilities in an economy where unemployment was a common experience and always a distinct possibility.

There are things worse than war, I told Chris. In a shooting war there is at least sharing of hardships and dangers and the casualties have an honored place. But in the economic struggle the losers are held in contempt and people are forced to fight their own battles for survival in lives of "quiet desperation." I may not have used those exact words but that was the thought I conveyed. He seemed to agree.

Neither of us expressed any special fears or feelings about Bombiana. We didn't know how strong the position was. I hoped the lead company would be able to take it without our help. Sometimes it happened that way. You could always hope for the best.

On the fateful morning of Friday, October 13, we got up early, had breakfast, saw to our weapons again and waited. The brief artillery preparation went in on schedule. When it slackened, we knew the company ahead of us was on its way.

I talked later to a noncom in the company leading the assault. He told me the Germans had an outpost at the foot of the hill with a telephone line leading up to Bombiana. The artillery preparation and the American advance scared off those manning the enemy listening post, but the phone line was still in place.

The sergeant picked up the telephone and gave a couple of rings. When a voice at the other end of the line said, "Ja?" he knew he was connected with a German CP at the top of the hill. The sergeant had very little German and he used most of it now.

"*Kommen Sie Hieraus,*" he shouted. "*Krieg Kaput! Kommen Sie Hieraus*!"

There was a moment of silence although the sergeant could detect confusion in the background. Then another voice, in an English not significantly better than the sergeant's German, came on the line and delivered an unmistakable string of epithets, insults and threats. The sergeant interpreted this as a negative response to what he had thought was a polite offer to accept a surrender. Linguistically unable to pursue the argument, he gave what was probably the only appropriate response.

"*Vir Kommen*! *Vir Kommen*!" he repeated. And up the hill they went.

Back in Porretta, we heard the sounds of an expanding fire fight but couldn't tell what was going on. Even when the volume slackened a bit, we didn't know whether the company was taking the hill or was being driven back. We wanted very much to believe the former; we feared the latter. After a wait of about thirty minutes or so and with fire from both sides increasing again, our company was ordered forward. We judged that the lead company had been halted but was trying to move up once more. They needed our help.

Frank would lead the first two platoons. I would remain at the CP with company headquarters and the reserve platoon awaiting further orders. It was all very standard, very orthodox.

In a short while Frank radioed back instructing me to bring the rest of the company forward. We started forming up in the street. I would lead off with company headquarters. The reserve platoon would follow.

There was some milling around as we got into place. Chris, with the radio strapped to his back, was standing three or four paces to my left front. His assistant was about an equal distance to my right front. We had not yet dispersed on both sides of the road.

BAM!! An enemy mortar round landed just in front of us. No one had heard the "plop," and just as Antonio had warned in the informal lessons of long ago, when the round struck the pavement, there was nothing to absorb its fragments except human flesh. Simultaneously, it seemed to me, I heard Chris scream, felt fragments striking me, and heard the sound of additional fragments slapping against what has stuck in my mind as a large wooden garage door behind me. Chris and his assistant were knocked to the ground. The rest of us went down as an automatic response. As I hit the ground, I heard the "plop, plop, plop, plop" of additional mortar rounds on their way. The enemy had our range and was firing for effect.

Chris needed immediate attention. He had taken most of the lethal fragmentation from the first round in his body. I crawled over to him as additional mortar rounds began to impact. He asked for his mother. He called on God for help. He looked me in the eyes and begged me, pleaded with me, "Don't let me die! Don't let me die!"

Almost immediately he struggled for air. His breath came in loud, strangling gasps. In a fraction of a second his face drained of all color and turned black. He was dead. There was no mistaking that. I had seen the life go out of him. No need to yell for the medics.

Fielding's cries for help had activated another friend, the platoon sergeant of the reserve platoon. While the rest of us hugged the ground, the sergeant jumped to his feet and ran forward to help. I and others yelled for him to get down. It was too late. The incoming barrage caught him before he could reach us.

The enemy gunners stood down. I got to my feet and hurried back to where the platoon sergeant lay. One of our medics came up. Again it was too late. The sergeant died without making a sound.

Two other men had been severely wounded but were still alive. One of these was Fielding's assistant. He had also been hit by the first round and had also taken fragments in my place. I don't know who the other man was and never found out when he got it.

By this time two or three dozen civilians, almost all of them men, had come out of hiding and into the street. Most of them wore clerical garb. There must have been a religious order housed behind the closed shutters of a large building we had seen but hadn't tried to enter. One of the priests had such an expressive, wide-eyed look of grief, sympathy and horror on his face I have never forgotten it.

Shocked as they were, the clerics were not immobilized by the scene stretched before them, this eloquent example of the waste and futility of war. They offered sanctuary for our wounded in the building they occupied. I accepted. There was little else to do. Our radio was out and the wounded men were in urgent need of attention. At least we could provide them temporary shelter. I sent someone to the rear for an ambulance but was prepared to use the company jeep if safer and more comfortable transportation didn't arrive soon.

My own injuries were slight. I had been splattered with fragments but one had done real damage. My left hand was stinging and I now examined it more closely. A mortar fragment had perforated my ring finger. It was a bloody mess, hanging there apparently damaged beyond repair. I assumed I would lose it, but what a small price to pay! A kind of schadenfreude which I always felt when other people were killed and I was spared helped me temporarily to forget about Chris, the sergeant and the others.

Since the reserve platoon was now without a sergeant, the senior squad leader was moved up to take over. The platoon and company headquarters were reorganized and sent on their way to Bombiana. Medical assistance arrived. The wounded men were taken back and I followed them in the jeep.

At the aid station the small fragments which had struck the lower parts of both legs and around the right knee were quickly taken care of. Only the finger was deemed to require additional medical attention.

When I learned they were sending me back, I didn't rage and demand that I be allowed to return to my outfit immediately. I don't recall voicing even a small protest. Instead, I accepted my fate with manly courage and inner exultation as I was evacuated for the third time.

This time I was sent to a rather small hospital near the coast rather than to a general hospital in the big city. Shortly after I arrived, I was examined and prepared for the surgery. As I stretched out on the operating table, I asked the surgeon if he was going to amputate my finger. No, he told me, they were going to try to save it.

A likely story, I thought. From what I had seen, there wasn't much to save. And why treat me to the bedside manner? I was a big boy now and they didn't have to play games with me.

To my pleasant surprise when I woke up, the finger was still there. A steel peg had been inserted through the lower joint and protruded on either side. Rubber bands had been attached to this anchor and the finger put in traction. There was some kind of a sling under my left forearm. The surgeon had told me the truth. They were trying to save the finger.

I heard now for the first time about a new wonder drug called penicillin. There were dangers of infection, I was told. They sentenced me to a round of penicillin shots, one to be given every four hours for seven days. They stuck in the right arm, in the left arm, and in both sides of my butt before I told them to go back to the arms again. They woke me in the middle of the night to administer the treatment. If I happened to be off the ward for some reason, they chased me down to stick me. I threatened to hide in the men's room but there was no escape.

The cost to the American taxpayer of saving that finger must have been considerable. If I had been in the armed services of any other major power, Britain, Germany, the Soviet Union, Japan, or whatever, I suspect I would not even have been sent to the hospital. They probably would have chopped off my finger, bandaged me up, kept me at the aid station perhaps overnight and then sent me back to duty. It would have been cheaper that way. But, of course, this was a kind of waste to which I had absolutely no objection.

At least I was not taking up bed space which could have been put to better use by other foot soldiers. There were very few infantry men in this hospital. Its principle clientele came from a rather sizeable P-47 air base nearby. From the air force people I met and from the hospital staff I learned that all kinds of accidents were taking place on the airfield. Men were injured in line of duty, but rather infrequently as a result of enemy action. Most of those injured in combat never had a chance of reaching one of our hospitals.

One evening while I was still on penicillin two pilots from the base came over to visit my roommate who was in their outfit. They were so late he had just about given them up. When they finally showed, he asked what had kept them. I heard one explain they were all assigned evening classes in map reading because a "couple of yo-yos" had mistakenly bombed American troops "up around Bologna." Ah ha! So these were the ones.

I made inquiries, but they could tell me nothing further. What did they know of Bombiana, Silla, or even Porretta Terme for that matter? To them twenty or thirty or even fifty miles on either side of a line would be "up around Bologna." They seemed embarrassed by the inquiry. I let it drop but was sure their "yo-yos" had bombed my company.

Neither the bombing incident nor identification of those responsible changed our love-hate relationship with the air corps. We loved the pilots when they helped us; we cheered them on their way to strike the enemy. But in good times and bad we also maligned them, resented them, were jealous of them and insufficiently aware of the courage it takes to fly through heavy flack or to bring a wounded plane in "on a wing and a prayer" as the song tells of it. We knew the fly boys were considered "the very cream of American youth" while the government regarded us as the most expendable of the expendable. We felt bitter about that as well as about a lot of other things. And as the war progressed, the bitterness hardened.

One of the worst times for me came after the first few days in the hospital when the shock had worn off and I had time to think. My feelings had little to do with the air corps. It was the total situation which got to me. I brooded, refought the old battles, went over all of it again and again in my mind. In dreams I saw the blood drain from Fielding's face, heard again his scream, his desperate pleading, his death rattle. When variations on the same nightmare came two or three times during the week, I almost dreaded going to sleep. But wide awake I relived the chilling experiences of the wadi country, recalled the direct hit on my dugout in the pines, the sudden explosion which sent me to the hospital on the breakout. When I thought about what could have happened on that landing at Pontedera, I felt weak. When I thought about Porretta Terme, I wanted to cry.

I had been extremely lucky and had no difficulty reaching the conclusion that my luck was just about played out. No one could go on like this forever. Chris couldn't; neither could Ellis nor Cheney nor any of the rest. It was just a matter of time. There was no reason for believing that God had chosen me to defy the odds. "Stay alive 'til forty-five" had seemed a possibility when I first heard the slogan, but that was before I had been hit the third time.

I didn't confide my forebodings to anyone. Instead, I tried to conceal them as Ellis had taught me to do. But bitter, gloomy, sarcastic, complaining entries began to permeate my journal notes.

There were no large cities to visit in the vicinity of the hospital. I wrote letters, tried to work on my journal, tried to study Italian but my attention span was short. Soon I became almost frantically immersed in the distractions which the hospital offered.

The hospital personnel were universally tolerant and kind, although I know some were scandalized by my behavior. I had access to the officers' lounge and got drunk there with some frequency. And I am talking pissy assed drunk, dead drunk, sick and sickly drunk. There are things I don't remember as well as things I would rather forget. And it was not just the drinking which raised eyebrows. I was a frequent visitor in the nurses' quarters, sometimes at odd hours.

Everybody must have thought I was cracking up. The nurse on ward duty gave me a back rub almost every day. Never have so many back rubs been lavished on such an undeserving but receptive back. A few nurses, not on the officers' ward, came around individually to visit. One of them read poetry to me. Another let me borrow a pair of her dress slacks so that I could attend officers' parties. They buttoned on the side but she said I would just have to learn to "swing it." In short, I became a member of the family and behaved no better than a spoiled little boy who takes kindness as no more than his due.

Thinking about it now, I am convinced that someone gave orders that I be coddled or at least tolerated. I don't know who it was but I am grateful to them and even more grateful to those who carried out their instructions so faithfully. It must have been painful duty at times.

My fellow patients provided male companionship. One of these was an air corps dental officer, a young major who had been in the hospital on several previous occasions complaining of lower back pain. Some of the hospital staff thought he was just trying to get out of the army. Whatever the truth of the matter, the major was always kind to me. He examined my teeth and reported that I was in urgent need of dental care but suggested that it would be the gravest possible error to allow anyone but him to do the work.

I agreed to let him fill a couple of teeth. He reserved the dental facility one night and hobbled alongside me, in a semi-crouching imitation of the Hunchback of Notre Dame, down to the work place. There he performed with great skill the task he deemed essential if I was to have a "bright dental future." I was much more worried about having any future at all.

I don't recall the major as a participant in any of the lively crap games on the officers' ward. Perhaps his back wouldn't allow him to get down on the floor with the rest of us. In any case, I pretty well ended this form of entertainment by winning all of the available cash, a total of well over a thousand dollars. I lost some of that in a poker game with a shrewd air corps lieutenant colonel but was able to send most of it home. There was nothing to spend it on where I was.

Late one morning the hospital was warned to be prepared for a flood, and by nightfall the high water had reached us. I never knew whether this new danger was a natural result of the autumn rains, as seemed entirely possible, or was due to German destruction of a dam up in the mountains as one rumor had it. Whatever the case, all hospital personnel including the medical staff were involved in moving hospital equipment and records to the upper floors. My doctor sought me out and asked to borrow the waterproof mountain boots I had been wearing when I was hit. I, of course, gave consent and went down on the stairway landing to watch him and others slosh through water several inches deep on the first floor. Fortunately I was observing the flood at its crest. By morning the water had subsided and begun to go down.

When my outfit got off the line, a group of company officers came over to visit. Pathfinder, wearing a pencil thin, black mustache which made him look a bit like the villain in an old-fashioned melodrama, led the group. Norm, spruced up almost beyond recognition and showing no trace of five o'clock shadow, came along. They brought two replacement officers with them. One of these, Lieutenant Johnson, a giant, jolly man, had special talents which would take him shortly to a reassignment with Service Company. The other, Lieutenant Nansen, stayed with Frank's company and quickly became a favorite with officers and men alike.

Nance, at five feet, five inches tall, was the smallest officer in the battalion. With his light blonde hair and deep blue eyes, he didn't look more than eighteen years old. All of us felt somewhat protective of him, I think, even when he demonstrated that he could more than take care of himself.

I would find Nance to be the neatest soldier I had ever known. Off the line his trousers were always sharply creased and perfectly bloused in his well-shined boots. Even after a week at the front, someone said, Nance looked better than the rest of us when we dressed up in the rear.

But he was not what some of the kids today call "a neat freak." That would have been fatal to his future in a line outfit. He served as an example but was no more demanding of spit and polish than the rest of us. He governed his platoon with a light but sure touch. At first his man may have been amused by him, but they were always respectful. It would be too much to say they "worshipped him" but they liked him more than a little and the probabilities are high that they would have followed no matter where he led. Nance drew his share of tough assignments but I never heard either him or his men complain any more than was normal.

All of my visitors that night, veterans and replacements alike, must have made the trip because they had heard I had an "in" with the nurses. I don't recall being in contact with anyone in the company, but perhaps memory fails. I may have enticed them to visit with extravagant promises. It is a bit difficult for me to believe that someone in the company tracked me down through bureaucratic channels just to say hello.

The visit worked out much better than such things usually do. When I introduced them to the nurses, Pathfinder and Norm quickly latched onto partners as if it had been prearranged. Johnson, a bit too particular, perhaps, played the field until it was too late. Nance, who apparently had no intention of pairing off, chatted amiably with several girls, many of them larger than he. It may or may not be of significance that the veterans made contacts while the replacements did not.

The Pathfinder, who had been a radio performer before the war, was the star of the evening. He sang something called "Giannia Mia" to the delight of, it must be admitted, a slightly inebriated audience in the officers' lounge. It was the first of several such performances during the winter after I got out of the hospital in which we visited the nurses or they came over to visit us.

There was little serious discussion that night but I did learn that the battalion had taken Bombiana on the day I was hit. Norm told me I could have helped repel the counterattacks if I had stayed around. I told him I was truly sorry to have missed it. Everybody hooted their derision.

In the course of the evening I became reconciled to the inevitable. For good or ill I belonged to the battalion and it was time to return. There was no place else to go. Besides, I was getting tired of the life I was leading in the hospital. No one in the outfit would believe that. When I told them, they said I was crazy and couldn't stand prosperity. Any number of volunteers were available to trade places with me.

When, the day after Christmas, I was released from the hospital, I presented my doctor with the pair of mountain boots I knew he coveted. I could get another pair if I lived long enough to need them. But we were still short of the Po Valley and the odds on my survival were, to my mind, less than favorable.

Chapter 11

Winter 1945

My outfit was more or less marking time in winter quarters around Lucca when I rejoined them. Fifth Army had suspended offensive operations around the first of November when it became clear the Allied armies would be unable to reach the Po Valley before the onset of winter. While the Gothic Line had been rolled up, the enemy backup positions proved almost equally difficult. In my company, indeed, there was never any distinction between the Gothic Line and the strong points to the rear. As far as any of us had known at Bombiana, we were still in the enemy's main line of resistance. Two facts were indisputable: we were still in the mountains and the *Tedeschi* were still there, as the soldier at Cassino had said, in "big by god bunches."

For two months there had been stalemate across the entire front. Over on the Adriatic coast the British Eighth Army was bogged down in the mud some forty miles from Bologna. In the center the Second Corps of Fifth Army, after breaking through at Giogo, had redirected its efforts up Highway 65 and had driven to within a half-dozen miles of Bologna before being halted. On the left in the Reno River Valley where Fourth Corps continued to operate, my battalion had moved some eight miles up Highway 64 from Porretta Terme but was stopped short of Vergato.

I had missed some hard fighting before the offensive was called off. After holding Bombiana against determined enemy counterattacks, the battalion had repeated its success at Plazzo, again taking significant casualties but gaining a Distinguished Unit Citation this time. In this area Captain Morrow's company sustained something like six counterattacks in five days. To break up one of these, the company commander called down artillery fire on his own position. It was a desperate chance but proved one well worth taking. The company was sheltered behind thick stone walls while enemy troops, swarming around outside, were unprotected. They suffered more than the company and the attack was beaten back. After this ordeal, the battalion moved back in reserve.

When I returned, Frank's company was for once oversupplied with lieutenants. Sandosky, the Pathfinder and Nance led the platoons. Norman was second in command. Johnson and Evens were attached to company headquarters awaiting assignment when somebody went down. If I returned to the company, I would be the third supernumerary. At that time I had a friend highly placed at battalion headquarters, a major I could talk to and rely on. On the day I returned he asked how I would feel about taking over the machine-gun platoon Ellis had commanded at Anzio. There was a vacancy and he thought I might be the man for the job especially in view of the fact that Frank's company was overstrength.

Actually, I didn't feel much of anything about it. I would hate to leave the officers and men of Frank's company, of course, but I had been in and out of the hospital so much maybe they didn't want me anymore. Maybe it was time for a change. It didn't matter much. I told the major no one could replace Ellis. He said he knew that but thought I could do a better job than any of the new men he had available. I doubted that and told him I was slowing up after the third hit. I thought it better to put it that way than to tell him I was a prime candidate for a Section Eight discharge, a classification broad enough to embrace emotional instability.

The major thought the new job might even be a bit safer than an assignment with a rifle company. I doubted that too, but since he obviously had the assignments all planned out, I told him I would take the job. Even if I had resisted, he probably would have made the change anyway.

Headquarters Company to which I was now assigned was a sprawling, highly decentralized entity which didn't know itself as a company. It was not a tactical unit. In addition to the customary headquarters personnel, it had two platoons of 81MM mortars and a platoon of .30-caliber light machine guns, units which in a straight infantry battalion of the day would have been assigned to a separate weapons company. As it was the mortars and the machine guns were most frequently attached to or assigned in support of one of the rifle companies. There were also two self-propelled assault guns as a part of Headquarters Company and a communication section led by Lieutenant Able, an officer I knew rather well.

I also had more than a passing acquaintance with the mortar platoon leaders. Both had been around a long time and each had been decorated for bravery. They were, however, quite different personalities. One was an outdoor, forest ranger type, very much at home in the field, cool, deliberate, reticent and soft-spoken. He smoked a pipe. The other smoked cigarettes and was outgoing, fun loving, convivial, talkative but also deadly competent as was his companion.

Their different personalities and talents were reflected in the performances for which each of them had, on separate occasions, received citations. According to the stories which circulated in the battalion, the forest ranger was alone on reconnaissance, as was his usual practice, looking for an observation post from which to direct mortar fire. Coming to a clearing in the woods, he was greatly surprised to see immediately ahead three German soldiers in relaxed postures outside a machine-gun emplacement.

The enemy saw him at about the same time and were equally startled. One member of the machine-gun crew took off running to the rear. The other two jumped into their emplacement and tried to swing their gun around in the direction of the ranger. He must have sensed immediately that he would be done for if he tried to run away. Instead, he ran forward, jumped into the position with the enemy, shot one with his carbine, and killed the other with his bare hands. If the incident ever preyed on his mind, he never let it be known.

The more outgoing and gregarious lieutenant was also on reconnaissance but, as was his usual practice, had his platoon sergeant with him. The two of them spotted a house some little distance to their front and decided to investigate. Whether they were in search of wine, as the lieutenant told me, or were seeking more worthy military objectives as the citation indicated, was never clear. When they got to the house, they didn't find whatever it was they were looking for. They found instead something which surprised them quite as much as the ranger had been surprised.

After banging around in one of the rooms, the lieutenant and his platoon sergeant entered the kitchen and found several German soldiers, their weapons out of reach, smoking cigarettes and relaxing with their boots off. The sergeant, not recognizing they were enemy troops, is reported to have said something like, "Uh, oh. We've got company." The lieutenant recognized the situation immediately and just as immediately decided to bluff his way through. He placed his arm affectionately around the shoulder of the startled German noncom who seemed to be in charge and called upon him to surrender. Then, pretending to have the place surrounded, the lieutenant went to a window and signaled his imaginary troops, ordering them to keep down and maintain concealment. The act must have been a good one. The *Tedescho* in charge of the enemy contingent was persuaded and called to people who were sleeping upstairs to come down. As I recall the story, they rounded up some fifteen prisoners.

The lieutenant said he had only two rough moments. The first one came just outside the house when he ordered the prisoners to form up in a column of twos. When no other American troops put in an appearance, the German noncom, realizing he had been tricked, showed signs of resistance. A fierce growl and a tommy gun pointed at his belly soon persuaded him that it was too late. After warning battalion outposts to be on the lookout for a group of German prisoners coming toward them, the lieutenant and his sergeant took their now reluctant captives back through the lines. The second rough moment came when the action had been completed. The knowledge of what he had done was enough to make his hands shake and his body tremble. Not until he had been given a stiff slug of cognac was he able to unwind. And still, the lieutenant said, he had nightmares from time to time. They required more cognac.

There were also noteworthy characters in the platoon I now commanded. The platoon sergeant was equal in competence to the best I ever had whether in Italy or the States. He had a complete technical knowledge of all kinds of automatic weapons, German as well as American, a competence which I couldn't claim. A big man without bluster, he looked capable of punching out any member of the platoon but had neither the inclination nor the occasion to demonstrate that ability. He was, in addition, most cooperative and sensitive to the division of labor between us. We seemed to develop an unspoken agreement. I would support him on disciplinary and housekeeping issues even if I sometimes thought he might be wrong. He, in turn, would see to it that all my orders were carried out promptly even if he had reservations. We would consult with each other when appropriate and possible.

The section and squad leaders of the platoon were much like those I had known in Frank's rifle company. Most of them were good, some, due to attrition, had been promoted beyond their level of competence and would either grow into their positions or have to be replaced. The platoon sergeant knew who they were and I soon learned.

The platoon as a whole no longer had its bad-boy, elitist image. That had gradually eroded after Ellis was killed. Disciplinary problem cases were no longer automatically assigned to us, and many of the rough and ready oldtimers were gone, their places filled with ordinary soldiers who had learned to use machine guns proficiently. There were still enough veterans around to remember the old days and to carry on some of the platoon's traditions. But they were not bad men in the sense of being hardened killers. None of the men I knew, whether veterans or replacements, in the platoon or in the battalion seemed to enjoy killing. The story was told after Porchia of how one of the first men to the top of the hill, upon seeing the backs of enemy soldiers in flight, yelled out, "Don't shoot! They're running away!" While his plea went unheeded by those more hardened to war, no one ever gloated over this or any other kind of a kill or sought to claim credit for one.

There was another story in the battalion about a platoon leader in North Africa who, feeling himself in a desperate situation, shot two German prisoners after his platoon sergeant had refused orders to do so. While there were those who defended his action as an operational necessity, he had become something of a controversial figure with both officers and men.

One of the most notable of the veterans in the platoon when I took over was my runner/interpreter, a private of about my age and size. Although he didn't speak German, he was fluent in Italian and could be of great help in questioning civilians we met. But in this as in many other things, it paid to watch him rather closely.

By this time I knew enough Italian to realize that Runner frequently took liberties in passing on messages to the natives. In his translations my requests were likely to come out as commands filled with more menace and threat than I had intended. You didn't need any Italian to recognize that. The gestures told the story. One time he delivered a request more or less accurately but concluded by saying something like, "Porque se no. . . ." and followed that by drawing his hand across his throat in a cutting motion. I had to instruct him to tone it down, but once he knew his performance was being monitored, we had no more difficulty on that score.

It didn't take me long to learn a number of other things about Runner. Our jobs brought us into close contact and he was not at all reticent about his rather checkered career. At the outbreak of the war, he told me, he was accused by the civil authorities in his native state of killing a man in a barroom brawl. He was given a choice, or so he said, of either standing trial or volunteering for the army. Runner chose the army, and here, if his story is true, we have an almost literal example of the "handcuffed volunteer" which people used to talk about.

After serving with the division in North Africa, my runner/interpreter had been over the hill for several weeks in the winter of 1943–1944. It was not that he sought to avoid hazardous duty. He had met a girl in Naples and had concluded that a warm bed was preferable to freezing in the mountains. I could relate to that. In Naples he became connected with an Italian black market gang. He described with many gestures how he had misdirected and distracted American truck drivers while his partners had pilfered various items from the backs of their trucks. Apparently the gang lived rather well.

After a couple of months the adventure turned sour and Runner broke up with his girl. The separation produced no particular trauma for him. Women were easy to find, but he became increasingly concerned that, this being wartime, he might be charged with desertion in the face of the enemy, an offense the military seemed to condemn most severely. Desertion was the furthest thing from his mind. He fully expected to do his duty, and, after some deliberation, turned himself in.

The resulting court martial convicted him of something, I'm not sure what, but surely it could not have been for the worst offenses he freely confessed to me. He was sentenced to a forfeiture of pay and allowances, of course, and in addition was given a jail sentence to be served at the end of hostilities. It was under this suspended sentence that he came back to join Ellis and the platoon.

I believed most of Runner's story but was alive to the possibility that he might be trying to intimidate me by showing what a very bad man he really was. His confessions caused me to reflect on matters I had not considered since coming overseas. In the States, junior officers had sometimes discussed the possibility of a platoon leader being shot by his own men in the heat of combat. We had heard it happened in World War I and thought it entirely possible that some bad dude with real or imagined grievances might, if given the opportunity, try to settle old scores with a shot in the back. It was not thought of as a major problem, only as a possible problem.

Overseas it had appeared to be a nonproblem. No one ever mentioned it and I suspect we would have questioned the emotional stability of anyone who did. Line officers had a lot to fear but not from their own men. There were many reasons why. The vast majority of our men were good soldiers, just as scared as their officers but also just as determined to do their jobs. We shared the dangers and hardships of campaigning. We dressed alike. Even off the line there were no blouses and pinks, no Sam Browne belts, no low cut shoes to distinguish the officers from the enlisted men. Saluting was limited to more formal and ceremonial occasions. Many of the remaining privileges of the "officer caste" such as socializing together were, we thought, functional necessities. We tried to maintain a proper social distance from the men without setting ourselves too far apart.

Very few men ever tried to overstep the invisible line. No one ever called a platoon leader "LT" to his face or "ninety-day wonder" or addressed him by his first or last name except in rare instances where the platoon leader told them to. Runner always called me "Tenente" or "Signor tenente" as the Italians did. That was OK with me.

Most line officers I knew tried to avoid "chicken shit" discipline. We practiced a "strategic leniency," ignoring petty regulations and deciding for ourselves what had to be enforced. And, above all, officers and men made common cause against higher headquarters and all other outsiders. Only those, actually not nominally, entitled to wear the Combat Infantry Badge belonged to our fraternity. It was "us against them."

Runner was one of us. I really didn't think he was capable of shooting me in the back but, under the circumstances, thought it best to put him on notice before he tried to get away with things short of murder. I told him his earlier career was no part of my concern. That was all in the past. But, I said, I had my own problems and responsibilities and if he ever let us down or I had to come after him for any reason, I would do my damnedest to see that he was put away for good.

He protested rather mockingly that he had learned his lesson, that I had nothing to worry about, that he was a new man, etc. I very much doubted that and hoped he had heard about the earlier disciplinary cases I had won. I refrained from mentioning them. The threat would come with greater force if he found out for himself. Actually, when he was sober, I didn't have anything to worry about in his case. Despite his rather wild behavior and self-confessed lawlessness off the line, Runner was by no means without redeeming qualities. Under fire he displayed courage, toughness, tenacity and a capacity to meet hardship with good humor. He did his job; that was enough. He could be generous and kind as well as surly, cruel and unpredictable. And for both good and ill, there was no better scrounger in all the Fifth Army.

Sometimes his enthusiastic acquisitiveness got him into trouble. I had heard about an incident which took place before I joined the platoon in which Runner had been chasing chickens around the barnyard of a farmhouse between the lines when a sniper shot him in the throat. To my knowledge that was the first and only time he was wounded in action.

He may have regarded the sniper's bullet as a minor occupational hazard. The incident failed to make any observable difference in his behavior. He continued to go out of his way to collect items useful for comfort or barter. On Easter Sunday of 1945 we were on a remote mountain top a mile or so past the point where the pack mules had to stop when he appeared before me with an offering of a hardboiled egg. When I expressed reluctance to take food intended for his own mouth, he fished in his pocket and brought forth a duplicate which he had saved for himself. I thanked him for the treat and we sat there eating silently. At least there was no talking. I didn't ask Runner where he had obtained his treasures. There were some thing I really didn't want to know.

In the middle of January we began a long period of intensive training devoted to tank-infantry cooperation in anticipation of spring operations in the Po Valley. Most of it was old and boring activity for the veterans, but there were replacements, both officers and men, who had never been through the drill. They quickly became bored too. We repeated the same exercises over and over in the hope, I suppose, of eventually getting it right, but, more important, to be fair, in the interest of setting up predictable, automatic responses when we faced the real thing.

Some aspects of the training paid off; certain refinements were simply ignored. Since line troops are not supposed to have too many smarts, higher authority had prescribed for our training in some detail. They even provided us with an innovative set of commands. To get the infantry down from the tanks, for example, the command would be: "Doughs, Down!" with "Doughs" as the preparatory command and "Down" the command of execution. When we first heard that one, we speculated on the age and competence of the officers who had dreamed it up. As far as I know, American infantry had not been called "Doughboys" since World War I. And did the plans and training people think we were fighting this war by the numbers? Didn't they understand that the troops would be happy to dismount from the tanks without command? And to get them to climb aboard, it was necessary only to say, "Let's Go!" or "OK. Let's haul ass."

Around the first of February with the company still involved in training exercises, I and one officer from each of the other companies in the battalion went back to rest camp in Florence for five days. My favorite nurse came down to rest with me. I didn't get out of the large, luxurious but still old-fashioned hotel during the entire time.

A new generation of junior officers crowded the bars. Most of them seemed a lot younger than I. Shoulder patches from the Eighty-eighth, Eighty-fifth, Ninety-first, and Thirty-fourth divisions were predominant. I saw no one from the Ninety-second and would have been greatly surprised if I had.

I gravitated toward the men of the Thirty-fourth, hoping to get word of my friend Dono who had toured Naples with me so long ago. After making several inquiries, I learned that he had been killed in the drive for Bologna. This news was not only enough to make me want to cry. It added to the feeling I had outlived my time. There weren't many left of the group which had come up from the repple depple a year ago. After five days, I returned to the company. The training continued. We were grateful for the fact that it kept us out of the mountains during the worst weather, but at some point sheer boredom can become almost intolerable. The change when it came was not welcomed enthusiastically by any means, but it was acceptable.

Around February 20 we were ordered back into the mountains above Highway 64 for an extended tour of duty at the front. Our initial positions were on a barren peak with but few trees and nothing to provide a windbreak. It was the tail end of winter, but the weather was still cold and unpredictable. In the first week we had a day and night of cold rain, sleet and snow during which we struggled to keep warm and to keep the weapons dry. After that the weather cleared a bit but there was always the cold, penetrating wind to make us wish we were back at Lucca. At night in exposed positions where we couldn't risk a fire, we huddled together for warmth, pretending it was only the cold which made us shiver.

I saw no reason to enforce standing orders that the men keep themselves as clean as possible. The stench of our bodies was never a major concern, winter or summer. It is said that the stink inside the lodges of the Sioux Indians on the western plains was almost unbearable to strangers but seemed perfectly natural to the tribe. And so it must have been with us.

Captain Yount, who didn't limit himself to the acquisition and analysis of intelligence, chewed out a couple of my men because they hadn't shaved. When he and I were alone, I took as much exception to his action as I thought prudent. While I didn't tell the captain so, I thought it ridiculous to require men to shave dry or with cold water in freezing temperatures. I seethed inwardly at the time but now conclude that he was right. It is an elementary proposition of conventional military wisdom that personal cleanliness has a more or less subtle influence on morale. Soldiers who have cleaned up as much as possible feel better and perform better. If I had been older or closer to my frontier heritage, I would have known that. At one time, as I understand, everybody knew that if you didn't curry your horse, you would have a cranky horse to deal with.

Except for patrol activity, our sector of the front was relatively quiet. Both sides seemed content with the stalemate. On our side artillery ammunition was rationed and we were cautioned to use mortar and small-arms fire sparingly. No longer could an infantry officer almost automatically call down artillery fire on the mere suspicion that the enemy occupied a position to his front. Now there was talk of "more lucrative targets" and of "defensive fire missions" which had priority. The artillery continued to lay down harassing fire but on a noticeably more limited scale.

To be "ammunition poor" on orders from higher headquarters was a new experience for us. What had happened? Could it be that the arsenal of democracy was at last empty? Had the strain of providing supplies for a global war been too much? Were there problems of transportation we knew nothing about? Were we stockpiling ammunition for the spring push? Were we getting our fair share of what was available? We very much doubted that. We always felt ill used.

As if to make up for the ammunition shortage, Fifth Army, or somebody on high—but not that high—had earlier provided us with artificial moonlight. High-powered lights were bounced off the clouds, weather permitting, to illuminate the surroundings below. While this operation did not exactly turn night into days, it did improve visibility. But, of course, the synthetic moon, like the rain from heaven, fell on the just and the unjust alike. We had a better chance of seeing the enemy but they had an equally good chance of seeing us. Still, the advantage lay with our side. Our magicians had only to say, "Let it be dark," and, lo, it was so, while theirs didn't have that capability.

A considerable part of my time in this position was spent climbing up and sliding down mountain trails made slick by mud and melting snow. The machine guns were parceled out to different locations. We had four guns in firing position on the front lines and the remainder of the platoon in reserve at the CP near the bottom of the reverse slope of the hill. Each night I went up the hill to visit the front line units, trudging from one location to another. I usually spent the night up there but returned to the CP at daylight. The trails received harassing fire early in the evening when the enemy knew there would be more traffic, but the fire was seldom heavy or of long duration.

The *Tedeschi* seemed to be hoarding ammunition too. Their fire was even lighter than ours. While I was still a little gun shy and fearful of getting a mortar round in my hip pocket, I adjusted to the situation better than I thought I might, probably because the hardships were greater than the dangers.

But there would be no more extended rest periods for us. After about ten days in these positions, we were pulled out and sent a bit further up the mountains on the east side of the highway. With but one brief exception for refitting, we would be at the front until the end of the war in Italy.

Chapter 12

Holding the High Ground

For the next several weeks the battalion occupied positions on the fringes of an area where Nazi SS troops had carried out a sickening massacre of Italian men, women, and children some six months earlier. One of our platoons was deployed around what showed on our maps as "Casa Creda" while other units looked down on Pioppe di Salvare, a small factory town still held by the enemy. Both places figure prominently in Jack Olsen's remarkable book *Silence on Monte Sole* (Bantam, 1969), a work which must rank with the very best ever written on war atrocities.

Before the war, Olsen tells us, Creda was one of the most prosperous farms on the mountain, but on September 29, 1944 a contingent of SS troops came up, drove some ninety men, women, and children into a shed, and fired long bursts from a heavy machine gun into their midst. Anticipating correctly that some of their victims had survived, a few troopers entered the shed to finish them off with pistol shots to the head. After that grenades were thrown into the mounds of human flesh, and still a few survived to tell their stories.

At Salvaro several dozen Italian men were summarily executed and it was the same or worse on other parts of the killing ground. For three hellish days and nights the storm troopers worked their will, killing, raping, looting, and burning. When the SS had finished and the American Fifth Army had moved through, there was "silence on Monte Sole," a silence interrupted only from time to time by the detonation of explosives which the warriors on both sides had left behind. The mountain remained virtually uninhabited for at least twenty-five years.

When I read Olsen's book for the first time, my excitement mounted as I encountered familiar place names and realized that my battalion had been close to the area when the atrocities occurred. Close but not nearly close enough. I compared my dates with Olsen's. When the Nazi raids began, my outfit had just started down Highway 64. Before we got to Porretta, still a dozen or so miles from the scene of the slaughter, hundreds of people had been killed, some of them partisans with whom the German command had legitimate concern.

There were other American and British units closer to Mt. Sole at the time, but Allied shelling and bombing served merely to complicate the problems of the doomed mountain people by increasing the indiscriminate violence inflicted upon them. An indeterminable number of casualties was inflicted by "friendly fire."

By the time we moved into our positions, there remained few signs to indicate that this place was special. If I had known what to look for, I might have seen more. We were warned for the first time since Pontedera to be on guard against an uncommon number of mines and booby traps but were given no explanation for their presence. There were the remains of civilian corpses in the wreckage of one of the farmhouses in my sector, a most unusual occurrence, but we avoided the area and didn't try to find out why, or how many people had died. The smell of death was no worse here than we had experienced elsewhere. I had never seen so much damage to real estate in such a remote area but I attributed most of that, probably correctly, to Allied bombing and shelling. In addition to the rubble of destroyed houses, the ground was littered by an unusual amount of debris, mostly tin cans, ammunition and rations crates, discarded equipment and other traces of infantry troops.

In early March of 1945 this front began to heat up in more ways than one. There was a gradual increase in artillery, ours and theirs, and a noticeable increase in small-arms encounters. Patrolling became more aggressive on both sides. The *Tedeschi,* to judge by the noises coming from their lines, were becoming downright exuberant. At night we could hear once again those guttural voices calling out, sometimes playfully, to each other across the valley. I never got used to those sounds. Every time I heard them, I was chilled by the feeling that there were giants out there in the dark thirsting for my blood. Fi, Fi, Fo, Fum!

Initially my platoon was in reserve on the reverse slope of a high ridge close to the battalion CP. On March 5 I was ordered to meet a lieutenant from Captain Zeller's company at 1930 hours on Pt. 516. In the afternoon I made a short trip up to the end of the jeep trail to see a part of the route I would be traveling. Neither the map nor artificial moonlight was an adequate substitute for daylight reconnaissance. I couldn't go beyond the end of the jeep trail in daylight and didn't need to. From the top of the ridge a guide would lead us forward when darkness came.

The path had been widened by military traffic. The wheel tracks of jeeps were in evidence and scattered piles of dried mule dung testified to earlier use of pack animals to supply units on the other side of the ridge. While the incline was not exceptionally steep, there were boulders and rough spots along the way. The trail had suffered natural erosion which revealed the rocky subsoil.

At dusk I had three people with me at the top of the hill, my platoon sergeant, my runner and one of the section leaders. We started for Pt. 516 but the guide got lost twice and we had to retrace our steps. When we got to what the guide said was the appointed place, we had to wait an additional hour for the lieutenant.

I was fuming. Being lost on a front which was supposed to be extensively mined was not exactly my idea of a good time. Besides, what assurance did I have that the guide had finally found the right place? Before coming up, I had heard the old man didn't trust the rifle platoon leader I was supposed to meet. During the long wait, I began to wonder whether the lieutenant would show up even if we were in the right place. I got so mad I almost forgot to be afraid.

The lieutenant finally showed up and, without explaining the delay, took us over to the left to a place called Caposena.

It was in ruins. Only the foundations of the few houses could be seen under the wreckage. There was a ledge to our left front and, on our right a path leading downhill to Serra and on to the Reno River. Unfortunately this path, like so many others, ran both ways. From the enemy's point of view, it led *up* from Serra to our positions on the hill. Our mission was to assure one-way traffic, all of it going down.

The platoon leader from Zeller's company had orders to dig in here. I would relieve him on the following night with a section of machine guns. But why should one machine-gun section relieve an entire platoon of riflemen? I never found out, but I sent the old man a request for a rifle squad to help us.

The next night I led my section up to Caposena, no rifle squad, no word from the old man. The artificial moonlight helped us find the way. My CP was a two-man foxhole which I shared with Runner. It was reasonably warm, if a bit cramped. I knew there must be a safe basement somewhere in all that rubble but, in view of the warnings, I was not about to go exploring by moonlight.

I had fourteen men counting myself to protect the path. For the first time since Anzio, I pulled guard on post with the rest. The enemy was whooping it up down below, firing their schmeissers, roaring and yelling.

On my two o'clock shift I could have sworn I saw a *Tedesco* crawling up on me. It turned out to be a rabbit and I was glad I hadn't embarrassed myself by opening fire. Behaving no better than a trigger-happy recruit could be damaging to the reputation of a platoon leader. Ellis would never have made that mistake.

Just before daylight I sent word around telling the men to empty their bowels if they could and to stay in concealment all day. There was no use attracting the attention of the enemy artillery unless we had to. The reminder was unnecessary. Most of the men would have followed these instructions without being told. They were veterans and it was their lives as well as my own.

After daylight I studied the surrounding terrain as well as I could from the vicinity of my foxhole. We were on the edge of a plateau a mile or so down grade from the head of the jeep trail. The ground dropped off sharply to my immediate left front but slanted more gradually down to the river on the path we were outposting. Captain Zeller's company occupied Pt. 516 and other scattered elevations over to my right. Across the valley to our far left rear was Pt. 826, the highest peak in the sector. I could see Casa Creda and part of the trail leading down the valley between it and 826. The upper part of the trail was crucial to battalion operations. It was our supply line, our route of evacuation, the only way out if we had to leave in a hurry. The lower segment down by the river was owned by the enemy.

The battalion's so-called front line consisted of a most irregular series of scattered strong points. Few of the positions were mutually supporting. Mountain valleys separated companies and even some platoons within companies. Squads, sections, platoons and small outposts were pretty much left alone to fight their separate little wars.

After seeing all I could from the foxhole, I crawled out on the ledge to my front under partial concealment from a brush pile. From there I had a view of the Reno Valley from Pioppe di Salvaro on the left to Serra and Casa Nova on my right. Nothing was moving down there. I crawled back to my original shelter.

A radio message came through during the afternoon instructing me to report to the head of the jeep trail after dark. Good. That must mean the old man was going to give me that rifle squad I had requested.

At dusk I tramped back up the hill to find the rifle squad waiting. It was from Frank's company, commanded by a sergeant I knew and trusted. I led them back down to Caposena and put them in place. Since the number of people on hand had just about doubled, I didn't need to pull guard on post. Things were looking up a bit.

Shortly after we got settled in, Pathfinder came through with a reconnaissance patrol. He headed for Serra but ran into enemy on the trail below and after a brief fire fight, disengaged and came back through our lines.

I managed to get several catnaps next morning. In the afternoon I learned from the telephone that another patrol would be moving through our positions after dark and that some of Lieutenant Quinn's platoon would be coming in to relieve the rifle squad.

It struck me as a bit unusual to have so many units rotating through this position. Caposena was neither a hot spot nor a rest camp. The old man must have other reasons.

Quinn and half of his platoon came in shortly after dark. The rest of his people were our nearest neighbors on the right flank. He didn't have far to travel. Since I had made a reconnaissance of Caposena, Quinn asked me to put his men in place.

Nance's patrol came through a little bit later. His mission was Pioppe di Salvaro. It would take a lot more men than he had with him to get through. I knew that, and Nance knew that. Probably battalion knew it too. In keeping with our usual practice, we attributed the decision to attempt this mission with a small force to the stupidity of a vague "higher headquarters." Nance didn't make it to Salvaro, but he didn't get any men killed either.

After seeing the patrol back through the lines, I dropped off to sleep in the hope that the war was over for the day. No such luck. I was awakened within the hour by the sounds of machine-gun bullets ripping over our foxholes. My ears told me the enemy was right on top of us but when I eyeballed the situation, I saw that most of the fire was coming from about fifty yards away. That was still much too close for comfort. I thought about asking for artillery fire but quickly dismissed the idea. The enemy was too close. All of us who had been around for a time knew the danger from "short rounds."

Our people had opened up with machine-gun and rifle fire at the outset. Within less than a minute it became obvious that the volume of our fire exceeded theirs, an indication that this was a patrol probing our lines unless, of course, the *Tedeschi* were trying to move in on us in the dark. I listened for the firecracker-like sound of enemy grenades and for other indications they might be coming in. I didn't hear any. Soon their fire slackened further. The enemy was moving back. Now we called for a mortar shoot well out to our front and on the trail in the hopes of catching some of the *Tedeschi* in the open. The mortars, eager to be of help, had their rounds on the way in short order. I couldn't tell whether they had the desired effect. The firing to our front ceased.

I visited our firing positions. No casualties. All was well. The men were still on an emotional high, but that was natural. I was too.

Now that we had tipped our hand, I rather expected enemy artillery the next day. Only a few rounds of harassing fire came our way. Maybe the enemy thought our positions were manned only at night. We hunkered down and once again traded comfort for safety. I was proud of the way the men behaved both in the action and in the waiting. I resolved to tell them so later.

Word came down that Lieutenant Reynolds, who was positioned over around Pt. 516, had been killed. He had gone out early that morning to visit one of his outposts. When he started back, he found that a German patrol had worked its way in behind him and cut him off. Reynolds was able to warn the outpost before a bullet hit him just below the eye and entered his brain. Evidently the enemy had been probing all along this part of the front.

At dusk I contacted Quinn. As more or less expected, he had found a safe basement and his men had been busy with sandbags and blackout material all day. He invited me and my CP personnel, consisting of Runner and Gimo, to join him in his shelter. We accepted eagerly.

As we moved in, Quinn was getting ready for a patrol. His mission was Serra, but he had decided to go overland, avoiding the obvious route where several other patrols had floundered. While his plan was well conceived, there were problems in execution. The terrain off the path was even more rugged than we had thought. The patrol made a good deal of noise and was driven back. It was a good try.

From looking at the map Quinn and I thought we had located one major source of our problem. We concluded that the enemy was operating out of houses in Casa Nova as well as Serra, sniping from them by day, patrolling from them by night. The map also showed a Pt. 247 located nearby which was also a probable enemy base. We directed artillery fire on all three places but couldn't tell whether it had done damage to anything except the houses.

In the middle of the afternoon, I received a message from battalion directing me to report to the head of the jeep trail at dark or "as soon thereafter as practicable." When dusk came, I made the distance in record time. By this time I knew the path so well I could almost negotiate it in my sleep. My platoon sergeant, a section chief, and a guide from Captain Zeller's company were on hand to meet me.

The old man wanted a section of machine guns near Pt. 516 to support the outpost where Reynolds had been killed. We looked for positions from which we could deny the enemy access to the route they had used to get Reynolds and, at the same time, places from which we could fire into a wadi which was giving Zeller trouble.

It took a little while to find locations which would satisfy all requirements. To get a better view of the field of fire, I moved too far out in front of a possible site and almost got myself killed by my own people.

Since we had experienced comparatively little difficulty with artillery fire, I was wearing a soft forage cap which in the synthetic moonlight looked very similar to something the *Tedeschi* wore. When my silhouette came into the line of sight of one of the men, he thought we were about to be hit by another German patrol. When I heard him click the safety off his weapon, I hit the ground and cried out. He didn't fire, and I never wore that cap again.

Once we had selected our gun positions, a detail of guard house prisoners was available to dig the emplacements with orders to have them completed by daylight. The platoon sergeant would bring the section up the following night.

I was back at Caposena shortly after midnight. Quinn and I stayed up and talked while our combined CP personnel brewed coffee for us and the guards. The cellar was the only place we could have a fire and there was quite a bit of activity. After a tour on post, the guards welcomed an opportunity to come in and warm up.

Quinn was fresh from the States. This was his first action. He was a most likeable fellow, much more eager and aggressive than I. After Porretta Terme I had begun to wonder about the validity of the assumption that seasoned troops are better than green ones; and in observing Quinn and comparing him to myself, I found additional reasons for questioning such a broad generalization. Seasoned troops are more cautious, perhaps, because they know they can be hurt, but green troops are likely to be more confident and aggressive. I thought about what I had read of fresh American troops in the Argonne in 1918 and about the Eighty-eighth Division on the Italian front in 1944 when that division was young and unbloodied.

Around 0300 hours we spent a few anxious moments when an enemy patrol hit Pt. 347 where the rest of Quinn's platform was located. To judge from the sounds, it was a small force similar to the one which had set up shop outside Caposena earlier. Quinn's platoon sergeant beat them off without asking for any assistance from us. The firing didn't last over fifteen minutes or so.

Just before daylight Quinn and I made a short "racky," as the British would say, up to Pt. 420, an unoccupied hill on our left flank. From there we got another perspective on Salvaro and other places in the valley. In addition to Salvaro, we studied Serra, Casa Nova and Pt. 247 as best we could.

There was early morning movement around the church at Salvaro. A single enemy soldier came out on the path and reset a trip flare. At least I thought that was what he was doing. When Quinn and I saw him, we were afraid he had seen us so we came back down.

I slept until noon when Gimo woke me and offered a breakfast of hot coffee and warm meat and beans. We received harassing fire from enemy artillery that afternoon. We were lucky it was nothing more.

Runner and I took off at dark for Pt. 516 where we found the platoon sergeant going into position. The guard house boys had done an adequate job of digging gun pits, but, of course, there were always improvements to be made. The sergeant would shoot in his fires before daylight. After seeing that all was well, I returned to Caposena.

Once again the enemy was running wild on the trail below us. They paid another call on Pt. 347 with a stronger force this time. After the firing had died down a bit, Quinn went over to investigate. He returned to report that some of the men were a little nervous in the service over there, having received company for two straight nights. We talked a little about the advisability of rotating them but decided it was not necessary.

My section at Caposena had been there a week when we received word we would be relieved the following night. The news was, of course, well received. Living in proximity to the *Tedeschi,* pissing in C ration cans, being cramped up to remain in concealment all day was not much fun. We got on each other's nerves even if we did manage to avoid casualties.

Relief came early the next evening. Jeeps were at the head of the trail with plenty of hot coffee. Our ten-minute break lengthened a bit but we didn't linger. All of us were eager to get down into the valley and the blacked-out farmhouses where everyone could find hot food and warm shelter.

I still had a section of guns attached to Frank's company across the valley on Pt. 826. After cleaning up the next morning, I slept the rest of the day and decided to visit them that night.

There was no jeep trail up to Pt. 826. It was a hard, steep, winding climb. At the top I found the section in good spirits, ready to spend the duration where they were. After making my rounds, I shacked up in Frank's CP for the remainder of the night.

He was sweating out a company attack into the Reno Valley scheduled for the following evening. No more screwing around with those small reconnaissance patrols. The company was ordered to take both Salvaro and Serra. Frank planned to do the job with two platoons. Norm would attack from the valley between Creda and Pt. 826 to take Salvaro; Nance would jump off from Caposena and go down the path to throw the enemy out of Serra.

The consensus was that Nance would take Serra without too much difficulty but that Norm would run into *"molti Tedeschi."* Frank planned to go down in the valley with Norm where the most trouble was expected. He asked me to serve on 826 as a communications relay station linking the platoons, the company and battalion headquarters. I appreciated the opportunity of being a spectator out of harm's way.

As the time of the attack approached, I stationed myself at the telephone in Frank's CP and kept a log for my own purposes. What follows is an almost verbatim account of what I wrote that night.

2400 Hours

I am writing this at midnight from Frank's CP on 826. Lieutenant Nansen left at dusk to go to his line of departure at Caposena. He wanted plenty of time for personal reconnaissance. Lieutenant Norman is already down in the valley near Salvaro. Captain Lebec is on his way down to join Norm. Somewhat unexpectedly, the old man has just come in to monitor operations from here.

0015 Hours

I have just learned of a slight refinement in the plan. Our old friend Lieutenant Quinn will precede Nance down the path to Serra. If his patrol finds Serra unoccupied, Quinn will occupy it until Nance arrives. But if, as we expect, there are *Tedeschi* in Serra, Quinn will try to cut the path leading in from Casa Nova to give protection to Nance's flank.

0030 Hours

Nothing new to report. We are waiting, mostly in silence. The old man, really a young man of average height, straight blonde hair and blue eyes, is all business. He is rather shy and difficult to know. There is anticipation in the CP and a normal amount of tension, but the feeling is nothing like it would be if we were sweating out a barrage or preparing to move forward in the attack ourselves.

0045 Hours

Quinn has reported on his mission. Got close enough to Serra to see lights in one of the houses and to hear the sounds of hobnail shoes on the trail leading in from Casa Nova. He is taking up positions to protect Nance's flank. Doesn't believe Serra is heavily defended but there are hostiles there. Nance will jump off in fifteen minutes. God I hope he doesn't get hurt! We are unable to contact either Frank or Norm.

0100 Hours

Nance sends word by radio that he is leaving the line of departure at

Caposena. We are still unable to contact Norm. He is scheduled to move out at the same time but we have no indication that he has done so. Norm is really the one to worry about. That's where the action is going to be.

0115 Hours

Both Nance and Norm are out of contact. We didn't expect to hear from Nance this soon but we should have had something from Norm or Frank. They have both radio and telephone down there but there is no response from either. The old man has asked the communications section to check the telephone line leading down to the valley.

0130 Hours

Nance is in Serra without firing a shot. They are laying a telephone line to him now. He reports by radio that the position is secure. Apparently the enemy took off at his approach.

Still nothing from Norm or Frank and it's much too quiet down there. We heard a few rounds of small-arms fire a little while ago but nothing else. There has to be something wrong.

0145 Hours

Frank has reported to me by telephone that Norm has cracked up and can't go through with the attack. The platoon is milling around in the dark. Frank and Welch, the platoon sergeant, are trying to round them up. Frank doesn't want me to tell the colonel just yet, but the old man keeps asking me for information. I won't be able to stall for long.

0200 Hours

The colonel has talked directly with Frank over the telephone. Don't know what Frank told him but I could tell the old man was pleading and pressuring Frank to get something started. Frank must have told him it was all over for tonight. The old man put down the phone saying only that the company would try again tomorrow night and that "the general" would be down. Don't know what general he meant. The commander of CCB? The division commander? Mark Clark himself? The old man just said good night and left the CP.

Good for Frank. I'm glad he couldn't be pressured into leading the attack himself. That's not his job.

That is the end of the play by play but the regular journal entry continues.

Frank returned to his CP at daylight, mad, tired, hungry, sleepy. We had some ten in one bacon warm for him along with the usual cup of hot coffee. Both of us went to our sleeping bags without saying anything about events down by the river.

I woke before noon and cleaned up a bit. Frank was already up and ready to talk. We went outside the CP to get a little privacy.

There really wasn't much to be said about Salvaro. Norm had been sent back to the aid station. Frank gave no details and I asked for none. No one wants to look in on the naked vulnerability of a longtime friend. I wanted to forget that anything had happened. I wanted it to be the way it always had been. Deep down I knew that if I had remained in the company, I might very well have been given the Salvaro assignment and more than likely would have been unable to carry it out. There but for the grace of God go I is a very good way of saying it.

Frank said that Welch, the platoon sergeant, was greatly embarrassed by the whole thing and was eager to redeem himself for what he considered a failure of leadership on his part. Neither Frank nor I blamed Welch any more than we blamed Norm.

More than anything else, perhaps, Frank was mad at the old man, mad at the army, mad at himself. He blamed the army and the old man for keeping junior officers on the line until they were either killed, wounded or until they cracked up. He blamed himself for failing to realize how shaky Norm was and for giving him an assignment all of us knew was most difficult.

I told him he was right about army policy but wrong about his own responsibility. A CO couldn't know everything and couldn't play favorites. It was just one of those things, the luck of the draw. If it was Norm's turn to go in, that was that. All of us were scared.

There was not long to dwell on the past. Frank's company now faced the necessity of another go at Salvaro. Perhaps to demonstrate the significance he attached to the enterprise and the pressure he was feeling, the old man sent down to the company what I referred to in my notes as "the battalion fire ball," a Lieutenant Karchmer from Morrow's company, to take over Norm's platoon and lead the attack.

Karchmer was something of a loner and a curiosity in the battalion, the only junior officer I ever knew who sought out dangerous assignments and seemed to have an active hatred of the enemy. I had met him for the first time in late February when he came by the platoon CP following a daylight reconnaissance patrol which he had initiated. He was an impressive looking fellow, above average height, well built, a two-hundred pounder. After we had introduced ourselves, he accepted my invitation to sit down for coffee. He did most of the talking.

The burden of his message was that we were too easy on the enemy. Even if we weren't ready for a major attack, we should be patrolling the Germans day and night, giving them no rest, denying them any possibility of recovering from our blows. And it was not just talk. He was more than willing to do more than his share.

Although a comparative newcomer, Karchmer had already made a name for himself. He had been decorated for his behavior at Palazzo where he literally drove some of his men back up a hill which they had started to leave under heavy fire. I was not there but Nance was, and, as he described it, Karchmer had a .45 in one hand, a grenade in the other, and a mean look in his eyes. The platoon held the position. It was rather widely reported that the men didn't particularly like him but they damn sure respected him.

As far as I know, Karchmer never said anything about his personal life. We were left to speculate. Some of us thought he might have personal scores to settle. While we didn't then know about Auschwitz, Dachau, and the rest, we knew enough to understand that people of Jewish faith and ancestry might feel deep personal involvement in the war against Hitler.

There was no arrogance in Karchmer's manner when he appeared at Frank's CP that afternoon. He was, instead, very professional, very cool and workmanlike. He conferred with Frank, studied the map, asked some questions and then was taken down to meet his new platoon and make his preparations. Frank accompanied him down into the valley while I stayed on Pt. 826 to man the relay station as before. We halfway expected some of the bigger brass to drop in, but no one came, not even the old man.

Contrary to one account I have read, Karchmer didn't take Salvaro that night, but his platoon got into the town and put up a stiff fight. His men reported they had permanently silenced at least one enemy machine gun. They got into some houses and onto the lower floor of the church which we all knew was the key to the Salvaro defense. An estimated twenty-five or thirty Germans occupied the loft and the steeple. From the steeple the enemy had all around observation. From the loft they sprayed machine-gun fire on the ground floor and bounced hand grenades off the helmets of their attackers.

Several of Karchmer's men were wounded, some very seriously. Sergeant Welch was killed. He more than demonstrated his courage that second night at Salvaro but paid for it with his life. At daylight the Germans allowed the medics to remove his body under cover of a Red Cross flag.

My machine gunners were relieved on 826 the following night. I led them back down the hill. Once again we came back to positions around the battalion CP with only occasional artillery fire to worry about.

Just above the CP the engineers were busy improving the trail leading up to the ridge on the way to Caposena. For a time their blasting gave us more trouble than the enemy. With every explosion the old house we were in would shake to its foundations. The first blast came on as suddenly as an earthquake. After that, when the engineers cried "fire in the hole," we took them seriously.

The trail was being widened and improved with a special purpose in mind. The old man wanted to get one of the battalion's self-propelled assault guns up the trail and down into the valley on the other side of Caposena for attacks on Casa Nova and Pt. 247. Our possession of Serra had relieved pressure on the trail above, but our platoon down there was exposed and lonely.

At about this time the commander of Headquarters Company went back to rest camp in Florence for a few days, and I took over as acting CO. The mortars and machine guns were scattered about at different locations in the battalion area and the assault guns were immobilized by the terrain. An efficient communications section was busy keeping its telephone lines in repair. The supply system was working smoothly; the kitchen was preparing what it had to prepare. The noncoms and the clerical staff had so routinized their operations that there was little left for me to do except sign my name occasionally.

I visited one of our mortar platoon positions to see if they needed anything—anything I might be able to supply, that is, and I rotated a section of machine guns back to Caposena. One night I served as battalion duty officer minding the radio and had one of my few opportunities of seeing the war from the battalion CP.

Most of the excitement that night involved Lieutenant Quinn's attack on Pt. 247. It was repulsed with heavy casualties. The old man had managed to get an assault gun up the hill and down the trail past Caposena to support Quinn's attack. Most unfortunately the S.P. got bogged down after it left Caposena and was unable to fire a single shot. Quinn's attack was already under way.

Casualties from the fracas were evacuated after daylight. I talked with some of the less seriously wounded. They confirmed what had appeared probable from our map reading, namely, that Casa Nova and Point 247 were mutually supporting.

To people directly involved, this was no "fracas." They might have taken 247 but must have felt as if the entire weight of the German army had hit them in the flank when enemy machine guns opened up from the Casa Nova position. If the S.P. had been able to get into position, it might have neutralized Casa Nova, and, perhaps, helped to clean up the entire valley including Salvaro. That must have been the colonel's plan. It was a nice try. But all we had to show for his good intentions were dead men, wounded men, and shaken survivors.

The Headquarters Company commander returned, and I rejoined my scattered platoon. This time I went up to Pt. 516. I had never spent an entire night with them. Captain Zeller called for assistance just before daylight, and we fired a fifteen-minute concentration into the wadi which was giving him trouble.

For a solid three hours later that afternoon, we were pounded by artillery and mortar fire. Our telephone line was cut during the initial stages of the barrage. And we soon became keenly aware of the weakness of our position.

Our CP was in the wreckage of an old house, but the roof of the dugout was thin. Several times when shells landed close by, pieces of masonry, rock, dirt and wood splinters rained down, some drawing blood. Mitch swore that if we got out of this alive, he would work like a dog to make our position bombproof. He offered me a cigarette. I grabbed at it, lit up, smoked and shivered. Soon my hand was trembling so much I had difficulty holding anything. I threw the cigarette away before my fear became too obvious. We prayed for darkness.

When the shelling was over, I was much surprised to find that the section had suffered no casualties serious enough to require evacuation. One of the new men was being blamed for attracting enemy artillery. He had built a small fire to brew coffee. I tried to tell everyone concerned that the shelling must have been due to other causes. The most likely explanation was that a German patrol in the wadi we had been firing on had reported our location. Or perhaps the enemy was simply firing off his stockpile of ammunition prior to a withdrawal. We didn't need any scapegoats. I was sure the new man had learned his lesson if he had a lesson to learn.

I was brought down from Pt. 516 late that night to serve as defense counsel in a series of courts-martial. This as routine duty, each officer serving his turn as defense counsel, trial judge advocate, member of the court, etc. Apparently higher headquarters had a backlog of cases they wanted to process prior to the spring offensive. Apparently, also, it was my turn to see to it that the rights of the accused were respected.

For the next few days I alternated between front line positions and attendance on the court. One day I would be groveling in the dirt and thinking survival; the next I wouldn't be thinking at all because almost all the defendants pleaded guilty. If a man elected to deny the charges, the court heard him out and then found him guilty anyway. What a war! And, I thought, but much later, what a travesty on justice. Some of the guys I was supposed to be defending may have been as innocent as an orthodox Mormon's coffee cup for all I know. I usually had from three to five minutes with each of the accused just before the trial opened, hardly enough time for me to put on a Clarence Darrow performance even if I had possessed the will, the knowledge and the talent to do so.

I, of course, made no objection to the arrangements, assuming, as I think other junior officers did, that the accused were guilty or they wouldn't have been charged. Besides, it meant for me time off the line, a chance to clean up and to get a couple of hot meals on the days the court was in session.

Late one afternoon after we had finished our docket for the day, Captain Yount wanted me to conduct him up to Caposena and on down to Serra so that he could get a firsthand look at the situation. What could I say? I would, of course, be delighted to have his company? Not true. The captain and I didn't like each other very well but I certainly respected his courage and competence. He didn't have to make that trip down to Serra.

The captain was accompanied by another battalion staff officer, Lieutenant Loving, a friend of mine. We stopped at Caposena and I checked out the machine-gun section. They had helped beat off another small-scale attack the night before, but the enemy no longer owned the path around Serra and their visits to our positions all along the line had become less frequent and threatening. Now, German patrols coming out of Casa Nova or from Pt. 247 had to bypass Serra and hit the trail further up the hill. Both the rugged terrain of the bypass routes and the possibility of being trapped between Serra and Caposena must have discouraged them. Our supply parties had always made it down to Serra and back without too much difficulty. From all of this I judged the path to be relatively safe, but, nonetheless, I borrowed a submachine gun and took a couple of grenades along for the trip.

We passed the place where our assault gun had bogged down. It was still there useless and at least temporarily abandoned. We approached Serra cautiously and were relieved when an American-speaking guard challenged us.

Serra was a scene of much activity. The supply party had gone back up the trail but details from Quinn's squads and outposts were in to pick up their allotments. Quinn himself, looking a bit like Brian Donlevy in need of a shave—somebody must have heard of Brian Donlevy, for God's sake—was giving instruction in a loud voice to a patrol just about to go out. His platoon sergeant showed us around the positions. There were lots of stone walls here and I looked for places to install machine guns. I assumed that was the main reason I had been "invited" to make the trip down.

The *Tedeschi* were located in buildings at Casa Nova less than three hundred yards away. To judge from the supplies coming in, Quinn's men were using up hand grenades at a rapid rate. What they really needed against those enemy positions was that assault gun the old man had tried to get down to them.

Our inspection trip completed, we started back up the trail. As we neared the halfway point on the way to Caposena, a burp gun opened up from the left of the path. We hit the ground. I feared the worst and was expecting to hear enemy fire coming down the path from straight ahead and from our right, an indication that the *Tedeschi* were trying to cut us off. My first thought was that we might be able to retreat back to Serra.

No additional fire came. The three of us decided that either the first shots were unaimed or had come from a small patrol installed to protect the enemy right flank while they attacked over by 516. But we faced a dilemma. If the enemy was close enough to see us, there was danger in getting up to move ahead. On the other hand there was equal or greater danger in staying where we were if our approximate location was known.

Loving solved the dilemma by going into a crouch and running up the trail. The captain and I followed. There was no additional firing, and, after resting a bit to catch our breath, we hastened on to Caposena without being further molested.

I stayed at Caposena while the captain and his assistant started back for battalion headquarters. Lieutenant Petri now commanded the rifle platoon at Caposena. His people had brewed up coffee and I waited around until the patrols had come back in. When they reported, we got one item of redundant information and another piece of news we wanted to hear. Pt. 247 was still occupied by the enemy, but our patrols had not suffered casualties.

I trudged through the darkness back over to our position around Pt. 516 to find that Mitch had kept his vow. With sandbags and rubble he had considerably improved our position. He swore it would take a direct hit from the 170 MM which had troubled us earlier. All of us hoped his boast would not be put to the test.

The next day we received a heavy mortar barrage but our renovated dugout lessened the strain. Like a householder when there is a storm raging outside, we felt some anxious moments but also a sense of coziness at being under shelter.

The more comforting feelings didn't last long. That night two events disturbed our peace of mind. First, we fought a battle with the rats in our cellar. One of them ran across my face in the dark. Eventually we had to light candles for a rat hunt. There were some big fat rascals.

But the other problem came on more gradually and proved to be more serious. A heavy rain had begun to fall at dark. Our shelter might or might not be bombproof. It was not well drained. Water trickled under our feet turning the dirt into mud. The trials became slick. On the short route from the CP to the guns and back, I fell down three times.

It rained harder next day. The CP became muddier and more uncomfortable. The guns had to be cleaned again. I called back for more oil and patches. I also asked that the mail be forwarded. The men were beginning to get on each other's nerves. Mitch quarreled with Runner and Runner, in a surly mood, quarreled with everyone in sight including me. I thought that mail from home might have a distracting and possibly a soothing effect. A German sniper kept pecking away at our positions. Here obviously was one man who had found ways of keeping his powder dry.

I knew the platoon sergeant was taking a section back to Pt. 826 that night. I wondered how they would make out on that slick trail. We had reports that a mule loaded with rations had fallen over the edge the night before. I hoped for the best.

In the midst of the deluge, I was called back to battalion for the last session of the military court. All the small talk back there was of an early end to the war. We were to be relieved by the Thirty-fourth Division, I was told, shortly after April 2. Some thought we were going back for a brief rest and refitting in preparation for the spring offensive. Others inclined to the view that we were going to take a boat trip. Where? They didn't say.

At the end of the day, I made my way back up to Pt. 826. If the machine-gun section had suffered an accident on the way up, I surely would have heard about it but I wanted to check for myself. Besides, 826 was becoming more rear echelon. No need to carry a heavy tommy gun up there; a carbine would do quite well.

When I got to the top, I discovered the section was doing very well, thank you. They had plenty of warm field rations, hot coffee, and cigarettes. Enemy artillery was no problem; neither were enemy patrols. What more could a soldier want? Silly question. I didn't ask.

From a particular point on 826 you could see the fronts of four different divisions. There was a great commotion over on Highway 65 the next morning. It was probably the Eighty-eighth Division giving the Germans hell and, perhaps, catching some itself.

The old man came up with a relief party a night or two later. There were a few air bursts around the CP as if the enemy knew a relief was under way. They did no damage. Our intelligence people were pondering a radio message intercepted that afternoon. When translated it said, "The dog has found the opening."

No one knew what that meant. I asked whether the message might not have been, "The *shaggy* dog has found the opening," but was assured, very gravely, that such was not the case. Maybe those guys had never heard a shaggy dog story.

I didn't ponder the meaning of this mysterious communication. When the relief was completed, we slid down the hill, giving no more thought to what the dog had done or left undone.

In a few more days the division moved back from the front. It had been a rather lengthy, uncomfortable tour, boring, exciting, and frightening by turns. But thanks to my new assignment, I had escaped responsibility for any of those patrols carried out by my friends in the rifle companies. I had reason to be grateful to the major who had arranged my transfer. He hadn't steered me wrong.

After getting back out of artillery range, I could see other things more clearly. Despite the enemy's apparent high spirits and tenacity, there were clear indications that the war was winding down. The noises the *Tedeschi* made were out of proportion to their numbers on the ground. While their patrols had hit our lines frequently, they were not following through as in the past. It was not at all like Anzio, not even like Pontedera. If we had attacked in full company strength on that first or second night at Salvaro, we would have taken the place. Of that I was sure.

As on the breakout at Anzio, I had no doubt of the success of a spring offensive. A full-scale attack would finish off the war in Italy. But some of us would never make it, and the odds hadn't improved in my case. They had become worse.

Chapter 13

The Last Offensive

Eight Days in the Mountains

When we got back from the front, there was only a week left to prepare for the opening of the spring offensive. That gave us little time for anything other than having our losses made good, getting resupplied, and trying to relax. The plan of operation for ending the war in Italy was complicated. As a junior officer I knew only that the British Eighth Army would go in first and we would follow in our sector a few days later.

The end of the war was so near and yet so far. I saw more clearly than ever now the probabilities of getting killed in the last push. I guess I had too much time to think about the odds. All the fears and feelings I had experienced after Porretta Terme came surging back stronger than ever. I tried to dilute a flood of powerful emotions with alcohol.

There were always people to help in that kind of endeavor. I shared with one of the mortar platoon leaders a large room on the first floor of a big house. We kept a plentiful supply of cognac, gin and wine on hand. Every night after the evening meal, we lined our bottles up on the mantle above the fireplace and held open house. When a group had assembled, either I or my roommate would officially open each session by taking a long drag off the bottle and yelling, "Fire in the hole!" After that it was every man for himself. The detonations would continue until after midnight. But still what Winston Churchill called "the black dog" refused to be frightened away.

On an impulse early one morning I sought out the old man. In actual age he couldn't have been more than five years my senior but in terms of maturity there was a great gap between us. He was a man; I was still a scared little boy.

There were no preliminaries to go through. The colonel and I were quartered in the same house. I simply went upstairs, knocked on his bedroom door, and heard him invite me to come in.

The old man was shaving. He asked what was on my mind, and I told him I wanted to talk for just a few minutes. He invited me to sit down while he continued to scrape the stubble off his face.

His informality put me at ease. I hadn't wanted an official audience. I still don't know what in the hell I did want from him and he must have wondered too. Some would say I was really asking the colonel to go easy on me this trip. Maybe so, but I had no conscious intention of asking that. Nor have I ever believed the old man thought that was what I wanted. I would like to think I just needed someone at his level to talk to.

It was a short interview as I had wanted it to be but I told him things I had never told another human being, things I had tried to conceal from my best friends. I began by saying I didn't know how I was going to react this time up. I explained how I had felt after Porretta, how I had thought everything was under control the last time at the front, but now, I told him, with the end of the war in sight, the old feelings of being doomed had returned stronger than ever. I concluded by promising that I would do my best and wouldn't bug out.

The old man was still shaving as he began his response.

"You really didn't expect to live through this war, did you?" he asked. He turned his head to glance at me briefly then looked back in the mirror, pulling at one side of his face to give it better exposure to the razor.

Startled by his question, I confessed that I had hoped and prayed for survival.

He finished his shave and toweled off but continued to stand, facing me now with his back to the mirror.

"If we do our jobs," he said softly, "There is no way we can live. Consider the odds. If we don't get it on the next hill, it will be the one after that or the one after that." And, he concluded, "After Italy and Europe, there is always Japan."

I told him he was probably right but it was most difficult to accept. He said he knew it was. Then he came over and sat down.

I had nothing new to offer. He asked about the platoon. I told him it was a good platoon and seemed to be ready. We exchanged comments on recent losses and the problem of integrating replacements into the outfit. I stood up and he did the same. I told him again I would do my best.

"So will I," he said and smiled. "So will I." He clapped me on the shoulder. "Thanks for coming in," he said politely. "And good luck to you."

"Good luck to you too," I responded. We shook hands.

Much later, James Jones in a book called *World War Two* reflected on the evolution of a combat soldier. The ultimate stage, the logical culmination toward which everything moves, Jones thought, was a stage in which the individual soldier gives himself up for dead. Having recognized that he can't survive, he is relatively free of fear, free to do his job, free to savor every precious moment he has left. Apparently the old man had entered the ultimate stage. I, quite, obviously, had not.

Preparations for the offensive were completed. By April 11 we were in a forward assembly area in the mountains west of Highway 64 ready for the attack to begin next day. The American Tenth Mountain Division had responsibility for taking the heights immediately to our front. It was a specially trained and equipped unit which had come over from the States during the winter and had already demonstrated its worth. All of us had heard about the February attack in which the division greatly surprised the Germans by putting an entire battalion on heights as sheer, it was said, as anything in the Alps. From our assembly area I got a good look at some of the Tenth Mountain troops. They were fresh, husky, confident young men.

The attack didn't go in on the twelfth. We were informed on the afternoon of the eleventh that the date had been postponed for a day because of bad flying weather. It will not have escaped your attention that after April 12 comes April 13, and it did not escape my attention that April 13 was on a Friday. That was a fatal omen. I was very conscious of the dates on which I had been hit. Of the last two times, one had been on Friday, August 13, and the other on Friday, October 13. Those were warning signs just as clear as the warning signs which precede a fatal heart attack. The old man was right. There was no way I was going to come out of this alive. Friday the thirteenth of April 1945 was my appointed time.

My gloom lifted a bit on April 12 when we learned that the date of the attack had been postponed again. We would not be going in on Friday the thirteenth after all. That was a good omen. The Lord God of Hosts, for reasons known only to Himself, had decided to spare me for yet a little while. I was grateful.

Lt. Howard "Fiesty" Able, our communications officer, came up with the ration party that night and visited my CP. He brought both good news and bad news. The good news was that we might not have to make this attack at all because the Russians were already in Berlin. As for the bad news, word had come in that President Franklin D. Roosevelt was dead.

I dismissed his good news as just so much wishful thinking. It was the bad news I took to heart. Roosevelt and I were oldtimers. We went back a long way. I had grown up with him as president and had been heartened by the comforting inaugural speech in 1933 when he had said, "The only thing we have to fear is fear itself." Now there were tangible grounds for misgiving. There were enemy soldiers out there with real guns. Roosevelt was dead and I was sure to be next. It was the end of an era. It was not that I was superstitious, you understand. Everyone knows there are signs and portents which modern science can't explain.

SATURDAY, APRIL 14

When the attack finally began on the morning of the fourteenth, I felt a sense of relief. It was a little bit like feelings I had experienced before a big high school football game where tensions were highest just before the kickoff. Once the first whistle blew and the action began, you could settle down, forget the crowd and play the game.

All that morning the artillery was booming as I had heard it do on the breakout at Anzio almost a year earlier. The big difference this time was air power. Ground-air coordination had been brought to a peak of efficiency none of us had ever seen. Capt. Abe Tucker, an air liaison officer, was attached to the battalion, furnished with a jeep, a driver, and a radio. At battalion request Abe could contact a "Rover Pete" hovering in the sky above; and Pete, in turn, could dispatch to our aid the nearest fighter units, a number of which were circling around like hungry predators looking for prey. I assumed that other battalions had the same capability. There was no reason to believe we were specially favored.

After a safe interval to allow the Tenth Mountain to clear, Sandosky and I accompanied Captain Tucker to the top of the hill behind which we had sheltered. In peacetime the view from the top would have stunned the senses. That morning it had an awesome added dimension. Every village, farmhouse, barn, shed or outbuilding had either been leveled or was smoking from the bombardment. I looked through the glasses trying to find a single man-made structure which had remained untouched. I couldn't find any. With support like that, how could we fail?

From the hill across the valley to our front, we could hear heavy small-arms fire, ours and theirs. Occasionally we could see smoke and get glimpses of tiny little figures going forward as the Tenth Mountain pressed its attack.

My machine-gun platoon was attached to the lead company of our battalion, a company now commanded by Lieutenant Dubak. That afternoon we moved up to a place called Riola. The old man led the way and set a sizzling pace as he usually did. Some of the overloaded machine gunners had difficulty keeping up. They cursed him and freely wished he had their load stuck up his ass.

We met a dozen or so prisoners coming out of Riola. They looked to be just kids, not over fifteen or sixteen years old.

The Tenth Mountain was making remarkable progress. We could tell from the frequency of our own forward movements. It was not at all like other times when we were in reserve.

After dark we moved out of Riola and down into the valley to our front. There was a considerable traffic jam down there. We got hemmed into a tank column which was also trying to advance. After we had struggled through the dust, the fumes and the noise for a little while, the old man led us off the road and into the field where we could make better progress.

We halted, waited, and then moved in behind our sister battalion commanded by Lt. Col. Samuel Urban. Their objective was Suzzano which was known to be a German strong point. After Urban's battalion had taken Suzzano, we would move through to attack first Mt. Radicchio and then Mt. Milano.

About 2230 hours Lieutenant Dubak's company with machine guns attached moved up to relieve a company of Colonel Urban's command. The remainder of my battalion dug in to protect Urban's flank and to be ready to go after our objectives when Suzzano had fallen.

Runner and I slept in an old shed. I didn't break out my bed roll. The way the attack seemed to be going, I thought we might be moving out at any time. That proved to be a mistaken judgment. Runner and I shivered under the only blanket he had brought along.

SUNDAY, APRIL 15

Urban's battalion jumped off for Suzzano at first light. Dubak's company and the machine-gun platoon stayed in place. We were told the company we had relieved the night before was on a wide, flanking movement against Suzzano.

As the morning progressed, the old man came up. He led us and the rest of the battalion forward, out into the bareassed open. Orders were to dig in. The men needed no urging. We were drawing enough mortar and artillery fire to keep the picks and shovels flying. Casualties from our sister battalion kept filtering back through our positions. I tried not to see or to think about them. I remembered Cheney.

Colonel Urban's battalion paid a heavy price, but by the end of the day they were in Suzzano although not yet in complete control of it. After dark we moved up to high ground overlooking the town and were ordered to dig in for the rest of the night. Lieutenant Dubak as company commander, assigned the field on the right of the road to Quinn's rifle platoon and the field on the left to mine. When we moved off the road, someone hit a trip flare which illuminated all of us in its harsh glare.

We hit the ground. The expected enemy fire didn't come, but in a couple of moments someone activated another flare and someone else yelled that we were in a mine field.

There was momentary panic with men running in different directions. A part of my platoon joined the stampede. It took us almost thirty minutes to round them up and even at that two men were still missing. When no mines exploded and there were no signs of an enemy counterattack, the panic subsided. We found ready-made shelter, posted guards and settled down in our foxholes.

MONDAY, APRIL 16

At daylight we got a good look at our immediate surroundings. We were in the midst of positions which the *Tedeschi* had prepared to defend Suzzano. There were trip flares, barbed wire, and booby traps on both sides of the road. No dead bodies. It looked as if the enemy had abandoned this position without a fight.

I had no casualties serious enough to require evacuation although I and several others had torn our battle dress on the wire. I still had two men missing but the platoon sergeant thought they had got lost of their own free will.

About 0630 hours we moved out for a new assembly area from which to launch the attack on the first of our objectives. The route was long and winding. We changed directions several times, going first north then west then north again and finally east, as we tried to approach Mt. Raddicchio from the flank. Our approach march took us over ground the Tenth Mountain had traveled in its drive. This area was sprinkled with dead bodies, some of them Tenth Mountain, but German dead outnumbered American on the order of three to one, a somewhat unusual ratio for troops in the attack.

In the afternoon we caught up with forward elements of the Tenth Mountain. They were busy fending off a German counterattack on the crest of Mt. Mosca. We went into an assembly area behind Mosca to await orders. It was almost 1700 hours before we were ordered over the crest and into the attack.

Dubak's objective was a village called Malfolle which sat back toward the rear of a long, rather narrow ridge. Artillery, mortar and sniper fire had pecked at us intermittently all day; but now, approaching the first elevation of Mt. Raddicchio, we got the undivided attention of whatever the enemy had left.

They proved to have plenty of artillery, mortars and sharp shooters left to say the least. As we moved forward through the valley, a heavy barrage caught us. I heard men scream. Some of them were my men. We left two casualties when we went forward. Only one was seriously hurt.

The machine guns were now in support of Lieutenant O'Neil's platoon. Since the trail leading to the top of the ridge would not permit a wider deployment, we were going up to Malfolle in a column of platoons, with Lieutenant Jarman's platoon in front, O'Neil's second, and mine third in line. At least that is the way we started out.

At the top of the first little hill, the terrain took a dip, slanted downward and then more sharply upward again. When I got to the top of the first hill, forward movement had stopped. I soon saw the reason why. Litter bearers were carrying someone back down the hill to our front. Word spread that it was Lieutenant Jarman. He had been with Frank's company at Anzio but was now working for Dubak. Jarman was lying face down on the litter, unconscious, bleeding from a severe wound in the mouth where a sniper had got him. I watched them pass and thought he was done for. Those goddamn Nazi sons of bitches!

We took a little time to reorganize. Jarman's now leaderless platoon came back. O'Neil moved to the point and my platoon was second in line.

O'Neil and I went up to where Jarman had been hit and forward progress had stopped. We established a new line of departure. O'Neil took off on the run. His platoon followed.

Waiting for his men to clear, I may have been a bit tardy in moving. My section leader at the head of the platoon with me inquired gently, "Do you want to go first, Lieutenant?"

In truth I didn't want to go first or last or anytime. But I bristled.

"You're goddamn right I want to go first. That's my job. Just see that you take care of yours." Later I was sorry I had reacted that way.

I took off in a run. A sniper opened up as I left the line of departure. I tried to run faster. But when a stream of machine-gun bullets burned past my face, I hit the ground. Looking back, I saw the platoon had followed my example. I could also see something else. A mortar barrage was walking its way up the trail toward our rear. We had been in similar situations before. Better to risk the small stuff in the front than the heavy stuff behind.

I got up, gave the signal, and raced forward. The platoon followed and none too soon. When I hit the ground and looked back again, I saw the barrage coming down where we had been. Most of it fell behind us.

When I caught my breath, we moved forward again. It was getting dark. The lead platoon halted and I went forward to contact O'Neil.

Our climbing was over. The ridge had widened out. We started moving forward more slowly; and as we approached Malfolle, I deployed a section of machine guns on the left flank to cover O'Neil's attack on the houses.

Warren Dubak, a company commander accustomed to being at the center of the action, came forward. He and O'Neil approached the first house together. They drew fire from a wadi to our left front. The machine-gun section fired into the wadi, and I heard what I must confess were satisfying screams of agony coming from the ditch. If they thought they could dish it out, this would advise them we could too. They had taken some of ours; now we had taken some of theirs.

We got into the houses, took a few prisoners, and heard sounds of men scrambling down the back side of the ridge. I left my machine-gun section in place on the left flank prepared to fire into the wadi again if that proved necessary, and with the rest of the platoon, entered a house on the edge of a cliff.

The former occupants had obviously fled this place in a great hurry. Our approach had interrupted their dinner. There was a table set for four. A large pot of soup sat on a still warm wood stove. There was a half-filled jug of *Vino Rosso* on the table with a plentiful supply of black bread.

The vino was passed around as far as it would go. We tore off hunks of the black bread and chewed them as if we were starved to death. I don't think anyone tried the soup. I wasn't a bit hungry but I ate the bread, and its flavor was greatly enhanced by the symbolism. This was our victory celebration, a final act asserting supremacy over people who had tried to kill us rather than let us come up here.

But were we in Malfolle after all? When things settled down a bit, a runner came down from the company commander indicating he thought he might have made a mistake. We might not be in Malfolle but in some other village. If we were not in the right place, I was informed, we would go for Malfolle in the morning.

I didn't have a map and didn't know whether we were in Malfolle or not, but it didn't matter much to me. We had won here and I had gained a small, temporary personal victory over fear of violent death. That was enough for the moment.

In all of the commotion the platoon sergeant and I found ourselves without either blankets or bed rolls. Not to worry. After scouting around a bit, we located a barn with lots of warm straw. Our only companions were a wounded pack mule and an undetermined number of rats. The mule was too weak to resent our intrusion and the rats scurried away at our approach. When we settled in, I found I had sprained my ankle somewhere along the line but the pain was not enough to keep me from sleeping.

TUESDAY, APRIL 17

The platoon sergeant and I counted heads in the morning and found a total of three men, including one section leader, unaccounted for. I didn't expect any of them to return although the section leader might. He could have gone to the aid station after running into some kind of trouble which no one noticed in the dark. Whatever the case, we made arrangements to get along without him and the others.

Before sunrise we were on our way to Malfolle number two. We met sniper fire along the way but nothing else of consequence. Our objective proved to be a very small place. We moved in and found we had one prisoner, a church, an onion patch and more black bread. Small wonder that Dubak had missed this place, whatever it was, in the dark.

The old man came up, and shortly thereafter Frank's company moved through to attack Mt. Milano. The men seemed grim-faced and abstracted. They made little response to our jibes and shouts of encouragements but they took their objective without serious loss.

Down in the valley on one side of us we could see all kinds of German vehicles and soldiers, milling about, looking as if they were confused and on the run. It was the first time I had ever seen so many of them on the loose without being deathly afraid. There was no way those people down there were going to counterattack and take our onion patch away from us.

That afternoon we moved off our objectives and hiked down the mountain to Vergato. This former German strong point had held us up all winter but had fallen to the Eighty-first Reconnaissance Squadron on the first day of the offensive. There was not much left of the place except rubble.

We could now see Pioppe di Salvaro, Pt. 826, and Mt. Sole from what had been the enemy's lines all winter and into the early spring. The high ground above their positions must have looked to the Germans as threatening as the Alban Hills did to us a year ago.

In our assembly around Vergato, the old man greeted me with about as much warmth as he ever greeted anyone. He was not a demonstrative man, but I knew he had been watching me as I had been observing him since the morning I had interrupted his shave. We chatted briefly, nothing memorable. It was shop talk, talk about the situation, the terrain, the weather. I'm sure he asked about my casualties; he always did. I understand now that the old man was shy and aloof only with strangers just as I was. But he and I were no longer strangers.

Our brief conversation was satisfying somehow. Quite apart from anything said, I felt bonded to him as a distinct human being with whom I had shared personal secrets. That was enough. Saying goodnight to the colonel, I crawled under a jeep and almost immediately went off to sleep.

WEDNESDAY, APRIL 18

We mounted half-tracks early in the morning and moved up Highway 64. Along the way I got another view of the church at Salvaro which had given us so much trouble less than a month ago. It seemed to me as if years had passed. Everything had changed. When I had studied Salvaro through the glasses in March, the church radiated menace. In the daytime it was exceptional to see anything move down there; and, except for artillery fire, all was still. The church and the town had appeared as major obstacles, problems to be studied and solved.

Now army vehicles moved up and down the road at normal speed, slowed from time to time by traffic jams. Routine human activity had been resumed. The church, still intact although said to have an unexploded artillery round in its belfry, seemed nonthreatening, even serene. People driving the highway and taking for granted the access it provided must have wondered what delayed us so long here. I wondered myself until I remembered how it was. I wanted to linger for a closer inspection, but we moved quickly by.

Unfortunately we didn't stay on Route 64. Shortly after passing through Salvaro, we turned left on a secondary road leading back into the mountains. Just below Suzzano we stopped, got off the half-tracks and were fed from the kitchen. Suzzano was another place which had changed greatly. A few days ago the enemy had punished our sister battalion severely for trying to enter the town. Now the place was swarming with American vehicles and troops.

We rested in the assembly area that afternoon but were alerted for a move to begin at midnight. The platoon cleaned and oiled the weapons again. I made notes for my journal, wrote letters home, and slept. At midnight we were on the half-tracks.

THURSDAY, APRIL 19

It was almost 0900 hours when we closed into a new assembly area. The movement, shielded by darkness, had been uncontested except for a few snipers.

I learned we were in the Samoggia River Valley and involved in a flanking movement against Mt. Ombraro, a German strong point which continued a fierce resistance with all arms in an area north of Tole. We would leave our half-tracks here and ride up to Ombraro on the backs of the tanks.

Riding tanks into battle was something we had prepared for but something we dreaded as a dirty and dangerous job. It was dirty because the dust from a column of tanks would mix with our sweat to produce a kind of mud which caked our faces. And then there were the fumes, likely to be especially bad on a full day of stop and go driving. We had been issued Plexiglas dust respirators but had thrown them away in favor of bandanna handkerchiefs tied below the eyes in the fashion of bad men out of the old west . The handkerchiefs were easier to carry and seemed to provide more real protection.

But there was no help against enemy artillery, mortar, antitank and sniper fire. These dangers were always clear and present when tanks were involved. It was impossible to conceal a column of tanks for long. They inevitably announced their presence to all who could see and hear; and their presence, almost as certainly, would bring enemy reaction with whatever force they had available. Infantry soldiers clinging precariously to the back of a tank made inviting targets for enemy small-arms fire; and the roar of the tank mortars, the clanking and screeching of their treads masked the sound of incoming artillery. Our sense of hearing had been sharpened by experience and we had from the beginning made friends with the ground. To be even partially denied these major sources of protection left us feeling naked and vulnerable.

We had at least seven hours on the tanks that day and were shelled almost all the way up. The closer we got, the more intense the enemy reaction.

Runner, Gimo, Mitch and I on the lead tank of the platoon clambered from one side of the turret to the other away from where the artillery seemed to be landing most frequently. Whenever the column halted for a few minutes, we dismounted in accordance with our training and went into hiding under the tanks. The sound of a driver revving up his motor was enough to bring us out regardless of what was taking place outside. No one wanted to be smashed up by the tank treads. We hoped the tank commander would wait for our all clear signal before moving, but we didn't have complete confidence in the system.

As we neared the end of our journey, an artillery round scored a direct hit on the tank immediately in front of ours. Everyone on that tank was either killed or severely wounded. I saw one man decapitated and not very nearly. I thanked God we had been spared. I thanked God for the interval between tanks and for the fact that none of the killed and wounded belonged to our platoon.

Late in the afternoon we left the tanks and dug in on high ground around Ombraro. From there we had our first really good look at Po Valley. No one was much interested. Heavy artillery and mortar fire continued to rain down on us until well after dark.

At dusk, thinking I would not be seen, I made a reconnaissance part way down the forward slope of the hill we were on and drew a frightening flurry of small-arms fire as well as fire from mortars and artillery. For a while there it seemed as if every gun in Ombraro had zeroed in on me. Once again I cursed my stupidity. So much, I guess, for the theory that the remaining enemy troops were nearsighted. I had to crawl back on my belly.

After dark I toured the gun positions and made a few adjustments.

Then I crawled under a light tank which was in partial defilade to get some sleep. It was warm under there, and the tank provided excellent overhead protection against air bursts. I was sure I would have adequate warning if the tank commander started to pull back. I could see no possibility that his movement would be forward.

There were no counterattacks and no enemy patrols coming in. I slept well, except for the fact that I was rather severely shaken up by an artillery round which landed just outside my place of shelter. My body bounced off the ground, my head came up, making contact with the underpinnings of the tank, and I saw a thousand little bright lights. The headache was gone in the morning; the lump on my head was a bit tender, but it soon went away too.

FRIDAY, APRIL 20

We remained in position all day. The men continued to dig. I had not seen so much voluntary digging since Anzio. Word spread down the line that Lieutenant O'Neil had taken a patrol into Ombraro last night and was missing in action. The best we could hope for was that he had been captured without having been seriously wounded.

After a full day of looking down on Ombraro, we were pulled back. The rumor which seemed most plausible to me was that the higher command had decided to bypass resistance here, letting Ombraro die on the vine, while we moved to its rear for more profitable undertakings.

My notes do not reveal how we made it out of there, whether on foot, by half-track, or some other means and I don't remember the journey. All I remember is that we moved to a somewhat sizeable village where I was ordered to report to a CP in a big, blacked-out house in the middle of town.

It must have been the forward headquarters of the Combat Command because Colonel Igo, a bird colonel, was there along with the old man and another lieutenant colonel I didn't know. When I reported in, I couldn't help thinking how unreal, how much like a Hollywood movie set it was. There were candles spluttering on the table, the rumble of artillery in the background. The bird colonel, the old man, and the other light colonel were talking quietly but intently and pouring over maps. We junior officers stood whispering in the rear as we waited for orders. Frank was there, looking haggard as he always did after the first three or four days, but ready to go on for as long as necessary.

The conference at the table finally broke up. I received my orders, no explanations, nothing more than a map showing me where I was supposed to go and how to get there. My assignment was to set up roadblocks on the other side of a town which showed on the map as Castello. I was to be supported by two medium tanks. Karchmer, the man who almost took Salvaro on the second try back in March, was to precede me with two light tanks. I was to relieve him and remain in place awaiting further orders. It didn't sound too bad. Better to relieve Karchmer at Castello than try to relieve the Germans of that town.

SATURDAY, APRIL 21

We mounted the half-tracks before daylight. Either they had come up during the night or we had ridden them in. Whatever. Before we moved out, I got the bad news. Karchmer's platoon had been stopped at Castello and he had been hit pretty hard in the shoulder. I was glad it was no worse. Some of us had been afraid he was going to get it. But with Karchmer down and his platoon stopped, we might have to try to relieve the Germans of Castello after all. That didn't sound good.

With one of the Sherman tanks in front, I felt a little better as we pushed off. Daylight was breaking as we neared the town. Just outside Castello about fifty yards off the road over to our right, we saw two German soldiers standing in a field. At least they wore German battle dress. Their behavior was more than a little strange.

The two men were facing each other, seemingly engaged in conversation. They appeared completely oblivious to our approach even when we fired over their heads. We scanned the fields for their companions. They seemed to be alone. Perhaps they were drunk. Maybe they wanted to commit suicide. We never knew. When they didn't heed our calls, we killed them with a long burst of fire from the .50 caliber.

The tank in front stopped on the outskirts of town. We could hear the crackle of small-arms fire up ahead. I got the platoon off the tracks and went forward on foot to contact Lieutenant King who had taken over when Karchmer went down. Runner accompanied me while the platoon sergeant directed the half-tracks into shelter and held the platoon in readiness to move forward when I sent for them.

We found King and his men in some houses on the other side of town. The enemy was set up about four hundred yards down the road in and around a big *Casa Colonica* and its substantial barns and other outbuildings. I sent Runner to bring up the platoon so we could relieve King's men. While waiting I helped guide the tanks into positions behind the houses we held. After we got in place, we settled in for an exchange of fire which lasted for most of the day.

At first I tried somewhat halfheartedly to break the stalemate by directing tank fire into the *Casa Colonica*. There was considerable damage to the structure and I thought we had inflicted casualties, but couldn't tell. The volume of enemy fire seemed to increase, if anything, each time the tank fired a round. Maybe the *Tedeschi* were taught to do that.

About the middle of the morning my friend and patron, the major at battalion headquarters, called me on the radio. While I don't have a verbatim transcript of the conversation, its tone and substance were substantially as follows:

"What are you guys talking about out there?" was his opening question. I put on my false face in preparation for my devil-may-care act and gave him the answer he expected.

"Booze and pussy," I replied. "What else is there to talk about?" He laughed.

"What have you got?" he asked seriously.

"Maybe a platoon, maybe a company," I answered.

"Not just a squad? Or maybe an old man and a little boy?" he chided.

"Have I ever lied to you?" I countered.

"Not lately. Not lately." And then seriously again, "Any little brothers or big brothers?" He wanted to know whether the enemy had tanks or assault guns.

"Not so far," I replied, "but who knows?"

"I do," he said. "We want you to hold what you've got. You probably hit a rear guard. Those people won't be comin' in."

At that moment a burst of machine-gun fire came through the window. The slugs buried themselves in the wall in back of me and brought down plaster. I scrambled to the floor.

"Did you hear that?" I shouted into the radio. "Did you hear that? That son of a bitch almost took my head off. You sure you know what you're talkin' about?"

"Have I ever lied to you?" he mocked.

"Probably not in the last two or three days." I had not seen him in a week.

"Trust me," he laughed. And then there could be no mistaking the fact that he was giving me an order.

"Well, hold what you've got. And another thing," he paused. "Be careful out there."

"You too," I said. I hoped he would.

After I got off the radio, someone directed my attention to a view from an upstairs windows in the rear of the house. I looked and saw something I had heard about and read about but had never seen. A considerable number of American tanks was deployed in a skirmish line and moving slowly forward across a field to disappear from sight over a gently sloping ridge. That had to be the main body of the combat command. We were outposting their flank, and this was the kind of terrain they had waited for since coming to Italy.

Early that afternoon during a lull in the firing, a middle-aged, portly Italian man, sweaty, puffing, disheveled and excited, made his way into our lines. He had slipped away from his *Casa Colonica* to seek our help. The *Tedeschi* were moving out, he said, but all morning they had been killing his chickens and butchering his livestock to take with them. He wanted us to drive these thieves and butchers out before they destroyed everything he owned.

I started to explain my orders but cut that short. I didn't want this man to carry tales to the enemy if we let him go back. He continued his efforts to get us to launch an attack. I told Runner to inform him that the entire Fifth Army would be up shortly and then we would most certainly round up his tormentors. After Runner had delivered some such message, the Italian gentleman went off muttering to himself, complaining, no doubt, that you could never find a policeman when you needed one. I got the impression that this *padrone* was accustomed to greater deference than he had received from us.

Late in the afternoon enemy fire dwindled down to occasional sniping. I was reasonably sure that the main body of the opposing force had moved back but was not about to go over and see. The orders to hold what I had suited me just fine.

At dusk we began to tighten up our defenses so as to provide all around protection for ourselves, the tracks and the tanks. I moved my CP from the house where the insistent Italian gentleman had confronted us. In the unlikely event that a German combat patrol came in now, they wouldn't find us exactly where we had been that afternoon. Besides, Runner had found a bigger and better house for the CP. It was a large villa having the look of a castle. There were no civilians in evidence, but there were honest to God beds made up as if to receive company.

With all my chores taken care of, I took off my boots and crawled between the covers. What luxury! But it was not to last. Just as I dropped off to sleep, a message came over the radio instructing us to rejoin the rest of the battalion. We were on the road all night.

Chapter 14

The Last Offensive
Twelve Days in the Valley

SUNDAY, APRIL 22

It was just getting daylight when we caught up with the battalion at a farmhouse out in the Po Valley. The old man, smiling broadly, came out to meet us. I reported and we chatted briefly. Again it was shop talk, but the old man's eyes and his manner seemed to say, "Well, you and I have made it this far, haven't we?"

There were lots of smiling faces and friendly greetings at headquarters. Even the dour Captain Yount asked about my casualties. All of us had reason for rejoicing. We were still alive and out of the mountains at last. The promised land lay before us.

We fed, rationed and resupplied the platoon. The track drivers and the service people saw to the needs of the vehicles. I had time to wash my face and eat a most delicious fresh egg sandwich before moving out with the rest of the battalion about 0800 hours. And I received an informal briefing.

The German front had been broken. Our mission now was to win the race against enemy columns retreating northward to the Po. If we could get behind them before they had a chance to set up a new defense line, the war in Italy would be over. If enough of them got across the river, all bets were off. Even a junior officer could understand that and could appreciate the need to bypass strong resistance along the way to the Po.

But "racing for the Po" was for newspaper headlines. It would be a contest between cumbersome military units engaged in a deadly marathon over a complicated obstacle course rather than a dash by world-class sprinters running on the flat. The rate of our forward progress would be problematic. Apart from the obvious limitations of men and machines, we could not be sure of the opposition we faced. It could range from old men and little boys at one extreme to fanatical, true believing Nazis on the other. In between were ordinary German soldiers, many of whom could be counted on to stand and die, but also to kill, even in a hopeless cause.

We couldn't afford to take the opposition lightly. Those at the head of the column had to be on the alert for ambushes by determined rear guards with antitank weapons in the hands of people prepared to sacrifice themselves to delay our progress for as much as an hour or two. And then there would be mined roads and blown bridges, not as numerous and significant as in the Apennines but still a factor.

Back in the column where I was, sniper fire was the primary concern that first day in the valley. We took a few mortar rounds early on, but most of them missed the column completely. The snipers were different. They were numerous and almost always at least close to what they were aiming at. No one from our platoon was taken out, but we heard of sniper casualties both up and down the line.

On my track no one believed that such armor plate as we had would stop a bullet from a high-powered German rifle. We hunkered down, nonetheless, when sniper fire came in. Sometimes a track to the rear of the sniper's target could get an approximate fix on the sharp shooter's location and spray the area with .50 caliber. To give ourselves a little edge, we loaded a couple of prisoners on the hood of our track to discourage enemy fire. I don't know whether it worked or not. Sniper fire seemed to ease a bit after that, but perhaps the enemy was just running out of snipers.

We continued to roll forward all day and through the night. Fatigue became a problem. Tired drivers usually dropped off to sleep when the vehicle in front stopped for a few minutes. Sometimes they failed to see the column move out. It was almost morning when one of the incidents threatened serious trouble.

A driver, two vehicles in front of my command track, woke up and, finding the column gone, followed a cloud of dust which turned out to be a German convoy trying to escape to the north. Recognizing his mistake, the driver halted some few yards to the rear of the enemy column and started to back out. This maneuver alerted the *Tedeschi* and they opened fire. So did the American troops immediately at hand.

When I heard the sounds, I assumed we had hit an ambush. From straight ahead above the crackle of small-arms fire, I could hear German officers bellowing commands, while from a parallel road to our right came sounds of additional vehicular movement.

When the firing began, most of my platoon jumped off the tracks without command. I got them into defensive positions with some facing the fire to our front and others aligned to take under fire anything coming from our right flank.

About that time Major James materialized out of the semidarkness. I remembered having seen him at battalion that morning. Perhaps I had even been introduced to him, but I was very surprised to see him now and never did find out where he had come from.

The major told me, somewhat excitedly I thought, that those troops on the right were not ours. I had hoped they were. He was absolutely sure they were not. As he saw it, there was not a moment to lose. He wanted me to take the lead in my command track and barrel down the road straight ahead where the battle seemed to have died down.

I didn't refuse to obey a direct order from a superior officer, but how do the lawyers put it? I demurred. It was the first time I had ever seriously challenged an order. I didn't know who this major was nor what he thought his job was supposed to be. I did know there were German troops somewhere down the road ahead and thought it unlikely, even if they had pulled out, they had not left some kind of a rear guard behind. Even one or two men hiding in a ditch by the side of the road with a *panzerfaust* could cause considerable damage. I wanted to wait until we checked out that column on the parallel road.

As we stood there arguing, or discussing, depending on your point of view, Frank came up from the rear of the column. He supported my position. It was getting light enough to see a little better and some of our men on their own moved far enough to identify the column on our right as friendly. James and I went out to see for ourselves while Frank went back down the road to his company. To my very considerable relief, the report was accurate. When I turned around, the major had disappeared as mysteriously as he had come.

As I began looking for a route by which we could rejoin our friends, it suddenly struck me with the force of a blow to the solar plexus that the major had told me something which, in the excitement of the moment, I had simply ignored. He had said that the old man had been killed earlier in the evening while looking for a place to take the column across a stream which lay in our path. A German sniper had shot him squarely in the chest at close range. I was told later the old man died instantly.

I remembered how he had looked at daylight twenty-four hours earlier and how he was as a battalion commander. He was not an inspirational leader. He didn't make fiery speeches. He didn't strike heroic poses. There was not a bit of bluster or bombast in his makeup. He was no daredevil. He had nothing to prove. But he was cool, ever so cool, under fire, and he was daring when the probabilities of success were reasonable and the possible payoff high enough. I had never known him to make a serious mistake. At the front I had always seen him going quietly where he thought he needed to go to do his job. He was killed while making a personal reconnaissance in the face of the enemy, a task crucial to his job because it enabled him to know the kind of terrain his men had to deal with. I have never had greater respect for a superior officer.

As much as anything, perhaps, I appreciated the old man's honesty. He certainly hadn't given me a pep talk that morning I bared my soul to him. He hadn't told me to cheer up, that everything would turn out all right. He hadn't told me to "have a good day." Instead, he had spoken the brutal truth as he saw it, and he had done me the honor of taking the incident at face value. My assignments on this offensive had been neither less dangerous nor more dangerous than they were before. The only difference was that he and I were about to become friends, for I think he was beginning to like me too. Now the old man was dead and the battalion would never be the same.

MONDAY, APRIL 23

With the death of the old man, the battalion executive officer took over. The king is dead. Long live the king.

We moved on toward the Po. By this time the troops had adapted to the routine. There were unexplained stops and no one ever knew how long we would be detained at any one of them. We used these times to relieve ourselves, to stretch, to sleep.

As we rolled forward, we dozed in sitting positions. Although frequently jolted awake, not many things could hold our attention for long. While more prisoners were coming in, a long line of defeated *Tedeschi* had become so commonplace we barely noticed. Even the snipers had difficulty getting our attention. Many of us simply slid further down in our seats and ignored them unless they left a calling card in our immediate neighborhood.

But now we began to encounter a new kind of excitement which never failed to bring us to life. Italians, men, women and children were coming out in increasing numbers to greet us with cheers, wine, fresh eggs, cheese, flowers, kisses. Having been stopped on the push to Rome, I had never experienced such a welcome. It was a remarkable stimulant.

In the middle of the afternoon a report filtered down that "the general" wanted to reach the Po by daylight; and, moreover, "the general" had said that he was willing to sacrifice "half of the vehicles" to do it.

That report failed to inspire us. Part of the general's problem was that "half the vehicles" were not willing to be sacrificed. Stubborn critters, those vehicles.

Night came on. Our admirers left the streets and the byways. We continued to roll forward at the same jerky, stop and go pace, general or no general. And then shortly after midnight, disaster struck.

I was dozing in the front seat of our command track when the platoon sergeant shook me and said, "Lieutenant, we've run into something."

The column had stopped. At first I heard nothing but a few rifle shots and thought it was the usual sniper resistance. Suddenly an explosion punctured the night air and flames shot up into the sky. Almost simultaneously the rippling sound of the schmeissers and the deep staccato stutter of American automatic weapons confirmed the sergeant's assessment. We had run into something much more serious than sniper fire.

There was another explosion and then another. The track in front of us started to back frantically. We did the same but were unable to move more than a few yards to the rear. I pulled my vehicles out of the column and into a field on the right.

An expanding fire fight was shaping up over a little rise in the road. An excited voice yelled over the radio that they were getting the hell bazooked out of them. Adding to the confusion was the fact that there were vehicles moving around on three sides of us. Those in the rear had to be ours and some of those in front must be, but over on the right I heard those spine tingling guttural voices shouting to each other. There was no way of knowing what was on the left.

I deployed the platoon in a semicircle around the tracks, leaving only the rear unguarded. We saw forms on our right front running toward the fight up the road. The machine guns opened up. We saw people fall. The chances are they were hostile, but I never knew for sure. At the time I was sure enough to empty a clip from my rifle in their general direction.

Receiving no orders or information on the radio, I moved up to the track in front of me. From there I could see three vehicles burning over the rise in the road. The small-arms fire had diminished, but ammunition and gas tanks from the vehicles continued to explode.

As I scanned the scene, Lieutenant Loving, the man who had led Yount and me back up the path from Serra, stood up literally at my feet from a ditch by the side of the road. Muddy, wet, cold, adrenalized, Love, as he was called, had crawled out of the fight. He told us something of what he had seen and surmised.

Coming out of road leading in from the right a mile or so behind us, part of a German convoy led by a tank had cut into our line of march. It was another case of mistaken identity. The tank and, perhaps, one other German vehicle pulled up close enough to Loving's jeep to recognize their mistake. It was a fatal one. Their options were severely limited by the presence of American vehicles to both front and rear.

Our battalion command track was immediately ahead of Love in the line of march. Captain Yount, riding in the front seat of the command track, recognized the German tank for what it was and tried to sound the alarm. It was too late. The enemy tank fired over Loving's head and into the rear of the battalion communication center. Love told me Yount was standing up in the front seat pounding on the hood of the track and shouting, "They're Germans! They're Germans!" when he was blown away.

After savaging our battalion staff with the first round, the enemy tank got off another shot for good measure before cutting out of the column and racing over into a canebrake where the fire fight developed. Its crew continued to fire into the thin-skinned American vehicles until silenced either by one of our tanks or one of our bazooka teams. Apparently some enemy soldiers abandoned their vehicles to take part in the shoot out, but most of them hurried away.

Love knew only that Captain Yount and Major James were dead, but couldn't see how anyone riding with them had escaped. He ticked off the names of people he thought of as probable fatalities. They included Captain Tucker, the air liaison officer, Lieutenant Able and two sergeants I didn't know. There was an undetermined number of other passengers which Love couldn't or didn't identify.

When the action subsided, two of our light tanks came back to guide us around the scene of battle. From our detour through the fields to our left, we could still see fires burning and hear ammunition exploding. The two parts of the column were finally reunited. The excitement was over for the evening. We dozed off again.

TUESDAY, APRIL 24

At daylight we pulled off the road to assess the damages and to reorganize the battalion command structure. Captain Yount, Major James and the two sergeants had, indeed, been killed along with others I didn't know. The Forest Ranger had escaped with a broken arm. Captain Tucker was missing and presumed dead, but "Fiesty" Able had turned up unharmed and more than willing to tell his story.

He had been dozing in the battalion command track when he heard a loud explosion and found himself lying on the ground underneath the vehicle. He remembered feeling around on the ground, very deliberately and in slow motion, for the glasses he habitually wore. He was, he said

"Damn near blind" without them. He finally found them; and although the frames were bent, the glasses were still serviceable. He put them on and only then did he venture forth.

"Fiesty" said he crawled out from under the track, got into a ditch at the side of the road, and then stood up, walking straight ahead in the opposite direction from that taken by Love. After a little while, still in something of a daze, he got out into the middle of the road and continued walking slowly in the direction he had started. He was completely oblivious to what was going around him. Coming up to one of our tanks which had buttoned up to ride out the storm, he pounded on the turret until they opened up and took him in.

I told "Fiesty" he was leading a charmed life and asked how many times he had drunk from the battalion cup. He said he and I were tied for the record and were both sure to live "a thousand yeahs."

What was left of the battalion command group was in considerable disarray. The survivors were people who had been riding in separate vehicles. There was so much bickering among the remaining barons of the battalion it was a bit difficult to know who was in charge. Several changes in assignments were made known to fill vacancies. I was interested in only three of these.

Frank was moving to the staff as assistant operations officer, an excellent choice for the job. The Pathfinder would take over Frank's company, again an obvious selection. On the basis of seniority, I was to become acting company commander of Headquarters Company pending return of its captain who was going back for treatment of a slight wound.

When the regrouping was completed, the battalion moved forward again. We took several more prisoners during the afternoon. Runner, with some of his cronies to help, promptly relieved them of all their money and personal possessions as they had been doing every time they got the opportunity. I didn't much like the rough treatment they were dishing out to helpless prisoners but didn't say anything. It was no worse than I had seen many times before.

Toward sundown a platoon sized cluster of defeated men came out to surrender. They were not exactly the elite of the *Wehrmacht*. One little guy, evidently mentally retarded, could not seem to understand that we wanted him to put his hands behind his head. I think Runner would have shot him if the platoon sergeant had not intervened by knocking his rifle aside. I hastily dispatched another prisoner to explain to his comrade what we wanted him to do. Only later did I consider the possibility that we might have gunned down two mentally deficient soldiers at Castello. I hadn't pulled the trigger but I had given the command.

We came off the road early that night with a promise of a good night's sleep. By 2100 hours Lieutenant Johnson, now with Service Company, had set up two cots, one for me and one for himself, in a nearby shed. We hadn't seen each other for some time, but this was not an occasion for talk. All we wanted to do and all we did was sleep, sleep, sleep.

WEDNESDAY, APRIL 25

A lieutenant colonel had come down from G-1 (division personnel) to take over the battalion. There could be no promotion from within our ranks. That was most unfortunate as far as I was concerned. We still had a couple of likely candidates and I would have taken either of them in preference to an outsider. Still, I wouldn't worry about the decision. For all I knew, division might have had a number of unemployed or underemployed lieutenant colonels eager to get a line command on their records now that the war was about over. Or someone "up there" may have been unhappy because we hadn't reached the Po on schedule. In those days the ways of the military bureaucracy were inscrutable. It was a waste of time to look for reasons. I am sure things are quite different in the new army.

They let us rest until the middle of the afternoon when we began to move forward again. I was temporarily in command of Headquarters Company and, wanting no part of the battalion command track, started out in a jeep with a driver and a radio man.

Shortly after moving out, we met the largest single group of prisoners I had seen. There must have been six hundred of them, a strong, reinforced battalion sized unit if they were all combat troops. They seemed ordinary soldiers, not mentally or physically deficient, and neither too young nor too old to fight. Looking at them, I was glad they would not get to the other side of the Po to man a new defense line.

Part of the convoy was lost again that night. German units continued to move on routes more or less parallel to ours. The Pathfinder, new as a company commander, was a bit fearful that he was following an enemy convoy. As battalion duty officer minding the radio, I reassured him and he thanked me politely. After our experiences of the last two nights, all of us were a bit jumpy.

It helped to be working with friends. I could tell by his voice that the Pathfinder trusted me just as I would have trusted him had our positions been reversed. It was quite different from my earlier encounter with Major James.

At daylight two German soldiers came out of a ditch at the side of the road with their hands up and their helmets off. One of them spoke excellent English. He predicted the war in Europe would be over in a couple of weeks. As we talked, a middle-aged Italian lady came out from a barn to give me a cup of warm milk. I drank it gratefully although I had never had a taste for milk straight from the cow. Our prisoners seemed more hungry than I was, but I didn't feed them. After all the gift was intended for the Americans. I didn't know what, if anything, this lady had suffered at the hands of the enemy.

THURSDAY, APRIL 26

We arrived at the Po early that morning, a little behind schedule, perhaps, but we made it without sacrificing half of our vehicles. Several Fifth Army units were already across the river and had been for a couple of days. That was fine with us. We had no interest in racing the Tenth Mountain, the Eighty-eighth, or any other Allied unit to any objective whatsoever. The generals might be concerned, but there was no outcry for greater speed from the men on the line. I did think it made good sense to try to beat the Germans to the Po just as it had made good sense to try to beat them to Valmontone a year earlier. I knew we had beaten many of them this time.

There was an anticipatory bustle in evidence at battalion headquarters. They were preparing for company, a visiting party of brass from corps and division. The people at battalion wanted to be sure the visit went well. One of the items of preparation, and a not insignificant one, had consequences for me.

About three-quarters of a mile over on our left, an enemy contingent had made its way back as far as our side of the river but had been unable to cross. They had dug in behind whatever cover they could find in the river bottom land. From there they continued intermittent, long-range sniping at our location down stream.

No one at battalion knew what was out there. To hear them tell it, we probably faced at worst a very old man and a little bitty boy, but I knew better and had reason to be concerned. I was given the task of cleaning up that "little situation." We couldn't have our visitors roughed up by snipers, now could we? Why, some of them might have to hit the ground and get dirty.

But under the circumstances the mission as well as my assignment to it were logical. As acting commander of Headquarters Company I had special responsibilities for protecting the battalion CP; and since, after almost two weeks of combat, the battalion was short of rifle platoon leaders, I was given the job. I had no quarrel with that, but I was scared because of the uncertainty. This was no time to get killed. This was not a good day to die.

The battalion commander provided me with a rifle platoon from the Pathfinder's company as I had requested. They came up, probably cursing me if they knew I had asked for their services. The battalion assault guns were to be under my direction, never mind that I had never commanded such a unit before.

At the last minute it turned out this would have to be a half-assed demonstration project. The visiting delegation began to arrive just before I moved out to get in place. At this point I had much more urgent matters to worry with but I told my superiors that if they wanted a demonstration of how to do it, they had better get themselves another boy. I sure as hell didn't know how. They told me to get on with it and to stop bitching.

Contemptuous of the spectators and more than a little pissed off with the battalion staff, I led my detail forward and then off the road into a field. Leaving the platoon sheltered behind a levee, I crawled up top for a brief visual inspection of the enemy's positions. I could see nothing of significance even through the glasses.

Coming back down, I ordered the platoon to deploy in a skirmish line with rifles pointed over the top of the levee. They were to open fire on my signal and to remain in place until they received further orders. I placed one assault gun in partial defilade on the left flank, directing the crew to fire on targets of opportunity when the action started. Having no idea of what the recommended procedure was, I decided to go in with the other assault gun on the right flank if we had to go in.

On signal the rifle platoon opened fire. There was only feeble response from the enemy. It became evident very quickly that rifle fire alone was not going to be enough. I was afraid of that. We would have to draw their fire, and, perhaps, go in and winkle them out one by one.

I got inside the protective armor of the assault gun on the right flank and ordered it forward into the field, its .50 caliber blazing. The gunner, with increasing urgency, requested targets for his seventy-five. I saw none. Small-arms fire began to patter off our armor as if we were in a hail storm. I was praying the enemy didn't have antitank weapons. Evidently, they didn't. Becoming less choosy about targets, I directed fire on what could be a possible hiding place for the enemy. The other assault gun on the left flank fired a few rounds shortly thereafter.

That was enough to do it. The enemy began waving more or less white cloth, throwing off their helmets and coming out with their hands up. It had turned out to be what the British called "a piece of cake." The prisoners were ordinary soldiers with sense enough to know they had lost the war.

Even at that we lost one man killed. It was a death which only I, the platoon, and the man's loved ones would pay any attention to. A young guy, new to combat, had, contrary to instructions, gone forward to meet the enemy as the first prisoners drew near the levee. Perhaps he was eager to pick up a souvenir he had spotted; none of us ever knew. A German soldier to the rear of his comrades, a man who had not given up, drilled our man squarely between the eyes.

When it was all aver, we took thirty-five prisoners including two German officers. I ordered one of them to get his men in a column of twos ready to start for the rear. He gave me a broad smile as he hastened to comply. I didn't know how to interpret his attitude. I'm sure he was relieved to find we weren't going to shoot him after they had shot one of ours. Perhaps he also concluded that even as a prisoner he would continue to have command functions and privileges.

Before we started back, I informed the men that we had been observed and that we would go back in style. They made feeble, almost pathetic efforts to spruce themselves up a bit. We started back down the road at sling arms, our prisoners marching in front, an assault gun immediately behind them, with the rifle platoon and the second assault gun bringing up the rear. I was marching along to the right of our leading assault gun and could see most of our distinguished visitors standing on the right side of the road.

As we came near them, I gave the command: "Detail, Tensh-Hut!" and as the front of our column came abreast of the imaginary reviewing stand, I followed with, "Eyes, Right!" just as we had done it at Leonard Wood, Benning, Breckinridge and untold other places where we had been trained long ago. On the command I threw a snappy salute and executed the movement. I don't know what the men behind me did. We hadn't been through that drill in a long, long time.

When the detail had cleared, I gave, "Ready, Front!" and then "Route Step" to bring things back to normal. Directing the sergeant to take the prisoners to the rear, I left the column to start back up the road. I was much relieved the operation was over and thought we had done the job expected of us. I should have known better.

As I started back toward the reviewing stand, someone from battalion headquarters told me to report to the general. I looked around. Now that the show was over, the visitors had begun to break up and drift away. The only general I saw was still standing there attended by three or four other officers. I stopped in front of him, gave a snappy junior officer salute, and reported in the prescribed manner.

He gave me a casual, general's salute in return and told me to stand at ease. That was all. He was still looking down the road toward the rear of our column of prisoners.

It was clear this general didn't care about seeing me. Perhaps I had reported to the wrong one. I felt ill at ease, but hadn't been dismissed and didn't want to violate protocol further by taking off. I stepped back from in front of him and took up a position on his left in the nearest space available.

The general watched our column out of sight. Then he turned his head toward me and said, "Well, you've brought in some more people for us to feed."

"Yes, sir," I replied. That is usually safe when you don't know what else to say.

He turned his eyes more directly on me now and asked, but in a light, conversational tone, "Did you understand what I said? I said now we'll just have to take these people back to the stockade and feed them indefinitely."

"Yes, sir," I responded again. I gathered that I hadn't been guilty of a major offense but had contributed to an avoidable drain on military resources.

He gave a very slight shrug of his shoulders and walked away.

I saluted his backside as he departed. Had I heard that right? Of course, I had heard it right. He had repeated and rephrased it so that even one as lowly as I could understand. Had I been talking to an American general? There could be no question about that either. I had thought that I was shock proof where the rear echelon was concerned. Not so.

I shrugged it off. The memory stayed with me, however, and when, years later, I read of Lieutenant Calley, Mylai and Viet Nam, I flashed back to it again. But Mylai and the Po River were entirely different in every respect. Or were they?

To our considerable surprise, we didn't cross the Po that day. Instead, in the afternoon we moved back some little distance to our rear. I guess we had just come up to the river for the show. In the new bivouac area the captain of Headquarters Company appeared to resume his command. And, a momentous event which I recorded faithfully, we received our first beer ration.

We were fed and the tracks were serviced. After midnight we moved out again, mulling over rumors that we were crossing the Po and heading for Milano which was reported to be already under control of the *partigiani.*

FRIDAY, APRIL 27

We moved forward through the rest of the night in rainy weather. At about 0900 hours we stopped for breakfast and to refuel the trucks in an assembly area still on the south side of the Po. Here I learned that, despite the lack of enemy resistance, the Pathfinder's company had taken casualties on the road up. Lieutenant Nansen's command track had slipped off the road in the dark and turned over in a ditch. Two men were killed and the lieutenant's leg was broken. Little Nance. What a goddamn shit eatin' shame! I was looking forward to celebrating the victory with him. One other man, a comical little guy I was very fond of, had been pinned under the wreckage for a considerable period of time and would have to have a leg amputated. We had experienced similar accidents before, but none had ever struck so close to home for me.

Our stay in the assembly area lengthened by several hours. Since we knew we would pay for the delay with an all-night road march, we tried to stockpile sleep, the commodity in shortest supply.

Later in the afternoon we finally crossed the Po and headed north. There was no resistance, not even sniper fire. Partisans were in evidence at many road junctions manning check points. We stopped at one of these; and since I was not yet a heavy smoker, I gave them most of my cigarette ration. They seemed most appreciative.

It rained intermittently all night, so hard at times it was impossible to keep dry. We were still driving blackout, of course, and the miserable driving conditions combined with the memory of the previous night's accident added to my sense of discomfort and unease.

The general situation was almost a complete mystery at my level. I had yet to hear anyone high or low proclaim that the war was over and couldn't believe it was. To be temporarily out of contact with the enemy for several days at a time was not a unique experience. On the contrary, that had been a characteristic feature of various stages in the Italian campaign. Even at this point I would not have been completely taken aback if we had suddenly encountered another defense line and been told there was one more hill to take, one more position to breech before we could rest.

SATURDAY, APRIL 28

We got a rousing welcome in Brescia when we moved through shortly after daylight. It was still drizzling rain, but the people came out anyway. There were more cheers, more gifts, more kisses. At Bergamo which we reached later in the morning, the reception was even more tumultuous.

Around noon we pulled off the road just on the other side of Bergamo. The rain had stopped and we were beginning to dry out. The kitchen prepared the noon meal. The battalion CP was nicely located in a big house where I managed a quick shave and located a warm bed. I had my gear moved in and hoped we would be there all night. No such luck. Before I could take full advantage of the accommodations, I was ordered to set up a road block in a suburban area nearby.

With us "road block" had become a generic term. It could refer to anything from a physical barricade covered by gunfire to an outpost or checkpoint. At this stage of the war, I knew I was not expected to fell trees across the road or take other heroic measures in anticipation of a major attack. We would be out there to screen the main body and to alert higher headquarters to any unusual or threatening developments. It was not a bad assignment except that I had to give up the possibility of sleeping in that inviting bed.

I moved the platoon on the tracks toward the assigned position. We entered an area where the Germans had maintained some kind of supply depot. As we drove into the downtown, I was greatly surprised to see men in German uniforms still carrying side arms and casually strolling the street, paying no attention to us. This was a crazy war where anything could happen, but, I mean, armed enemy soldiers in the middle of a position I was supposed to occupy? That was too much.

I brought the column to a screeching halt, as they say, and got on the radio to battalion. After a considerable wait, I was told that everything was as it should be. The rear echelon *Tedeschi* had negotiated a surrender agreement and were under our protection. Under the agreement the officers were allowed to keep their side arms—for the "spring plowing," I presume—and the enlisted men their personal possessions. How very like the rear echelon! They were the same the world over. Too bad someone hadn't thought to tell us of the arrangement earlier. What would have happened if four guys had gunned down some of the friendly enemy? It probably would have hit the fan and might have meant a court-martial for me. The execution would have been too public.

We moved on through town to a crossroads on the outskirts where I had been ordered to go. There was some difficulty getting the platoon off the tracks and into position because of the curious and friendly crowds coming out to surround us and get in our way. They showered us with affection. One charming forty-year-old lady with a provocative figure and a delightful French accent invited me to her place for dinner.

It took us some time to extricate ourselves from these well-meaning folk. I finally posted tracks and guards at the road intersection and quartered the bulk of the platoon in nearby barns and sheds. That way we could obviate some of the problems with the spectators and still accomplish our mission. We would also have decent shelter if it began to rain again.

The hayloft I chose for myself compared most unfavorably with the real bed I had coveted at battalion. And, worst of all, I had to decline that invitation for dinner. Under the circumstances, with such invitations floating around, it might not be easy to keep the outpost guards on duty. I couldn't afford to stray. You have perhaps heard of cruel and unusual punishment.

At midnight I checked the outpost and returned to the hayloft. At 0230 hours I checked again. Everything was in order. It was obvious that some of the guards had been drinking but I had had a few little nips myself. I cautioned them to keep it under control, suggesting that they didn't want to screw up at this stage of the game. There were only a few people for me, the platoon sergeant and the squad leaders to be worried about. Runner and his friends had been warned individually that the Germans were under our protection.

Back in the hayloft, I felt heightened anger at those arrogant, rear echelon Nazi bastards we were supposed to protect. From what I had seen and what I imagined, they were continuing to live off the fat of the land, sleeping in warm beds, no doubt made warmer still by the presence of beautiful women, while I had to sleep alone in the barn.

SUNDAY, APRIL 29

After daylight we had an opportunity to explore the area further. Restrictions against robbing enemy personnel did not prevent us from appropriating equipment left behind by the German army. At least that was our interpretation. We took what we wanted. Someone called my attention to a deserted army office headquarters, and I came away with a portable typewriter, a new German P.38, and a few lesser items.

The typewriter was my great prize. It was new and the keyboard almost identical with the American makes with which I was familiar. Although a couple of the keys were transposed and there were one or two unneeded symbols, I had no difficulty adjusting to its idiosyncrasies. As soon as I got the opportunity, I began using it to type up the notes I had made for my journal.

As was to be expected, Runner and his friends were the most enthusiastic looters in the outfit. Among other things, they liberated a two-seated, topless German *Volkswagen* with an undetermined amount of gas in its tank. I told them as far as I was concerned, they could drive it until it ran out of fuel.

We were called back from our roadblock and had an early noon meal with the rest of the battalion. Shortly thereafter the column moved out in the general direction of Lake Como. I gave the *Volkswagen* space at the head of the platoon. Mitch drove and I sat in the front seat with him. Gimo and Runner occupied the back seat with Runner on the right as the center of attention.

He was decked out in a new *Luftwaffe* cap and a German officer's blouse. As we moved slowly along the streets, Runner accepted the plaudits of the crowd with grave dignity, waving a limp hand from time to time and inclining his head in a slight bow first to one side of the street and then the other. The crowd was delighted.

We didn't move far. As we closed into a new area, the usual crowd augmented by numerous partisans, came out to welcome us. There was no roadblock assignment for me. Nor was there any way of escaping the carnival atmosphere which permeated the bivouac.

The people told us joyfully that the war was "finito," that Mussolini was dead and his body on display in Milano. "Patriots" were said to be in control of Milan and all other key points in northern Italy. There were even rumors that surrender negotiations were under way.

That night there was a great celebration with drinking, toasting, singing and dancing in the streets and cafes. Conducted by our partisan friends, I and a few other junior officers made some of the rounds. We were received with embraces, cheers, and toasts wherever we went.

After a few drinks, I became emboldened enough to propose an answering toast. In my pidgin Italian I tried to tell our hosts that "*primo Fiume Po*" we had seen "*multi Tedeschi*" but that "*doppo Fiume Po*" we had seen only "*Partigiani* and "*amici Italiani.*" And I tried to express "*mille grazie*" for their help.

Whether they understood or not, they gave a great cheer when I proposed "*Viva Partigiani. Viva Italia*!" It was a most enjoyable evening except for the fact that one very desirable young lady I tried to liberate laughed and told me that she had a "fidanzato" while I had a Neapolitan accent. I knew that last part was no compliment in this part of the country.

The celebration seemed likely to continue into the indefinite future. All of us were invited back for the following evening when a really big blast was planned.

MONDAY, APRIL 30

We moved on in the morning, leaving our *Volkswagen* with the partisans since it was almost out of gas after a night of joy riding. I saw more wood-burning trucks and marveled that this mode of transportation was possible although I took the gasoline internal combustion engine for granted without really knowing anything about it either.

Along the way we received our most tumultuous welcome of the trip. There were *Partigiani* everywhere, riding captured German vehicles and carrying German arms. They sang, they waved, they yelled "*Viva,*" they asked for "*benzina*" and "*sigaretta.*"

Our part of the column pulled into the little village of Arbiate and created a sensation there. A crowd of perhaps five hundred people assembled to watch one of our sergeants perform the commonplace task of shaving, using a helmet filled with hot water drawn from the radiator of his half-track.

In our new location we found a most acceptable CP which once again featured real beds. But once again we were not allowed to take full advantage of them. Shortly after midnight we moved out heading for Milano to reinforce elements of the Fourth Corps which had moved into the city that morning.

From the briefing at battalion, I gathered that our primary mission in Milan was to maintain order. Several days prior to the entry of our troops, the partisans had, indeed, driven the German garrison off the streets and into a number of well-fortified strong points in various parts of the city. From these positions the German command held out in anticipation of the eventual arrival of regular army troops. They refused to surrender to the *partigiani*, partially for reasons of pride, I suppose, but more important because they could not be sure what the irregulars would do to them.

For their part the partisans were content to keep the enemy contained. They, too, awaited the arrival of our troops. In the meantime partisan bands roamed the streets, settling old scores with Italian fascists, alleged fascists, German collaborators and alleged collaborators. The rumors were essentially correct: the mutilated bodies of Mussolini, his mistress, and leading members of his cabinet had been on display in Milan the previous day.

Advance elements of my division and other units of Fourth Corps were slow to enter Milan, probably because General Truscott, now Fifth Army Commander, recognized that sealing off routes to the Alpine passes had a higher priority. That realization was in refreshing contrast to the strategy involved in the "race for Rome" the previous spring when other counsels had prevailed.

Once a token force from Fifth Army had entered Milan, a German surrender was quickly arranged. But it might take more than a token force to restore order. We were reminded at battalion that we would be going into Milano on May Day, a traditional occasion for communist celebration. The American high command apparently feared that disorder would reach a peak and possibly involve clashes between armed bands of communist and noncommunist "freedom fighters."

I had been vaguely aware that the Italian Resistance Movement was internally divided along ideological lines, but had no idea of the seriousness of the cleavages. From what I had seen, the communist elements were clearly the more numerous, the more cohesive, the better disciplined. On my way up I had given most of my cigarette ration to a unit which flew the "Bandera Rossa." Our partisan friends who had taken us to the cafes around Bergamo were probably communists too. I hadn't noticed; it didn't seem important. Didn't someone say that the enemy of my enemy is my friend? Only as we moved through the night toward Milan did I begin to reflect on this mystery of Italian politics.

TUESDAY, MAY 1

When we rolled into Milan about dawn, I counted three bodies lying in the gutters. They were civilian casualties, quite possibly victims of the previous night's excesses. Otherwise the situation seemed reasonably quiet.

It didn't remain quiet long although there was no violence to disturb the peace. We bivouacked in a park in the center of town and were soon surrounded by a large, friendly, but essentially curious crowd. At first they didn't know whether we were British or American, but when the word spread, their enthusiasm seemed to increase. Our guards couldn't hope to keep all of them out of the area without using more force than we were prepared to use. We let many of the bolder, more insistent ones come in. They didn't seem to want anything except to look around, to talk, and perhaps to pick up a few souvenirs. We had just had mail call and they clambered for the stamps.

In the manner of policemen riding in separate squad cars, I and other junior officers cruised the area in radio-equipped jeeps supposedly to gauge the mood of the city, to maintain a presence, and to identify potential trouble spots. We enjoyed that duty immensely. It gave us a chance to swagger, to show off while sightseeing and girl watching.

From what I observed, earlier fears of a "communist takeover" or of "deadly confrontation" were ill founded. It is true that well-armed bands of partisans, mostly communists, careened rather wildly through the streets, some striking heroic poses as if they were on an urgent mission of utmost importance. But most of those I saw were just celebrating, singing "*Avanti Popolo*" and waving the "Bandera Rossa." Neither they nor anyone else seemed in an ugly mood.

I talked briefly with people on the streets. One pretty young lady hoped the Americans would stay in Milano a long time. She was fearful, she said, of what might happen when we left. But her fondness for Americans had its limits. With a polite little smile she declined an invitation to visit our bivouac.

The communists I talked to were outgoing and friendly, although one of them in a brief discussion tried to get me to admit that there were grave injustices in my country while in the Soviet Union people were "*tutti egali*." For once I had sense enough to refuse the bait. With my best Neapolitan shrug I said, "*Non capisco*."

He smiled, clapped me on the back, and offered me a drink.

The battalion moved out of Milano at dark amidst rumors that the German Fifth Mountain Division, still intact, was approaching from the west. Whatever the truth of the rumor, I noted that we didn't move in the direction of Como.

WEDNESDAY, MAY 2

We moved west through Novara and Vercelli into the path of the German division said to be coming up. In the early afternoon we stopped in the little village of Asigliano where I successfully negotiated with an elderly Italian couple for a night's lodging, one bedroom for me and one for Frank, now close at hand on the battalion staff. The lady of the house seemed favorably disposed toward us and showed me rather proudly the neatly kept rooms which she could place at our disposal. The man, a bit older and in poor health, said nothing. I brought them some real coffee and a few other items from our kitchen. They seemed delighted.

THURSDAY, MAY 3

It was in this little village we first received official reports of the surrender of all enemy forces in Italy. It was no longer a rumor. The Italian war was "finito." We could rest awhile.

The news, for me at least, ranked as the greatest anticlimax of all times. I didn't feel the great sense of deliverance, the inordinate joy, or anything else I had expected to feel. As a matter of fact I didn't feel much of anything except numbness, a sense of letdown, a curious sense of depression.

Perhaps I had expected too much, or perhaps the long anticipated event had come on too gradually. The war just sort of petered out. Or, God help me, I may have become addicted to the adventure, the excitement of never knowing what might appear around the next bend in the road or over the crest of the next hill.

I thought about those who didn't make it, especially the old man killed in the last push. Somehow I felt almost ashamed I had survived when better men had gone down. Maybe I hadn't even done my job.

At least I had a real bed for the night. Frank and I turned in long before midnight. There were a few sounds of celebration floating in on the night air, but not many and they didn't last long. I slept soundly until morning.

Chapter 15

That Italian Spring—May–June 1945

The day after the German surrender, we were assigned responsibility for disarming the enemy's Fifth Mountain Division, the unit about which we had heard disturbing rumors earlier. That division had, indeed, come up by forced march, somehow managing to escape the destruction inflicted on other large enemy formations. Their infantry regiments were still unbroken and, it was said, spoiling for a fight. If they had come up a few days earlier, we might have been forced to accommodate them. As it was, the Fifth Mountain would lay down its arms with all the rest. My outfit was to stay in place to assure they did just that.

The end of the war in Italy was followed by numerous personnel changes all up and down the American chain of command. At my level, a few battalion officers rotated home either to be relieved from active duty or, as many of us suspected, shipped out to fight the Japanese following a short leave. A few others were transferred upward, outward, or downward to different units. For those who remained, there were a number of shifts in assignment.

My patron at battalion headquarters, still looking out for my interests, had me assigned as of May 6 to the battalion staff as S-1, battalion adjutant and personnel officer. Since platoon leaders would now be performing mundane garrison and guard duty, I at first welcomed the changes. But then began to receive questions from division asking what we were doing to implement directives I had never even heard of. This duty alone was almost enough to make me wish I was back as a platoon leader.

Much of my time in the beginning was spent processing papers relating to battalion personnel who would have to stand trial by court-martial. One of our men was accused of raping an eighty-four-year-old woman; another of robbing an Italian householder. But most of the defendants faced charges for strictly military offenses. In each case the battalion personnel officer had responsibility for "causing a search to be made" for any evidence we might have bearing on the alleged offense.

All in all I began to wonder about the "favor" my friend had done me. Other platoon leaders were making frequent trips into Torino, while I was working overtime to get on top of the paper work. Some favor. Some friend.

Less than a week after I took over the new assignment, we moved a short distance to the little town of Cavaglia. The battalion headquarters was located at Rapallo in the commodious summer home of a prosperous businessman from Biella. The villa overlooked Lago Viverone, a minor body of water in the Italian lake country. I thought the view from our balcony was most impressive until I saw Lago Maggiore. Perhaps the Biella tycoon had a residence there too, but Maggiore was not in our area of operation and the place we were in served our purposes very well. I shared a large bedroom with "Fiesty" Able and had my office downstairs in a room close to the kitchen.

On Lake Viverone I undertook one of my more interesting assignments. The German Fifth Mountain Division was bivouacked across the lake from us and a date had been set for a formal, but very simple, surrender ceremony. As battalion adjutant I had responsibility for coordinating activities from our side. The Fifth Mountain sent over a captain to serve as liaison officer. Since he was my opposite number, he was quartered with me for several days.

Herr Hauptmann arrived early one morning wearing green shorts, looking tanned and physically fit. He was about my age and size. With him was his orderly, a young lad who didn't look to be over fourteen or fifteen years old. We had moved an extra cot into the large bedroom for the captain's use. One of our noncoms saw to the needs of the orderly.

When I returned from work late in the afternoon of the day he arrived, I found the captain reading Washington Irving in German translation. He told me he had struggled through *The Legend of Sleepy Hollow* for an English assignment in school but never until now had he understood and appreciated the story. He had grown up on the adventure tales of Karl May, he said.

After the evening meal, we sat in the bedroom drinking Italian wine, American beer, and German schnapps which the captain, with great foresight, had brought with him. We got along well. He told me fabulous war stories, some of which I believed.

On the Cassino front, he told me, his people had trained their pack mules to go to ground when a bombardment came in and the mules had become so quick in anticipating danger soldiers frequently took their cues from them. The pack animals had even learned to dig their own "mule holes." When I expressed some slight doubt, he informed me that he was trained as a forester and knew more about the capabilities of mules than I did.

I did accept at almost face value his story about how the men in his regiment cried when Colonel Ernst, their commanding officer, told them they would have to lay down their arms. They were not defeated and wanted to continue the fight, so Herr Hauptmann told me.

They probably cried, I thought, but who knows why they cried? There were many possible reasons. The only German soldiers I had met who wanted to continue the fight in the closing week of the campaign were people such as those in the rear echelon near Bergamo who had something to gain and little to lose by continuing the bloodshed.

Next morning as the captain and I went down to breakfast, we met one of our sergeants herding two German soldiers who had been detected moving through our chow lines. We stopped on the path. The German enlisted men braced themselves to attention in front of the captain.

He made a number of sharp inquiries; they gave brief response. When the captain had all the information he needed, he ended the brief encounter with a stern admonition. The men saluted smartly and moved off.

He told me these were "bad soldiers" and he had ordered them to return to their units. I gathered they were deserters who had decided to make their way back over the Alps to Germany and home. That prospect must have been most tempting to all of them. If the American and German positions had been reversed, would we have been able to hold our men in place? I very much doubted it but I didn't tell the captain so.

Our guest had spoken of his fondness for American films, and we now had new ones to show every two or three nights. We, of course, invited him to attend the showings which were presented at dark in the open air down by the lake. He was a bit hesitant at first. While he did enjoy American films, he wanted some assurance from me he would not be exposed to American propaganda if he accepted our invitation.

I knew there was a short "informational" film which usually preceded the feature attraction. The then current favorite was called "Two Down and One to Go." The burden of its message was that those international criminals, Mussolini and Hitler, were dead and now the invincible American military machine would go forward to the destruction of Hirohito and all his works. Suspecting that Herr Hauptmann would not appreciate that kind of "information," I suggested that he remain in his quarters until I sent word that the danger of ideological contamination was passed and the feature about to begin. That was agreeable to him and that was the way we did it.

The night before the surrender ceremony, I came home from a hard day at the office to find my guest sitting on his bed with a glass in his hand and a half-empty bottle of schnapps on the floor within easy reach. He was staring morosely off into space. His life was over, he told me. He might spend several years as a prisoner of war, but that didn't matter. There was nothing to go home to anyway. His family was dead, his country in ruins. There would be no jobs, no army, no forests to protect, no future. He envied me, he said, because I would have the opportunity to "hunt Japanese game."

I could understand his emotional state. He had good reason to be distressed. I joined him for a drink and tried to change the subject. That proved to be of no help. He was becoming more formal, excessively polite, bitterly sarcastic. When I asked him if he was ready to go down and eat, he replied that he was "the lieutenant's prisoner" and that if "the lieutenant" wanted him to go eat, he would eat. I told him the lieutenant did want him to eat and let it go at that. I could have said much more, but what was the use? He came along and ate in silence. After dinner he refused an invitation to another film and went straight to bed.

On the morning of May 15 the captain conducted me to the place where his regimental headquarters would stack arms. We joined a sizeable convoy of vehicles in which other American and German officers were going to other units of the Fifth Mountain on identical missions. It must have been a rather strange looking convoy, a mixture of American jeeps and trucks and German scout cars. The Italians on the streets looked somewhat bewildered. Not knowing whom to cheer, they remained silent.

At the end of a short trip, I was ushered into the reception room of a rather large villa. Several officers of the regimental staff were already there. After brief introductions, we stood quietly on our dignity. I was glad my boots and brass had a high shine and that my uniform was neatly pressed. The German officers wore dress shorts with knee-length stockings after the British fashion.

We didn't have long to wait. The fabled Colonel Ernst, the regimental commander about whom the captain had told me so much in such a short period of time, appeared shortly after we had assembled. He was a tall, gaunt man and looked a bit like Ichabod Crane.

When the colonel appeared, his staff officers were galvanized into action. They began to "talk it up" with short little exclamations of solidarity and enthusiasm as they congregated around him in the middle of the room. He extended both long, skinny arms into the middle of a semicircle and there was a "laying on of hands" such as I had only seen with an American basketball team about to take the court for a crucial game. It was all over in a matter of seconds. The circle broke, the officers stepped back and clapped hands briskly, rhythmically in a manner once again similar to what I had witnessed at athletic contests in the States.

Looking out into the courtyard, I could see, and we could hear, German noncoms dressing the ranks. The German officers waited, just as American officers always waited, to make their appearance. When all was ready, we followed Colonel Ernst outside.

There must have been close to two hundred German soldiers assembled. They looked exceptionally sharp despite the fact that they wore mixed uniforms. Some were in shorts, some in baggy combat pants while others appeared in more conventional parade attire.

The colonel stepped dramatically out in front of his troops. He roared something and the men gave a loud response in unison. This staccato question-response routine was continued several times. Colonel Ernst then gave a sharp command; the troops executed an "eyes right" and a "ready front" with more precision than I had ever seen on an American drill field. The colonel next gave the equivalent of "at ease" and spoke just a few quiet words to the troops.

After that a German noncommissioned officer took over and began to call the roll. As each man responded to his name, he came forward and piled his rifle into a waiting American truck. Side arms were placed in separate piles on the ground. I stood watching, maintaining a position of "parade rest." Some of the men gave me a friendly glance and a slight smile; others an appraising stare, but the majority looked straight ahead.

When it was all completed the troops were marched back to their billets. The German officers shook hands with the colonel and with each other. They clicked their heels, saluted me and departed to go their separate ways. Their liaison officer stayed at our headquarters until the following morning. When he left, he also performed the heel clicking routine, saluted and wished us "good hunting."

I went back to less interesting duty, concerned now with completing plans for Memorial Day exercises. We sent a detail to Anzio for the dedication of a military cemetery and planned to hold our own ceremony down by the lake.

My duties in those days took me not infrequently back to headquarters in Novara. It was a pleasant ride in the warm Italian sun through a blossoming countryside, and I sought excuses to get out of the office. When I arrived at Novara on one of these trips, I was given an urgent message from two of our soldiers lodged in the stockade awaiting courts-martial. They had not asked for me specifically but for any battalion officers who came within hailing distance.

The men were not from my company, but their names and cases were somewhat familiar because the court-martial papers had crossed my desk earlier. They were accused of "oppressing prisoners of war" or some such thing, which meant more specifically, looting a convoy of German prisoners being transported back to P.W. cages. A search for evidence had been made in the battalion but had turned up nothing.

When I went to see the men, I was surprised at the warmth of their greetings. Mine was the first friendly face they had seen since their arrest, they said. After shaking hands with some enthusiasm, they got to the point immediately. They wanted me to represent them as a special defense counsel. Yes, they had spoken to the regularly appointed defense counsel, but he had simply advised them to plead guilty. And what was wrong with that advice? Well, they both insisted forcefully, they were innocent of the charges. And, they reminded me, they could get as much as twenty years and a dishonorable discharge if convicted.

I reminded them in turn that I was not a lawyer and that these things were almost always settled with a finding of guilty as charged. They knew all that, they said, but the stakes were very high. Any defense would be better than no defense.

I asked them to tell me the whole story without dressing it up. I wanted to believe them. And what they told me was neither altogether implausible nor shocking.

They had been joy riding in a captured German vehicle. This was not an indictable offense; I had known others who had done the same. They had been drinking and had run out of wine. That, too, was a common experience and not grounds for locking people up. But now we came to the crucial part of the story.

As the defendants told it, they were driving along talking about various possibilities for alleviating their dry condition when they overtook a truck convoy which had pulled over to the side of the road to give its German prisoners a piss call. On one of the trucks, according to the young man telling the story, a prisoner waved a bottle of wine at them. "So, naturally," he concluded, "we stopped."

The bottle was passed around and they stood there for awhile fraternizing with the former enemy. At some point, both defendants admitted, they had climbed up into the bed of the truck, but, they insisted, the prisoners had voluntarily given them the money they were accused of extorting. One of the prisoners was reported to have said, "We won't need this where we are going," or words to that effect. Whether this thought was conveyed in German or English was never made clear either to me or at the trial.

In the midst of this touching example of human brotherhood, if that is what it was, the convoy commander came up and placed an entirely different interpretation on the scene. He preferred to think of it as additional evidence of man's inhumanity to man. He brought charges.

Despite a few doubts, I pretty well accepted the softer version of events. Besides, these men were family. If the battalion didn't look out for their interests, who would? Even if they were guilty as charged, they seemed to have done little more than my runner had done with impunity while the war was on. The possibility that these soldiers might receive a long prison sentence and a dishonorable discharge for such an escapade struck me as outrageous. Subsequent leniency, even if it could be counted on, would come from the grace of higher authority. These soldiers deserved something more

After a few more questions, I told them I would take their case but warned them I could make no promises. They seemed greatly relieved that they would be able to put on some kind of a defense. We made our only preparations on the spot.

For the trial, I told them to get short haircuts and to be prepared for the most important military inspection of their lives. They were to wear all of their campaign ribbons which I knew included two Combat Infantry Badges, at least one Purple Heart, and one citation for bravery. I also informed them that I would put them on the stand to tell the story exactly as they had told it to me, taking care not to omit that statement about how, "naturally, we stopped," when they saw the wine waved in their face.

I went back to battalion and reexamined the papers in our files. My clients, if not model soldiers, had never been in serious trouble before. They may have been subjected to company punishment, but there was no record of that and it would not be admissible as evidence in any case. I read again the deposition of the convoy commander. There was nothing else in our file, but I couldn't believe that I had all of the prosecution's evidence. If I did have it all, I reflected, we just might win this case.

From somewhere I acquired the manual on court-martial procedures, read, and marked the relevant parts. I made no attempt to memorize what I had read because I planned to take the manual with me to the trial.

Consciously and unconsciously I was following the example set by Lieutenant Ellis who, along with the old man, represented for me the ideal infantry unit commander. I did not deceive myself into believing I was in their class, but I had seen Ellis in a court-martial at Anzio defending one of the least worthy of his men and I took my hearings from that.

On the day of the trial, I, too, had prepared for the most rigorous military inspection of my life. I, too, wore my Combat Infantry Badge and other ribbons, and I, too, sat beside my men in easy comradeship just as Ellis had done.

The trial judge advocate, as the prosecutor was called, put on his only witness, the convoy commander. I would like to report that I demolished his testimony with a brilliant cross-examination which brought applause from the court, but that is not the way it happened. I attempted no cross-examination at all. In truth I was somewhat afraid of the witness who, after all, was a staff officer in the division and might be in a position to do me harm when I wanted to go back to the States. I was taking some chance as it was. Why compound the problem?

When it came our turn to put on a defense, I called only two witnesses, the defendants. To show, as if that were necessary, that I was just a good old combat soldier defending his men and not some slick lawyer brought in from outside, I got up with my manual of procedure in hand and more or less read from it just as Ellis had done.

"If it please the court," I intoned, or whatever equivalent phrase the manual told me to use, "The defendants have been informed of their rights and have elected to take the stand in their own defense."

I put my main man on first. When he told how "naturally, we stopped" when the bottle of wine was waved, I saw a slight smile come over the face of at least one member of the court and knew we had a supporter. The second defendant came on and told what was essentially the same story. The money in question had been freely given.

Both defendants answered questions on cross-examination from the court and the convoy commander with seeming openness and honesty. They were excellent witnesses as I told them later. It was their word against that of the convoy commander, but there were saving features on our side which I, in my inexperience and timidity, had failed to emphasize. There was no evidence that my men were armed, no evidence that they used physical force, and I don't believe there was evidence that my clients had taken anything except the money and, perhaps, a few "souvenirs."

The prosecution's lack of supporting evidence and the demeanor of the defendants spoke for themselves. We won an acquittal. The defendants were relieved and more than a little joyous. I was pleased; the convoy commander was outraged. But that was that. Justice had prevailed, as far as I was concerned, but I took great care not to gloat and was glad I heard nothing more about the case.

If, up to this point, I have left the impression that in my new job I had no time for anything but work, I must now correct that most erroneous view. Never in the world would I have let that happen. My journal notes indicate that I did, indeed, get into Torino, a little behind the other junior officers, but I got there. Apparently I was much impressed with the lovely girls, the broad avenues, the electric lights, the big stores, etc. It is a bit strange that I have so little recollection of that trip, but it was greatly overshadowed by pleasures which I wrote about much more fully. As will presently appear, I enjoyed that Italian spring more than I had enjoyed a springtime since the beginning of the war. But the time was so short.

Around the middle of June we were officially informed of plans to move the division into Germany as part of an army of occupation. Many of us had the option of rotating back to the States, but that opportunity still carried with it the possibility of only a short leave at home and a long trip to the war in the Pacific. Lacking the apparent enthusiasm of the Fifth Mountain Division's liaison officer for "hunting Japanese game," I quickly elected to stay in Europe. I would go to Germany in preference to a trip to Japan by way of the States, but I wanted more than anything else to stay exactly where I was.

By this time I had been in Italy some eighteen months and had acquired what was to be a lifelong interest in and appreciation of the country and its people. During the war I had seen Italy at its worst, but in the few weeks since the German surrender, I had begun to see the country as I knew it could be. I didn't want to leave the show at the very start of the happy ending.

For me there is at times an almost unbearable feeling of sweet sadness in remembering how we were in that brief but glorious spring in Italy immediately after the war. I sensed it then as one senses moments which can never come again; I feel it much more strongly now some forty plus years later. Let me try to explain.

From our positions around Viverone, the Alps stretched across our front, but we had no concern for enemy observations, no fear that our movements would bring down a devastating artillery barrage. No longer did we have to strain our ears listening for the telltale "plop" of the mortars; and there would be no enemy patrols coming in, firing their burp guns and shouting to each other across the darkness. We were at peace.

But there was much more to it than that. The magnificent lakes of northern Italy, Maggiore, Como, Garda, invited us to use them as our playground and we had already found time to take limited advantage of their hospitality. In the daytime a benign sun looked down from a cloudless blue sky and the nights, as Alan Paton has written in an entirely different connection, were beautiful "beyond any singing of it." With the full June moon shining on the lake, the gentle waves lapping at the shore, and the sound of soft music in the background, who could doubt that we had, indeed, reached the promised land? And, besides, I had fallen in love with Silea.

But that was crazy! We hardly knew each other. When we first met, Silea had almost no English and I was not what you would want to call a spellbinder in Italian. While Silea was fluent in German, I knew barely enough of that language to say, "Kommen Sie Raus! Hande Hoch! Macht Schnell!" phrases hardly calculated to facilitate romantic courtship or to deepen intellectual or emotional understanding. But these are trifles when you are young, single, and hungry for the honest affections of a beautiful girl. I had found Silea and my Italian spring was complete.

The owner of the summer house we occupied on Lake Viverone had served as matchmaker. Shortly after we arrived on the lake, he invited my battalion commander, me as battalion adjutant, and one or two other officers to his expensive home in Biella where we met Tina, his niece, and Silea, Tina's friend. Tina at once took charge of the battalion commander as I am sure had been planned. Silea was intended for me, and I certainly had no objections or reasons to complain.

I have a tendency to remember her now as some kind of sex goddess, the ultimate pinup girl; but I have her picture before me and, while it doesn't do her justice, I must admit, it comes closer to the truth. It shows a very pretty girl who combines features of both northern and southern Italian beauty. She had the ripe, full-bodied figure of a Neapolitan girl and the merry, mischievous blue eyes of someone from further north. Her hair was brown, her complexion neither dark nor fair but an attractive blend. I judged her to be about my age and, what was more important, several inches shorter than I.

It would be difficult to characterize the exact nature of my relationship with Silea. If an "affair" requires the physical consummation of love, this was no affair, I can assure you. It was more like an old-fashioned, tempestuous high school romance which stops short of ultimate gratification.

Due in part, but only in part, to language barriers, Silea and I seemed to have an almost uncanny talent for misunderstanding each other. That much was apparent on the night I met her. When we were alone, the very first thing she said to me in timid, tentative, faltering English was, "I luffa you."

Somewhat taken aback by this opening gambit from a respectable girl, I laughed and, with my customary tact, informed her that her statement was ridiculous.

She was devastated. What was the matter? Had she not said it right?

Yes, she had said it *almost* right, but the statement could not be true. She got angry, insisting in a torrent of Italian that she did so love me no matter what I thought of her. She was so cute and the situation so preposterous I laughed again. Perhaps still smarting under the mistaken impression that I had been convulsed by her effort to speak English, she offered the opinion that my Italian was not of the best either. I told her I was, oh, so well aware of that, and we both laughed. She agreed to teach me Italian; I promised to help her learn English. It was a beginning.

In the latter part of May Silea and I began to see each other rather frequently. She and Tina would ride out from Biella on their bicycles on Sundays, and the major and I would go over to see them on weekday evenings when we had the opportunity. Sometimes Silea would bicycle out to the lake by herself, and sometimes I would go into Biella without the major.

In early June she and I took long moonlight walks through the otherwise dimly lit streets of Biella. We swam and boated on the lake at Rapallo. We sat and talked, drinking wine and smoking cigarettes. We tried to learn each other's language.

In a brief and carefully controlled audience, Silea presented me to her father. He was an elderly man, somewhat infirm, and must have viewed me with considerable misgiving, realizing that he was gradually losing control of his grown daughter. But he hadn't surrendered all of his traditional prerogatives. In a degree which was never clear to me, he controlled the times and purposes for which Silea might leave the house.

She never in any way expressed complaint or resentment against her father but seemed to have devised various schemes for evading his edicts. She advised me that on those occasions when she was housebound I could call and talk to her at "Tre, Tre, Otto, Sette." I tried that but it didn't work out. I got the number without difficulty but found myself tongue-tied when Silea answered. I hadn't realized how much my meager Italian depended on gestures, body language, and visual feedback.

There were other things which didn't work out. Up to the last week Silea and I quarreled frequently, made up, quarreled and made up again. The sometimes stormy scenes were my fault; for I, her god, was a jealous god, whose first commandment was, "Thou shalt have no god but me." Once while rowing on the lake, the vivacious Silea tried to strike up a conversation in German with two men in another boat, men looking suspiciously like enemy soldiers, although I couldn't tell because they wore swim gear. My date seemed to be inquiring as to the whereabouts and welfare of a third party. The men could provide her with no information. They seemed embarrassed by the encounter and eager to get away. Silea persisted; I was furious.

But interspersed with our foolish spats were periods of sweet tenderness and carefree enjoyment. One unforgettable Sunday we double dated with the major and Tina for a trip to Lago Maggiore. It was a breathtaking ride, enhanced, no doubt, by the fact that we were in an open jeep in perfect weather. After lunching at a little café overlooking the lake, we drove on in to Stresa where we found a secluded beach and lolled in the sun for several hours. Silea and I laughed, petted, and talked only of pleasant fantasies.

Two days later, acting the part of a jealous schoolboy, I said goodbye forever. This time Tina intervened with the battalion commander on her friend's behalf; and the major gave me the "orders" which, after two days, I had secretly longed for: to go back to Silea, kiss and make up.

Somewhere in all of this we had declared our eternal love for each other. And we told each other outrageous lies. I swore there was no one waiting for me at home; she insisted that I was the first and only man in her life. My parents were rich beyond the dreams of avarice; her people were equally well provided for. She loved American sports; I liked nothing better than listening to Italian opera. We would get married, live in the States, but return to the lake country on frequent holidays. We would, of course, have children and live happily ever after without a care in the world. But she wouldn't take her panties off until the time was right.

After I told Silea I was going away within the week, there was permanent peace between us. She could not get out of the house for a couple of days, but on June 22 her father left Biella for the country. Apart from necessary battalion duty, the next four days and nights would be ours.

The night her father left, the major and I picked up the girls at Biella and brought them out to the lake. Silea and I sat in the big lawn chairs at the water's edge and reiterated our vows. We would write to each other, of course. It wouldn't be possible for us to forget. There was too much love between us. This was only a temporary parting, etc.

On Saturday night I had a date with Silea for the last battalion officers' dance. It was the usual raucous affair, but I didn't drink too much and Silea hardly flirted at all. We were polite to other people but our knowing smiles and loving looks were for each other. I took her home and lingered until daylight.

She was out on her bicycle by 10:15 the next morning. We spent the afternoon on the lake where Silea made sure I would never forget her. She appeared now in a daring two-piece bathing suit, the first I had ever seen. It was modest attire by contemporary standards but it was, without doubt, a major source of my lingering image of Silea as sex goddess.

We had supper together and attended an American film. It was well after midnight when I took her home. Was I imagining it, or had her

English greatly improved under my tutelage? Despite her flirtatious behavior and the lies between us, could it be possible that she really loved me? Was there a chance for us? Do fairy tales really come true? On that night I halfway believed they did.

Monday evening was our last time together. I got into Biella early and found Silea waiting. We had a drink with Tina and sat talking to her while I said the less painful of my goodbyes. Then Silea and I went for our last long walk in the moonlight.

As we strolled hand in hand through the quiet streets of the little town, we reinvented our fairy tales and renewed our vows, both of us trying to make the parting as easy as possible. But the big moon and the heartbreak inherent in the situation kept getting in the way. We both realized that this might be the last time for everything, the last drink together, last cigarette, last tender glance, last kiss. When finally, I just had to leave, we clung to each other and cried; for I think we both knew we would never see each other again.

Chapter 16

The End of Everything

My body was with the convoy as it left for Germany next morning but my thoughts were still with Silea. I knew I couldn't tell anyone I had fallen in love with her. Even my best friends would have laughed. They would have made jokes. They would have said things like, "Never lose your head over a little piece of tail." They would have asked, "Whatever happened to find 'um, fool 'um, fuck 'um, and forget 'um?" And they would have prescribed the only antidote they knew for a man with my delusional fancies: copious doses of alcohol, administered preferably by a variety of beautiful girls both before and after bedding time. I didn't need the advice of those cynical, misguided wise asses.

At the close of our first day on the road, we bivouacked around Lake Garda. Somehow the water no longer seemed as blue nor the lake as inviting. Garda compared most unfavorably with Maggorie, I thought, especially that part of Maggorie up around Stresa.

The second night's bivouac was worse. We were in Bolzano for our last night in Italy. The springtime was gone. There was no perfume in the air, and we saw only patches of snow and bleak mountain peaks ahead. The wind was chilly. We started shivering long before the sun went down.

In our encampment at Bolzano we were reminded once again that the concept of "collective guilt" had found lodgment in official policy. There was to be absolutely no "fraternization" with people in the conquered territory beyond the Brenner Pass. When we requisitioned billets to shelter our troops, all civilians were to be moved out regardless of age, sex or health and without regard to the presence or absence of other structures capable of affording shelter. Even fraternization with small children was proscribed. There was a sixty-five-dollar fine for any one of us caught talking to a German woman unless he could prove the conversation was required in line of duty. I saw fit to record the specific amount of the penalty. It caused considerable discussion among the men in the convoy.

Next day we, as a unit of the conquering army, moved through the Brenner Pass. If anyone had expected dramatic changes on the other side of the border, he must have been disappointed There was little new to see. The Italian side had been plastered rather heavily by the Allied air forces. Immediately on the other side there was relatively less damage, but Innsbruck was flattened. At one time I might have been gratified by that sight. No more. I, for one, had seen enough war damage to last me a lifetime.

For the most part, the people in the conquered territory simply ignored us. From time to time small children, blissfully unaware of the taint they bore, would wave. At first the men ignored these seductive provocations, but within a couple of hours, common courtesy, common sense, and human decency reasserted themselves. The men began to wave back and then to throw hard candy from their field rations in the direction of the little enemy. There were no officers or noncoms to stop them.

Later, as we moved into Bavaria, we found the roads clogged with recently demobilized German soldiers on their way home. Most of them had packs on their backs; some were hobbling along with what must have been fairly recent wounds. Relaxing the nonfraternization ban a bit further, I picked up one of the more pitiable of these poor devils for a ride in the jeep.

My passenger had no English and I no German, but he had been on the Italian front and we found we could converse in pidgin Italian, making heavy use of the infinitive and ignoring grammatical constructions. Believing, I am sure, that the statement was self-evident to all who had been there, he opened the conversation with the observation, "Italiani soldati niente bono."

I reflected on our guide at Pontedera, the partisans who had sacrificed their lives and especially those who had saved us casualties by neutralizing opposition in Milano and in other places north of the Po. These were Silea's countrymen he was talking about. I was tempted to suggest stringent qualifications of his assessment, but he was my guest, a wounded and a defeated man. I simply responded with a nod here, a "Si" there, and tried to change the subject.

On a rainy, cold, miserable and otherwise totally unsatisfactory day on the last of June, we arrived at and were billeted in the tiny Bavarian town of Satteldorf. There was war damage even here, but we were assigned to a big farmhouse which, with its well-kept outbuildings, was still intact. I was grateful the advance party had already dispossessed the elderly farmer and his wife of their lodging, since under our directives, it had to be done. I had no stomach for such a task, but as Silea would have said, "What to do?"

The next morning the farmer approached me as the only American officer in this little town with a modest request that we move some of our vehicles which were blocking access to one of his fields. The old man, in all probability a veteran of World War I, had white hair, a white handlebar mustache and a military bearing. With a very slight click of his heels and a slight respectful bow, he stood before me in an unobtrusive but still unmistakable attitude of attention. He addressed me as "Herr Leutnant." There were no traces of obsequiousness in his manner. His military training had provided him with a dignified way of dealing with superior authority.

Impressed by his manner, the reasonableness of his request, the difference in our ages, and feeling guilty for having been indirectly involved in his consignment to the barn, I overreacted with a profuse apology, probably a breach of military orders, and quickly directed that the vehicles in question be moved.

A little later I had occasion to make a request of him. He had a fine crop of corn immediately across the road from the house we occupied. It was tough, field corn, but we had our hearts set on supplementing our ration by roasting a few ears. I thought it appropriate to ask permission before allowing it to be picked. He readily acceded to my request, but with white eyebrows upraised, expressed amazement and some slight hint of disgust that we planned to eat that which was fit only for cattle.

Once again I felt on the defensive. Who were the conquerors around here anyway? So what if he was old enough to be my grandfather? I resolved in future to maintain the dignity of my office. Next time I would have him brought before me. Never again would I go out to see him.

Even before we moved into Bavaria, another shift in battalion assignments was being considered. In part changes were necessitated by the fact that the military planned an extensive educational program for the benefit of soldiers who might be stationed in Germany indefinitely. Under the program men could earn high school and even college credit.

At battalion level this meant a new staff office for coordinating and implementing the program. The battalion S-2, normally in charge of intelligence, was transformed into what was essentially an information and education officer; and I was transferred into the restructured position with a first responsibility of reporting to an army headquarters in Paris to be schooled in the grassroots administration of the program. That was

Paris, France if you can believe! My friend at battalion had done me one last and much appreciated favor.

My trip got off to a fast start. In keeping with one of its more endearing traditions, the army didn't tell me of its plans until 0800 hours on the morning they expected me to leave. Well, no matter. There was no way they were going to keep me off balance on this one. I pulled back the cleanest part of my laundry, grabbed some toilet articles, borrowed $100, and took off more or less on time with a captain from another unit in the division who had a jeep and driver at his disposal.

We drove west through the great rubble mounds of what had been Stuttgart, crossed the Rhine on a temporary bridge near Strasbourg, and spent the night in a transient officers' facility at Nancy. Most of the buildings on the French side of the border were standing, but the military presence was still overpowering. The few subdued, grim-faced civilians on the streets were lost in the dreary world of military men and machines.

I saw Paris for the first time the next afternoon. We had been driving since early morning when finally the Eiffel Tower loomed in the distance. It was an exciting moment, additional evidence we were approaching civilization.

When we drew closer, the driver stopped and consulted a city map. There was no problem in locating the University of Paris, our ultimate destination. After we reported in, the captain and I hastily spruced up a bit and headed for town. After all school didn't start until next morning.

By guiding on the Arc de Triomphe, we soon found what we called "the main drag." Our first stop was at a rather posh civilian bar where the gin was potent but inordinately expensive. We knew we could do better in an officers' club.

When we found one, I ended my barhopping for the evening. The captain, a man of about thirty-five, quickly struck up a conversation with three or four French women of approximately the same age. In passable French, he invited them to our table. Soon he was in jokingly serious negotiations with them.

While I couldn't follow much of the interchange, I could tell I was weakening his bargaining position. The ladies expressed shock at his proposal. They argued among themselves in very rapid French, throwing sidelong glances in my direction from time to time. It was evident they didn't think I was old enough to take part in what was being planned. I felt much as the smallest kid on the playground feels when the teams quarrel about which side is obligated to make a sacrifice and take him in.

No matter. A group of Second Armored Division officers at a nearby table was buying drinks for an extra girl nearer my age. At their invitation, I joined them. My companion of the road soon disappeared in the company of one of the women he had been negotiating with. I never saw him again until we started back to Germany.

There was much coming and going at the big round table where the men from the "Hell on Wheels" division had set up their CP. Couples would leave, unattached males would drop by, and a number of unclaimed females continued to circulate. I couldn't understand why some of the girls were not making out until the attractive young lady I was now buying drinks for revealed what you might call "the bottom line." She would let me spend the night with her for $60 American.

I was aghast. My God! That was well over half the money I had to make last a week! The dreaded postwar inflation had struck! How could a man on a fixed income hope to survive? I shook my head sadly, bade the young lady goodnight, and went back to the university to sleep alone.

When school convened next morning, I discovered that the intellectual content of the curriculum would be within my grasp. Each of us was handed a rather sizeable stack of papers; mine told me all I needed to know about the program and more. But to supplement the written word, they had us assemble each morning in a large auditorium where lecturers, both military and civilian, made extensive use of visual aids to underscore points they thought worthy of emphasis.

Toward the end of the week there were speeches of an inspirational nature. But, it was summer, and need I tell you, the auditorium was innocent of air conditioning? The audience proved most difficult to inspire. Indeed, it was almost impossible to keep many of us awake. One fiery civilian speaker, recognizing the situation, kept a handbell on the podium and wielded it vigorously to alert his audience to an upcoming statement of special import. When this flamboyant performer rang the bell to signalize the onset of his peroration, I was jarred awake just in time to hear him declaim: "But what the hell? I say UP with capital and UP with labor. I say UP with Democrats and UP with Republicans. And I say UP with Negroes and UP with white people. . . . And I say UP WITH AMERICA!"

He sat down to a considerable applause in which I joined. I am sure it had been a very interesting and worthwhile message.

The night after my first day in school I started out to explore Paris on my own. Enough of those joint negotiations. Enough of communal matchmaking. I wanted to roam freely, to be by myself for a little while.

The blackout in Paris was now the stuff of legend. The city was several days away from celebrating the first Bastille Day since 1939, but it looked as if the celebration had already begun. The Champs Elysees was crowded with soldiers and civilians, men and women. They were celebrating something, acting as if it might be New Year's Eve. The bars, both civilian and military, around the Etoile and up and down the nearby streets filled up early. Increasingly boisterous patrons shuttled between them.

From many of the night spots in the vicinity came the sounds of music. Two songs from that night seemed to etch themselves on my brain. I heard them wherever I went. One was a popular French song of the day called "Le Petit Vin Blanc," the other a powerfully haunting Russian number which I knew as "Meadowland." Occasionally a band would strike up "Dog Face Soldier" and I would know there were friends from the American Third Division on the premises if, unlikely prospect, they had not already made their presence known.

And then entering an American officers' club, I saw Leigh. She was sitting on a stool at the end of the bar, the blondest, sweetest-looking girl I had ever seen. She couldn't have been more than five feet three. Her simple but pretty summer dress, her pert little breasts and her fashionably slender figure gave her the appearance of a teenage model, but I decided she was about my age.

She was sitting alone, waiting for someone, I assumed, a lieutenant colonel, perhaps or even an air corps bird colonel. It was unthinkable that she should be there unescorted or waiting for anyone below the rank of major.

I made my way to the bar with absolutely no thought of trying to obtain the unobtainable. Ordering a cognac and water, I was soon involved in conversation with some Thirty-sixth Division officers sitting and standing nearby.

It was always good to say hello again to old friends, and anyone with a Thirty-sixth Division patch on his shoulder was an old friend, especially if he wore cross rifles on his shirt collar as these men did. No matter that none of those I talked to that night had taken part in the heartbreaking effort to cross the Rapido in the prehistoric age out of which I came. It was disappointing but almost inevitable that they could give me no information about people I had known in their outfits. That was almost always the way it was now whether I talked with guys from the Thirty-sixth, Thirty-fourth, Third, Forty-fifth, or whatever. But my attention was always attracted to a familiar division patch. I tended to forget how unlikely it was that I shared friends with its present wearers.

As I talked to these young kids from the Thirty-sixth, my eyes strayed frequently down the bar to where this delightful little blonde person was sitting. Occasionally she took tiny little sips from a drink I couldn't identify. I noted her attitude of aloof disdain, her haughty, abrupt dismissal of the men who came her way. I waited with considerable interest for a look at the lucky guy who would appear at any moment to take her away from all this. No one came.

After my second, or perhaps it was my third, cognac and water, an overzealous captain staggered against her, spilling his drink down the back of her dress. While he tried to make profuse apology, her eyes met mine in what I thought was a plaintive appeal. So, naturally, as my witness had testified in that memorable court-martial at Novara, I moved to her side.

We found a table. She had noticed me too, she confessed in a rather heavily accented English which I found irresistible, dismissing with a distinctive shrug the numerous suitors who had come her way.

Leigh was employed in an office on the Champs Elysees, an office we later visited, but on this night she offered only to show me Paris after dark. How could I refuse? Here was a beautiful girl who was not put off by my unlined face, someone who wanted to be with me and had not yet, at least, put a price tag on our relationship.

Shortly before midnight we started out. Our first stop was in Montmartre at an out of the way restaurant where she took me to sober up. I was the only service man in the place. At Leigh's suggestion we ordered big bowls of onion soup which I found delicious and inexpensive by Paris standards. Leigh insisted we take glasses of the house wine rather than a $20 bottle of what was supposed to be the finest champagne.

There was a piano player in the place who improvised what must have been funny remarks for the amusement of the diners. I suspected some of his barbs were aimed at me, or at us, but no matter. Leigh told me he was drunk and that I shouldn't pay any attention to him. We lingered over something which tasted a little like coffee, getting acquainted and smoking cigarettes.

Then we toured Montmartre. She pointed out places where famous artists had worked, taking for granted that I knew who she was talking about. I tried not to disillusion her. She took me to Sacre-Coeur where we stood for quite some time. The famous church was still bathed in floodlights, although at this hour we were the only tourists abroad. Romantic sentiment welled up inside as I turned to her and said tenderly, "I love you for bringing me here." She came into my arms, murmuring she loved me too. It wasn't love at first sight. It had taken us two or three hours.

Leigh had told me in the officers' club that she had an apartment located on Chateaubriand near her work but couldn't take me there because of strict rules prohibiting the entertainment, however innocent, of male guests. And that, I learned at Sacre-Coeur, was that. Lacking a place to make love, we strolled and petted until daylight when I returned to the university and Leigh went back to her apartment.

After that I was with her every day, usually from the middle of the afternoon until early next morning. She showed me Notre Dame, the Louvre, the Place de la Concorde, the Opera, Pigalle, Moulin Rouge. We walked arm-in-arm along the banks of the Seine; we sat in sidewalk cafes, classifying people and feeling sorry for anyone who wasn't in love.

For me Paris meant Leigh and life and love and great good fortune. And how could it have been otherwise? I had survived the war. Fate had brought me to this fabled city to celebrate a glorious moment in history, and fate had sent me a gentle enchantress.

I wanted to hold back the passage of time or at least to minimize it by acts of will. I rationed sleep, decided against laundering my clothes, and pondered ways of evading the dull duty which was the major problem.

But my little sorceress used her magic to hold me on a prudent course. She kept me in school and out of her apartment. But as a tour guide, she was by no means unbending. Recognizing when I had become satiated with sightseeing, she led me frequently to the Bois de Boulogne where we rested and petted with the intimacy of young lovers everywhere.

We spent all of one afternoon in the park. What with lectures in the daytime and being out late every night, I was exhausted. She let me sleep for a time with my head in her lap while she protected me from the wolves which, she said, were known to abide in the area. But I was her very own wolf, she said.

That night Leigh suggested we go to the *Folies Bergères,* not that it was prime entertainment but it was inexpensive and something any self-respecting military tourist ought to do. We went and sat in the least expensive balcony seats, holding hands and snuggling together. There seemed to be some kind of performance on stage.

By this time I had found a partial solution to my "cash flow" problem. Leigh had known from the beginning that my funds were limited and, on the second night, generously offered to pay for her own dinner. I refused because, I told her with a thank-you kiss, there was a better way.

The American military, wise in the ways of soldiers in Paris, had conveniently located finance office kiosks in various parts of the city. I went to one of these, showed my papers, and drew the maximum amount of advance pay allowed me. Then, on the theory that the left hand of the military wouldn't know what the right hand had done, I made my way across town and successfully repeated the operation. If that wasn't enough, I would try again.

Although I never found out much about Leigh's past, I conjectured a good deal. She was very much on her own. Her parents were dead and the rest of her family living far away. And despite her carefree manner, I sensed a wistful sadness at the core of her being. Perhaps she had lost a lover or a husband in the war; and perhaps that almost-too-thin figure was in part a matter of necessity rather than choice. I knew food had been scarce under the occupation.

There were indications that Leigh had been close to the resistance movement and was still involved in Gaullist politics. When she took me to the place she worked, I found one inside wall of a rather large office dominated by a poster showing the great man in a typical heroic pose. The office supervisor, Leigh's superior and friend, was a slender, vigorous lady in her forties who had lost an arm just above the elbow. Her unaccented English was excellent and her admiration for de Gaulle apparent in her conversation. It was a bit difficult for me to know whether I was in a commercial establishment or a Gaulist headquarters. I concluded it was a little bit of both.

During the afternoon in the Bois, Leigh told me things suggesting insider knowledge of the resistance struggle, things I didn't read about until at least twenty years later. Just before the Normandy invasion, she told me, they had listened eagerly to the BBC for coded messages which would bring the resistance out into the streets all over France. One of these signals involved the broadcast of certain lines from a Paul Verlaine sonnet. Leigh recited all fourteen lines in French. I didn't understand a word, but it was thrilling to listen to the sound and cadence of her voice.

While she was much better educated, more cultured, more sophisticated than I, she was no cultural snob. Her fondness for good literature and art didn't prevent her from liking American popular music. In her soft little voice she sang for me the lyrics of a then popular song called, "I'll Be Seeing You," and at my request, repeated the performance several times. It was done with that devastatingly, heart-melting accent in which many of the words came out as American baby talk. I wouldn't have changed a syllable and it is her version which comes back with special poignancy whenever the music is played. She would be seeing me: ". . . in zat sma' café, zuh pawk ac-woss zuh way, / Zuh child-wens ka-wo-sel, zuh Chin-est twee. . . ."

I always stopped her at "zuh Chin-est twee" for a big hug and kiss.

On the night before Bastille Day, we made our way up the Champs Elysées to see the rainbow-colored lights beamed down on the Arc de Triomphe. Moving on to near the base of the Eiffel Tower, we stretched out to watch a fireworks display. Then it was jostling through more crowds, our hands locked to prevent separation. Once, before discreetly turning away, we stared at an amorous couple less inhibited than most. This was New Year's Eve plus Mardi Gras. But we soon tired of it.

For our own private celebration, we went back to the restaurant where we had had onion soup on the night we met and where we could again visit Sacré-Coeur, which I fatuously, but very romantically, you may be sure, referred to as "our little church." Afterwards, at the risk of being dispossessed, Leigh sneaked me into her apartment and hustled me out before daylight.

And then time ran out. It was over. I had to go back to the outfit, and it mattered more than I had thought possible. I felt a great emptiness, a sorrow nothing could assuage.

When it was at least two hours past the scheduled time for me to leave Paris, Leigh came out to the university with me and waited outside on a bench while I went in to gather up my gear. We promised to write often and vowed we would see each other again. Her cheeks were wet when we kissed goodbye; there were big tears in my eyes too. Had I promised too much? Yes, as things turned out, but at the time. . . . ? Maybe I knew and just refused to know.

I sat in the jeep and watched her out of sight as she walked slowly back to catch the metro. The wind caught her dress, accentuating her slender figure. Her head was slightly bowed. I knew she was crying. The wide, nearly deserted boulevard made her look so small, so fragile, so helpless and alone. I had a powerful impulse to run after her, take her in my arms, kiss away her tears. But she never looked back. Goodbye, my darling. *Je t'adore, mon petit chou.* If only. . . .

The road back to Germany took us through Verdun, Metz, Manheim, places which ordinarily would have held considerable interest for me. But neither the situation nor my emotional state was ordinary. The war damage and the gray, rainy weather matched my mood.

Back at battalion there were so many changes it no longer seemed home. We had a new battalion commander, a West Pointer this time. A number of my friends had rotated back to the States. There were strangers to replace them. Some of the guys had applied for leave to visit Paris. Two officers I knew only slightly were celebrating their promotions to captain.

Fortunately, I had work to do. The day after I got back, I began speaking before different groups to publicize the educational program. Within a week I had appeared in all of the companies in the battalion.

After the original round of explaining the opportunities, I began making arrangements for the construction and location of bulletin boards for further dissemination of informational material which would be coming down through channels. We conducted a survey to find what possible additional courses the men would like to see offered. We compiled an inventory of in-house expertise so that we could know what kinds of courses men in the battalion might be prepared to teach. We began to enroll students.

Battalion units were widely dispersed about the countryside. The S-2 office and support troops were housed in the little town of Crailsheim, not far from Mochmuhl if that will pinpoint the location for you. The only things of interest in Crailsheim when I was there were a pretty English-speaking German school teacher in her late twenties and her family, consisting of her three-year-old son and a sister, a girl about my age.

No, I didn't "fall in love" with either of the two girls. Nor did I try to "hit on" either of them. While the spell of Paris couldn't survive the nitty-gritty world to which I had returned, I was still fully committed to Leigh. Or was I "fully committed?" What about my high school sweetheart? I hadn't seen her in two years but I still loved her too. As for Silea, I was now willing to admit that was a harmless infatuation helped along by the Italian spring. But it was all so hopeless anyway. It would be a long time before I could provide for a wife, any wife of whatever shape, complexion, character or nationality.

The attractive German teacher let me know immediately that she was "Frau Grun" and that her husband was a prisoner of war in Norway. There had been no direct word from him for over a year, but she prayed he was still alive and would soon be permitted to come home. She and her baby had lived in Stuttgart with her younger sister, Hilda, until the bombing drove them to seek safety in the country. It was also emphasized at the outset that Hilda's situation was entirely different. She was unmarried and unattached.

In the village Frau Grun was the natural link between the occupation forces and the subject population. As the officer in charge at Crailsheim, I had daily contact with her. The villagers could not travel over a few miles without a pass, even to visit a doctor, purchase supplies, or bring home a son wounded in the war. I think I signed every request for a pass which Frau Grun placed before me, although I was aware that her role gave her considerable power over her neighbors. Occasionally we were able unofficially to find transportation for applicants who seemed to be most in need.

In return for soap, chocolate for the little boy, modest quantities of flour, coffee, etc., Frau Grun and her sister took care of my laundry, cleaned my quarters, read German poetry to me and tried to accommodate my half-hearted and basically disinterested efforts to learn their language. I was more concerned to learn French and to figure out some way of returning to Paris.

While I admired Frau Grun's loyalty to her husband and, up to a point, enjoyed talking with her, I wondered about some of her personality traits. In important respects she seemed a rather overbearing lady accustomed to having her way. And the one time our conversation broached politics, I was somewhat disquieted by what I heard.

She started it by observing that Americans were so interesting "ethnically." She sometimes amused herself, she said, by estimating the proportionate racial mix in the heredity of the various Americans she met, a certain percentage Anglo-Saxon, German, Italian, whatever. She wondered if I did the same.

I was surprised at her question and told her that such precise calculations had never entered my head. I also told her I didn't think most Americans thought in those terms.

It was her turn to be surprised. I don't think she believed me. She politely asked the inevitable question, "what about the Negro?"

I had first thought seriously about that when the Ninety-second Division came up to our front on the Arno. Now I had an answer to her question.

I told her I wouldn't try to defend the indefensible. Our treatment of the Negro could not be justified. Neither could a lot of other things in my homeland. I professed the heresy that Americans were not God's chosen people, that the United States also had serious blots on its record, a wicked history as well as a glorious one. The last few years had taught me something about how the world works. It may have made me cynical and a little bitter; I prefer to think of it as the process of "getting real."

I asked her, in turn, about racial and religious persecution in Germany and about the "final solution" to what Hitler was pleased to call "the Jewish problem."

She was most defensive on those issues, concerned to exonerate herself and "the German people." She and other ordinary citizens were not "political," she told me. They had been completely unaware of what was going on in the concentration camps. They knew of the existence of such places, of course, and even the locations of some of them. There were rumors, she said, that prisoners "were not well treated"; but the citizenry didn't know any of the details and didn't ask.

There was a ring of truth about some of the things she said. I knew the location of prisons in my native state and had heard that inmates were not well treated. I didn't know the details and was not sure I wanted to. So far, so good. But Frau Grun's attitudes seemed different. In view of her curious racial consciousness and her failure to acknowledge, after I had been honest with her, the criminal nature of the Nazi regime, I could not help but wonder how much of Hitler's package she had bought.

After that we steered clear of politics. Frau Grun seemed much more concerned with promoting a relationship between me and Hilda. Apparently I had passed through the mysterious screening process which she used to establish racial legitimacy.

For the most part her efforts at matchmaking were obvious. She never lost an opportunity to extol Hilda's many virtues. The good Frau made frequent trips on her bicycle over to Mochmuhl to give English lessons, she said, but the lessons usually lasted until well after dark and I would be left alone with her sister.

Hilda was a very nice, very likeable girl, but rather plain, meek, and self-effacing. Our relationship never progressed beyond the handholding stage. Actually, I kissed her goodnight once, but it was a chaste little kiss which could easily be forgiven by my true love, whoever and wherever she might be.

A very sweet letter from Silea arrived shortly after I got back from Paris. It was written in English and I wondered with a strange kind of jealously who had written it for her. For some reason, I didn't think it was Tina. Should I respond to Silea? If so, in what language? And, if in Italian, where could I find someone to write for me. And what would I say? As I pondered these questions, my correspondence with Leigh began to develop.

Each of us wrote first. Our letters crossed in the mail. Men in the battalion were going to rest camp in Paris on a regular basis now and there was no problem in finding an emissary to hand-carry correspondence between us. I sent one letter to Leigh in this way and got two letters in return. Later on she sent me a bottle of French cognac. It was half gone when one of my last remaining friends in the battalion, Lieutenant Norman, now with Service Company, delivered it to me. I had to forgive him. He thought we were still living in the old days when we held everything in common. I doubt that he even sensed the depth of my feelings for Leigh.

And then in what seemed one continuous, marathon broadcast, the radio brought into the village momentous news from across the world. An atomic bomb had been dropped on Hiroshima. The Soviet Union declared war on Japan. A second bomb obliterated Nagasaki. The Japanese sued for peace, requesting only that they be allowed to keep their emperor. The Allies made that concession. The war was over. It would be safe to go home now, and time.

I don't know how they celebrated the news over in Mochmuhl, but in Crailsheim, we took it all in stride. My own joy was decidedly restrained. It would be good to go home again, of course, and I was glad the killing was over, especially since that meant "old Bitty Burr" would be safe. Even so, I didn't feel compelled to dance in the street, embrace total strangers and celebrate to the point of exhaustion. The world might be at peace, but I was trapped in hopeless dilemmas, largely of my own making, and beset by problems the vast majority of which I either didn't identify or didn't appreciate the significance of at the time.

The end of the war had found me with an addiction to cigarettes, an unrecognized dependence on alcohol, an excessive number of "significant others," a guilt-ridden conscience, an almost pathological fear of unemployment, an old-fashioned, overly romantic image of the "husband-provider," and a lifestyle which didn't bode well for the future. Otherwise, I was in the very pink of physical and emotional health, a stunning example of normality. But why did I feel so numb, so listless?

It took me a long, long time to sort things out, recognize my problems, and gain a better understanding of what had happened to me in that climactic, truly decisive, watershed year of 1945. Not until I began serious reflection on my journal notes, for example, did I appreciate the wrenching abruptness with which my spirits had been jerked up and down during that time.

On Friday, April 13, I had been up in the mountains near Bologna waiting for the spring offensive to begin and more than half convinced I would soon be dead. By the middle of May I had spent twenty up-and-down days on the line before watching the enemy stack arms. A few days after that, I had fallen in love with Silea; by June 16 I was preparing to tell her goodbye. Less than a month later, I had fallen in love with Leigh and said goodbye to her too. By the middle of August, the war was over and I was preparing to go home.

And that was not to be the end of it. Before the year was out I would break clean with my high school sweetheart, the girl I had once been absolutely sure I would marry, the one who had waited in vain for me to grow up. And this time I would be emotionally devastated as never before. Yes, 1945 was quite a year.

I hadn't planned to break with my first love. I hadn't planned anything at all. That was part of the problem. Without realizing it, I had acquired what Veblen would have called a "trained incapacity" for thinking about, let alone planning for the future. For some time the future for me had been tomorrow, the next day, or at most the next week and planning was something done at higher headquarters. I had become accustomed to going where I was told and to living by my instincts and appetites. On the line my instincts had served me well enough and off the line life was too short to be bothered about anything which didn't "feel right" at the moment. When my postwar prospects and choices proved too painful to ponder, I pushed them out of my mind and had another drink. It would be time enough to face the future when it became the present.

About the Author

Lloyd M. Wells (1919–2000) was Professor Emeritus of Political Science at the University of Missouri–Columbia. He was the coauthor of *The Supreme Court and Public Opinion*.